DEPP

NATIONAL LIBRARY OF CANADA CATALOGUING IN PUBLICATION DATA

Heard, Christopher,
Depp

ISBN 1-55022-470-0

1. Depp, Johnny. 2. Motion picture actors and actresses — United States — Biography. I. Title.

PN2287.D447H42 2001   791.43'028'092   C2001-900805-8

Cover and text design by Tania Craan
Front cover photo by Jean-Francois Robert/Outline
Author photo by Mary Marentic
Color section photo credits: N. Eno/Shooting Star, Steve Sands/Outline, Benito Gely/Globe Photos,
Theo Kingma/Shooting Star, Sonia Moskowitz/Globe Photos, Chris Helermmanas-Benge/Shooting Star,
Benito Gely/Globe Photos, and Steve Finn/Alpha/Globe Photos
Layout by Mary Bowness

Printed by AGMV

DISTRIBUTION

CANADA: Jaguar book group, 100 Armstrong Avenue, Georgetown, ON L7G 5S4

UNITED STATES: Independent Publishers Group, 814
North Franklin Street, Chicago, IL 60610

2   3   4   5

Published by ECW PRESS
2120 Queen Street East, Suite 200
Toronto, ON M4E 1E2
ecwpress.com

This book is set in Minion and Akzidenz Grotesk.

PRINTED AND BOUND IN CANADA

The publication of *Depp* has been generously supported by the Canada Council,
the Ontario Arts Council and the Government of Canada through the
Book Publishing Industry Development Program. Canadä

DEPP

Christopher Heard

ECW PRESS

For my brother, Peter S. Heard,
whose kindness and generosity
have always meant a lot.

Table of Contents

Acknowledgments

Writing this book has been a very enjoyable experience for me from start to finish, so some thanks are in order.

I would like to thank Janice Luke from Universal Pictures Canada for giving me the opportunity to sit down with Johnny Depp for our first interview and unwittingly providing the spark for this book.

Thanks also to Jack David and Jennifer Hale at ECW. I was a bit of a handful, but they were always supportive and encouraging, and that's what did it for me.

Thanks to Dara Rowland and Rob Firing for their efforts.

Special thanks to my editor, and a wonderful writer in her own right, Alana Wilcox, for making the book better in a calm, friendly, and easygoing manner.

Thanks to Vicki McKay; without her, my job would have been a lot harder.

Thanks to Shane Maxwell at the Hollywood Renaissance for all his help in finding some of the missing pieces of the puzzle.

Thanks also to Susan Smythe, Julia Caslin, and Mike Calnek at Alliance Atlantic for their support on this project and others throughout the years.

Special thanks to all those mentioned in these pages who shared their thoughts and remembrances with me.

Thanks to Andreas Kyprianou, my friend and fellow scribe. It is always nice having him around to talk to.

Thanks to my good friend and teammate on *Reel to Real*, Richard Crouse — I'm glad I'm on this magical mystery tour with you, Mr. Cool.

Thanks to my friends Mark Pauderis and Julie Vaillancourt, who both make me look good in their own distinct ways.

Special thanks to lovely Sylvie Lapointe, pretty face, sexy accent, and the one who arranged for me to see Paris. Sylvie, you are truly a beautiful woman.

Preface

This book is first and foremost about the life of an intriguing actor named Johnny Depp. But it is also about the cult of celebrity and our unquenchable thirst for details — true or untrue — of the lives of famous people and how, when the legends surrounding famous people and the facts of their lives don't always mesh, they become even more famous because of it. I am interested in separating the fact from the tabloid myth. In the case of Johnny Depp, the actual story is even more interesting than what has been fabricated. Tabloids have said that Depp dates only gorgeous models and actresses — true, but he dates only one at a time and is fiercely loyal and attentive to the woman he is with. Until recently, his relationships have always lasted between two and four years and almost always involved either marriage or engagement. And it's probably a surprise that Depp is a voracious reader — tabloids never seem to mention that. They'd rather tell you that he's a "bad boy" because it sells more papers. If, in telling his story, I tend to come down on his side more often than not, and if that may appear sycophantic, then so be it. I am a movie fan, a connoisseur of movie history and movie culture. For his contributions to the art form, Depp deserves respect and admiration, and I intend to show him both. I would rather tell his story as I uncovered it than take the position of a sniper. I am not particularly interested in peeling back layers of his skin to expose what is shameful or humiliating underneath; I want to clear away the dust and the dirt and allow fans of Depp to see the side of him that the tabloid press never seems to cover.

Johnny Depp is what I call an accidental actor. He didn't grow up idolizing James Dean or auditioning for commercials when he was five. He was a kid with humble beginnings who dreamed of being a successful musician — a passion he holds to this day. Were it not for a few minor decisions that yielded major results, he might never have been an actor at all. He is still somewhat bewildered by what he does, how much he is paid to do it, and how much wild adoration he receives for it. When people think of a "movie star," his picture is probably what they see, yet Depp has done his best to dodge that label. When asked about his reputation as a "bad boy," he is quick to retort, "The press developed that. They did that. The only reason they portray me as wild is because they need to have a name for the product. I'm a normal guy with a slightly strange job."

I happened to be speaking to a young Canadian actor recently who has a couple of movies and numerous TV appearances under his belt and was about to pack up and head to L.A. I mentioned to him that I was working on a book about Johnny Depp, and his eyes widened. "I love Johnny Depp," he enthused. I asked him why, and he launched into a passionate explanation of what an inspiration Depp is. "Depp does work that he chooses to do based on what he feels strongly about. It isn't about money and fame; it is about doing good, solid, memorable work." I heard that sentiment repeated often when speaking with actors, both famous and unknown, about Depp. He has managed to do it, as the song goes, his way. When you go down the list of films that Johnny Depp has made, you won't find any box-office hits, and you won't find any Oscar-winning movies. What you will find is a complete change of direction with almost every film. Why, then, is this guy on the cover of magazines the world over? Somewhere along the line, this geeky kid from Kentucky came to personify cool in the '90s. Another young Hollywood actor told me that the "Depp attitude" is one that he himself would love to project. In Depp's case, however, the cool is there without having to be cultivated as an attitude. One need look no further than the people from whom Depp draws inspiration — Jack Kerouac, Iggy Pop, and, later, his friend Marlon Brando — to see where his attitude comes from.

Before the idea of writing a book on Johnny Depp occurred to me, I had interviewed him on a number of occasions, and each time I was struck by the fact that the commonly held, tabloid-media-driven perception of Depp as a hell-raiser and a brat was far removed from the person I was with. In telling his story, I hope to expose both his darker, deeper side and his lighter, softer side — neither of which makes for splashy headlines. Yes, Depp has had problems with authorities that have led to a few overnight visits to jail, but he is also someone who dotes endlessly on his com-panion and their daughter, someone who actively supports charities (including the wonderful Make a Wish Foundation, a heroic organization dedicated to making gravely ill children's wishes come true), without holding a press conference every time he does. He is a loyal friend and, despite what the tabloids say, a faithful companion.

Depp is the story of an actor named Johnny Depp, who just happened to come along when the cult of celebrity had grown to epidemic proportions. He is an actor who resists Hollywood's professional traps but who has been known to indulge in the more personal excesses that come with movie-star status — a private person by nature who finds himself, not entirely unwillingly, in the glare of the spotlight. Depp has often been heard to say to photographers following him on the street, "Please, could I not be Johnny Depp for this one evening." As he nears 40, Johnny Depp has relocated to Paris to live with his companion, Vanessa Paradis, and their children. He seems to have found a new contentment in his life, which is being positively reflected in his work — always fascinating to watch because he takes it seriously. He continues to be in great demand, and, as the year 2000 rolled around, he was working on several projects back to back, but the well-being of his family is now clearly his top priority. Whether we like it or not, movies and television are the main channels in the development of our culture, and often these influential media distance themselves from the responsibility that comes with that. Johnny Depp is one of a few actors who refuses to walk into a project that will bear his name if he is not convinced that both he and his family will be proud of the result. The further I delved into the Johnny Depp story, the more interested I became. The slight similarities we share — among them, that both of us went through parental divorce at age 15, that Johnny is part Cherokee and I am part Cree — led me to be more empathetic toward how his story is told. Well, be it for die-hard fans or the merely curious, for movie freaks or casual fans, I want to tell his story in an interesting, entertaining, and informative way — because I care.

They don't know anything about me, they know absolutely nothing about me. There's a great quote, I think it was Jean Cocteau who wrote it — he wrote it or he said it . . .

"The more visible you make me, the more invisible I become."

Johnny Depp
November 1998

Chapter One

The Kids

"You're an actor."

Unnamed casting agent's message to Johnny Depp after his first audition

Owensboro is the third-largest city in Kentucky. It was first settled in 1780 by two explorers named Joseph Blackford and William Smeathers, and it was established as Owensborough in 1817 in honor of a local colonel named Abraham Owens. Owensboro is most well known for hosting the world-famous International Bar-B-Q Festival

Johnny in his Grade Seven classroom
CLASSMATES.COM

each summer. But a second claim to fame was added on 9 June 1963 — the date John Christopher Depp II was born there.

I was once asked to read a biography of the great Katharine Hepburn for a televised discussion. I'm an avid reader of Hollywood history, so I eagerly set about devouring this one. I found myself 160 pages into it without having read her name once. I knew everything there was to know about her ancestors, but I was bored stiff. It was Katharine Hepburn I wanted to read about.

So, to avoid miring this book down in that kind of excruciating history, I'll plunge right in with Johnny's parents.

When Johnny, the youngest, was born, Betty Sue and John Depp Sr. were living a lower-middle-class life. John was an engineer who worked for the city, while his wife waitressed in a coffeeshop, a job she would do with pride for many years. In fact, Johnny was deeply affected by his mother's dignity. He has even stated that his mother, along with her father, Johnny's Cherokee grandfather, PawPaw, have been his greatest influences. Depp has declared Betty Sue to be "the greatest lady in the world. She is my best friend, the coolest thing in the world." And he's not shy about showing it — his first tattoo was a red heart with "Betty Sue" written across it. When Johnny started gaining a foothold in Hollywood, he announced, "I won't let my mom wait tables anymore." It seems like that was the one aspect of his "teen heartthrob" status that made it all worthwhile. To this day, Depp continues to display characteristics inherited from his mother — she too is a chain-smoking, swearing, "I am who I am" individualist.

There is a fair amount of Irish and German in Depp's background, but it is his Cherokee ancestry that Johnny is most connected to. When playing with his friends as a kid, for instance, he always wanted to be the "Indian." He adored his Cherokee PawPaw and spent as much time as he could with him, picking tobacco or just sitting around together. PawPaw died in 1970 at the age of 102. His death affected Johnny deeply, and he continues to believe that his grandfather is with him in spirit: "There are times when I will dodge a bullet of some kind, and I'll think, 'How did I get out of that?' I'm sure that it is my grandfather staying near me and keeping me safe."

The cause of Native American rights remains important to Depp. He has been photographed wearing a black T-shirt emblazoned with a blood-red map of the United States with the words *Indian Territory* written underneath. And one of the several tattoos that now decorate his body is of an Indian wearing a ceremonial headdress. Native rights is a passion he shares with Marlon Brando, a devoted Native American activist, and he and Johnny have become close friends.

Johnny's childhood can be described as nomadic; his father would uproot the Depp clan frequently to follow better-paying job prospects. "I remember moving around a lot, it could have been as many as 25 or 30 times when I was a kid," said Depp. "It was really a transient existence; we would live in apartments and houses and hotels. It got so I would not even introduce myself to kids in the new neighborhood because I knew I wasn't going to know them long enough for it to matter." This feeling of isolation can be seen in his work as an actor. He is still drawn to characters who proudly remain on the outside. "I always felt like a total freak," he said. "I had the feeling of wanting to be accepted but not knowing how to go about being accepted as who I am."

Moving so often meant that Johnny and his siblings, older sisters Christine and Deborah and older brother Dan from his mother's previous marriage, were always the new kids in the neighborhood and the strangers in class. Despite that, Depp still maintains a fierce belief in the strength of the family unit. "Man, family is the most important thing in the world," he said. "Without that, you have nothing. It is the tightest bond you will ever have."

Depp's brother, Dan, would go on to write the screenplay for Johnny's directorial debut, *The Brave*. Depp describes his brother as a "genius." His sister Christi now looks after his schedule from her home in Florida. Depp relies heavily on her because she keeps him organized — something he simply can't do himself. Sister Debbie stays out of the limelight altogether.

When Johnny was seven years old, the family made a larger move, from Kentucky to the Florida suburb of Miramar in Broward County. Miramar is a working-class area that has a number of aerospace and aviation-based industries. The Depp family would end up living in a small motel there for the better part of a year while John Sr. searched for a well-paying and rewarding but elusive job in his field, engineering.

Like many kids of that era, Johnny was engrossed by the music and theatrics of KISS. But, although he conformed in some ways, he had some eccentricities that set him apart from his peers hungry for popular culture. He liked to keep lizards as pets — odd but not enough to label him a freak. He was suspended from school for mooning one of his teachers. Again, that's a bit on the rebellious side, but it's not a crime that should have earned him outcast status. But the way he chose to decorate his bedroom walls gives us pause. Most North American kids adorn their rooms with posters of movie stars and rock singers. The young Depp chose to decorate his walls with reproductions of the works of Vincent Van Gogh. And prominently displayed in the center of the room was the self-portrait of the earless artist.

Another person who would ultimately have a profound influence on Johnny was a friend of the family who was an evangelical preacher. He would travel around the South and preach in tents at revivals, drawing in large crowds of the faithful with his well-honed oratorial skills. Johnny would hang out in the tents and watch, mesmerized, as this man held these crowds in the palm of his hand. Also part of the revival was a gospel rock band that had a couple of Johnny's cousins in it. The preacher saw that Johnny was very interested in the band, so he often tried to coax him out of the shadows and up onto the stage. "My cousins' band was the first time I had ever seen an electric guitar," Johnny has said, "and I became instantly hooked."

In fact, Johnny talked about guitars and playing in a band so much that Betty Sue went out and spent a hard-earned $25 on an electric guitar for him when he was 12 years old. Johnny spent the better part of the next year locked away in his room teaching himself how to play by listening to records over and over again, trying to mimic the chords. By the time he was 13, he was reasonably sure that he was ready to take the next step. He decided to form his own rock band and become a rock star. His band was called Flame. Costumes were integral to his vision — he would borrow crushed-velvet blouses from his mother's closet and bop around the house as he wailed away on the guitar.

He and childhood pal Sal Jenco — a close friend to this day who still helps with the running of Depp's club, the Viper Room — once took this focus on performance a bit too far: Depp wrapped a T-shirt around an old broom and set it on fire, then filled his mouth with gasoline and attempted to do a Gene Simmons by spitting the fire across his yard in a dazzling display. Only the quick action of another friend, a skinny kid with long red hair and chipped front teeth known as Bones, kept Depp from doing serious damage to himself. Bones jumped on him and put out the flames with his bare hands. Depp would later repay Bones by immortalizing him on film, modeling himself on Bones in his role as Gilbert Grape.

This passion for music would remain with Depp throughout his life and would be responsible for some interesting twists and turns, taking him places he never dreamed of going and allowing him to form friendships with people he thought he'd admire only from afar.

I met Depp for the first time in 1987, during the second season of *21 Jump Street*. I was visiting a friend who was working on the series in Vancouver, and the three of us had lunch one sunny, cool afternoon. Talk turned to virginity and how monumental it can be to lose it, so Johnny told us the story of how he lost his at the tender age of 13. It happened in the back of a Ford van that belonged to one of the members of the band he was playing in at the time, and his partner was a 17-year-old girl who'd been hanging around the venue where they were playing. She described herself as a virgin too. The way Johnny described it, the event was completely free of fear and stress. They both jumped into it with wide-eyed enthusiasm; he said it was "wonderful fun" and remembered laughing a lot throughout it.

For many young people, high school is a difficult, awkward time, when identity is uncertain and fitting in is all that seems to be important. Johnny was one of those people — he tried things that were wrong for him, and he tried things that were just plain wrong. In an attempt to please his father, Johnny signed up for the football team, but he didn't enjoy any part of the experience. He quit, was talked into returning to the squad, quit again, then went back before he finally quit for good. He then fell in with the "bad crowd." His new pals' favorite pastime was burglarizing and vandalizing local schools. Drugs were also a part of that scene. When asked about it today, Depp makes no excuses for the indiscretions of his younger days: "I wasn't really a bad kid or malicious — I was just curious. After a while, when you see where that stuff has you headed, you decide to get out."

Depp's life in Miramar was dull beyond belief. Much of his performance in *What's Eating Gilbert Grape* was based on the time Johnny spent in the southeastern Florida town, which he describes as having "a Winn-Dixie store, a drugstore next door, and next to that a card and gift store. Across the street was a Publix store that had its own drugstore and card and gift store attached to it. You were just . . . there."

Johnny looked to his brother, Dan, for influence and inspiration — Dan read cool books and listened to cool music. "One day," Johnny remembers, "he gave me a book that was to become like the Koran to me. A dog-eared paperback stained with God knows what of *On the Road*, written by some goofball with a strange frog name that was almost unpronounceable for my teenage tongue." Depp was not a reader at that time. "Possibly the only things I'd read to that point were a biography of Knute Rockne, some stuff on Evel Knievel, and some picture-heavy books about World War II. *On the Road* was life-changing for me," he wrote in a piece he was asked to contribute to *The Rolling Stone Book of the Beats: The Beat Generation and American Culture*. He continued, "So much has happened to me in the 20 years since I first sat down and took that first long drag on Kerouac's masterpiece. I have been a construction laborer, a gas-station attendant, a bad mechanic, a screen painter, a musician, a telemarketing phone salesman, an actor, and a tabloid target — but there has never been a second go by in which I deviated from the road that ol' Jack put me on, via my brother. It has been an inter-esting ride all the way — emotionally and psychologically taxing — but a motherfucker straight down the pike. And I know that without these great writers' holy words seared into my brain, I would most likely have ended up chained to a wall in Camarillo State Hospital, zapped beyond recognition, or dead by misadventure."

Like most teenagers, Johnny went through many phases. He badly wanted to be the first-ever white member of the Harlem Globetrotters. Then he wanted to be a daredevil like Evel Knievel. He wanted to be Bruce Lee. But *On the Road* came along and grabbed him by the throat and would not let him go.

During one early interview, Depp went into a used bookstore with the journalist, and there he found a copy of a book on black history that had once been owned by Jack Kerouac. The margins were filled with Kerouac's doodles and notes. Depp spent almost a hundred dollars buying the well-worn volume. "It was like a piece of history," he marveled. "I would look at it every day." He also later bought a battered old raincoat that Kerouac had once owned.

Johnny with his mom, Betty Sue
LISA ROSE/ GLOBE PHOTOS

When Depp was 15, his life was rattled by the acrimonious divorce of his parents. He woke up one day, and all that he'd thought he could count on disappeared. It was made even tougher by the fact that he was the only child still living at home. After the initial overwhelming despair and depression, he found courage in the idea that hopes and aspirations can remain strong despite the immediate circumstances of one's personal life. Depp spoke to me about that time. "She [Betty Sue] got very ill over it. Her life as she had known it for over 20 years was over. Her partner, her husband, her best friend, her lover, had just left her. I felt crushed that he had left, but when you are faced with something like that it's amazing how much abuse the human mind can take. You just get past what you need to get past. On some level, I was thinking, 'Wait a minute, what happened to my family? What about stability, the safety of the home?' But my feelings were secondary to thinking about my mom. All the focus was on her getting through that time, which she finally did, and now everything is pretty okay. I'm even on good terms with my dad."

Depp's brother, Dan, nine years Johnny's senior, and his sister Christi, two years older, were already on their own, while his sister Debbie, seven years older, decided that her future was with her father and moved in with him. As often happens with kids who go through this kind of thing, the first thing that suffered was Johnny's schoolwork. Since Johnny wasn't really into school anyway, that was pretty much it for his high school career.

It was around this time that he became an uncle. He'd always had a fondness for children, but he didn't realize how intense it was. "My sister Christine had a baby when I was 17, and I was terrified about it because I had read a long article on crib death," said Depp. "I was nervous around the baby, and every night I would sneak into the room where she was sleeping and put my hand in her crib, holding her little finger, and sleep on the floor next to the crib just to make sure she would be all right. I thought the warmth of my hand might help — that maybe if she felt my pulse she would remember to breathe."

Johnny grew so close to his niece, Megan, that he included her in a photo shoot he did with hotshot photographer Bruce Weber for *Vogue* magazine in 1993. There were several shots of the two clowning around on a beach in an article on the up-and-coming actor.

Johnny's best friend at the time, Sal Jenco, had also recently gone through a family breakup and decided to move away from home. Having nowhere else to go, he moved into his 1967 Impala. Johnny, being a loyal friend and not wanting to see Sal live in a car by himself, decided to move into the Impala with him; they would listen to the car radio and play along on their instruments. Both still harbored dreams of having careers as musicians. In the meantime, they'd feed themselves by staging daring daylight raids on local convenience stores to steal submarine sandwiches.

But Johnny was driven to do better. "Nothing is permanent," said Depp. "When that dawns on you, it kind of messes you up." The one thing he'd always feared was being a loser, someone with no talent and no ambition. "When I left high school, I really didn't know what I wanted to do. The only thing that saved me was my band."

Johnny and a couple of his friends formed a band they called the

Kids. They were full of determination and youthful zeal and were committed to making a go of it. Through hustling and hard work, they quickly developed a reputation with local bars as a high-energy band that might be going places.

Attention begets attention, and soon the Kids were being asked to open for larger acts passing through Florida — bands such as the Talking Heads and the B-52s. They also opened for Iggy Pop. After that show, the Kids got drunk to unwind, even though they were all too young to legally drink. Then a drunken Johnny staggered over to Iggy Pop and made a fool of himself — first gushing all over Iggy, whom he greatly admired, then hurling insults at him. Iggy shrugged him off with a few well-directed insults of his own before shoving him aside and disappearing into the crowd. Years later Iggy would meet up with Depp again on the set of *Cry-Baby*, in which Depp was starring and Iggy had a featured role. The two became friends and have since appeared in a few films together. They have also performed together at the Viper Room, and Depp asked Iggy to score his directorial debut, *The Brave*.

Now Johnny was 20 and in a band that was doing well, or at least as well as a bar band in Florida can do, and his life was about to change again — Johnny met a pretty young woman. Her name was Lori Anne Allison, and she was an aspiring musician and the sister of one of the band members. Johnny was thrilled that she was musical and found the fact that she was a bit older — 25 — and more experienced quite alluring. Soon Johnny and Lori Anne were a couple. It was only two months before they decided to marry.

Johnny soon spearheaded a campaign for the Kids to move to Hollywood and take a serious run at a record contract. They were buoyed up by the confidence that their Florida club success had given them and decided it was time to put it all on the line.

Upon their arrival in Los Angeles, it quickly became evident that they were only one among hundreds of bands out there chasing the same recording contract. Many of them had developed local reputations in Seattle or San Francisco or Chicago, and many had even been top opening bands in their areas. There was nothing particularly distinctive about the Kids, nothing that would really set them apart from all the other bands hovering around Los Angeles. "There were just so many bands," remembered Depp. "It was impossible to make any money at all. We all had to take menial side jobs to avoid starving to death."

One of his jobs, which he'd speak of often in subsequent years, was as a telemarketer. His job was to con people into buying junky things over the phone — as he put it, "We got paid a hundred bucks a week to lie to people." Lori Anne found work as a makeup artist, which would end up being fortuitous for Johnny in a way he could never have imagined.

The band continued to rehearse and knock on doors. They changed their name to Six Gun Method because the Kids didn't sound like something an LA bar band should be called, and they finally managed to play a few gigs, including one that had them opening for Billy Idol.

The lack of consistent work and the stress that it was putting on all the band members led to their unofficial dissolution. But to this day, Depp considers himself a musician who became an actor: "I use music when I work. Listening to music is the quickest way to get to an emotional place I need to be in to act."

The stress also led to the breakup of Johnny's marriage after less than two years. But unlike the situation with his parents, this split was amicable. Johnny and Lori Anne decided that they'd had fun together and had grown, but they were ultimately moving in different directions.

Fourteen-year-old Johnny had been deeply affected by the writings of Jack Kerouac; in fact, he'd eventually grow into a modern-day version of a Beat poet. But at this point, he was a young guy struggling to make it in Los Angeles — broke, recently divorced, and dealing with the disappointment of his unrealized musical dreams. Soon, though, he was about to go on his own road — a magical journey that would take him from being an awkward, geeky kid to a reluctant pop culture icon of cool.

Chapter Two

Craven Images

"What were they going to write? 'Johnny Depp was great as the kid who dies'?"

Johnny Depp on never being mentioned in the reviews for A Nightmare on Elm Street

"It isn't what you know, it's who you know" — that old adage is never truer than in Hollywood. And it worked in Johnny Depp's favor.

While continuing to struggle as musicians, all the members of Six Gun Method had taken side jobs to make their rent. Lori Anne worked as a makeup artist, and one of the people she applied makeup to was a young actor named

ERIK HEINILA/SHOOTING STAR

Nic Coppola, who would soon change his name to Nicolas Cage to distance himself from his famous uncle, Francis Ford Coppola. Nicolas and Lori Anne even wound up dating for a while. Since she and Johnny were still friendly, all three would often end up going out drinking and partying together. Depp and Cage became regular drinking buddies.

It was during one of these drinking binges with Cage that Depp had his first brush with the law, which would eventually end up as fodder for tabloids intent on depicting him as a bad boy. After getting quite drunk one evening, the pair ended up at the Beverly Center, a big, gaudy mall in Beverly Hills. Shortly after, the police were called. They arrived to find two youths dangling several floors up on the outside of the parking garage. When asked about the incident, Depp shrugged: "I don't actually remember doing that, but it sounds like something I would have done."

During another of their booze-ups, Cage mentioned to Depp that he knew of a low-budget horror movie that was being cast, suggesting that Depp give acting a try. The music thing wasn't really working out, and Cage knew that Depp hated doing the odd jobs he was forced to do. Johnny fought the idea, arguing that he knew nothing about acting and that all he really cared about was music. Cage persisted, explaining that acting was easy and that Depp had the looks for it. Since it was to be just another low-budget horror film, he added, technique and acting talent would probably not be high on the list of requirements. "They [producers, directors, casting agents] keep their eyes open for a look — and you got that look, man" is how Nic described his pitch to Depp. Johnny continued to resist the idea — he didn't think he had the personality to be an actor. But he was in Hollywood, and it seemed that everyone was either doing it or hoping to do it. Depp's resolve began to wear down, so Cage went ahead and arranged a meeting between his own agent, Tracey Jacobs, and Depp.

Jacobs was impressed with Depp's look, even though Johnny had put no effort into his appearance — he went into the meeting just as he was. After a brief talk and a quick once-over, the agent sent him to an audition with a young horror director who was finally getting a chance to make his movie about dreams. His name was Wes Craven. Of his initial meeting with Craven, Johnny recalled, "I read the part of the screenplay that I was shown that described the character I was auditioning for, and he was described as this big blond surfer jock type, and here I was this little scrawny pale little guy with long dark hair starched to death with five-day-old hairspray."

Craven liked Depp, but he wasn't the one who got him the part in the movie. Craven had brought his daughter with him to the audition to read lines with the prospective actors. Johnny's audition was taped and just put in the pile with all the rest. But after Depp left the room, Craven's daughter couldn't stop talking about how "hot" he was, what a "fox" he was. Craven hadn't seen such an overwhelming response to any of the other candidates. He decided to go with his daughter's reaction, thinking that this guy had something other young girls would also want to see.

I have had the good fortune to speak with Wes Craven on a number of occasions, and I've always found him to be erudite, intelligent, and very interesting. As horrific as his cinematic images are, the man himself is distinguished looking — more like a college professor than a maker of horror movies. I asked Craven what he remembered about meeting Depp. "I would love to be able to say that I can spot talent in young actors," said Craven. "Just meet them once, put them in their first films, and then have them go on to international success, but. . . ." I pressed him on this because he has done this very thing a number of times — most notably with Depp. "Well, I guess I have," he admitted. "But with Johnny Depp, with the entire casting process on *A Nightmare on Elm Street*, I looked for things in each person that I thought would be appealing to the audience I was hoping would form my core group for the movie. I had seen so many actors for this movie I finally just ended up going on instinct. Depp wasn't even close to the way the Glen character was written. Johnny came in looking rumpled and peaked, but he had a gleam about him — he had that look that directors look for, even though I could never really explain what that look actually looks like. It was my daughter who really pushed me over the edge as far as my decision went. She just flipped for him — she found him hypnotically good looking and very charming. Her overanimated reaction to him made me cast him radically against the initial idea of how Glen would look."

I asked Craven about Johnny's acting in those early days — was Depp a quick study? Craven replied, "I remember him being very green. But he did pick it all up pretty fast and was very eager to participate in the process. He seemed to automatically understand what acting was and what creating a character was."

When I asked Depp the same question, he said, "I was being paid $1,200 a week for pretty much doing nothing for most of the day, then pretending to be someone else for a while, telling a few lies. I couldn't believe my luck."

Depp still thought of himself as a musician at the time — in fact, he would later admit that he saw this initial acting job as "a way of financing my music career. I thought I would be doing this acting thing for a couple of years at the very most."

When parts of a movie — a catchphrase or a word or a character's name — go on to enter the common lexicon, you know the film has had a major impact. *Psycho, Jaws, Halloween,* and *Friday the 13th* are examples. In 1984, Wes Craven entered that league when he created what would become the most wildly successful horror film franchise in history — *A Nightmare on Elm Street.*

The film is about a group of teenagers battling a nightmare demon named Freddy Krueger. Krueger was a real person at one time, a school janitor who was also a predatory pedophile. When the law fails to do anything about him, some parents form a vigilante group to see that justice is done. But Freddy returns as a hideously burned nightmare figure wearing a tattered, striped sweater and a special glove armed with knives at the ends of the fingers to terrorize the children of the parents who tortured and murdered him.

The adult characters were played by established actors. The role of Freddy Krueger went to Robert Englund, a veteran character actor and experienced stage actor with fair chunks of Shakespeare and Shaw under his belt. This role would make him a multimillionaire and hopelessly typecast. John Saxon, who has starred opposite everyone from Marlon Brando (*The Appaloosa*) to Bruce Lee (*Enter the Dragon*), played Lieutenant Thompson, the cop investigating the gruesome deaths that are weirdly connected to the late Freddy Krueger.

The three young leads in the film were played by emerging actors. The role of Rod was filled by Nick Corri, who was making his big-screen debut after a promising New York stage career. Not much has been heard from him since. Heather Langenkamp played the main dream warrior, Nancy. She fell into acting by answering an ad in a local newspaper. She was about to start studying at Stanford University when Francis Ford Coppola rolled into her hometown of Tulsa, Oklahoma, to film his adaptations of the Susie Hinton novels *The Outsiders* and *Rumble Fish*. Heather auditioned and ended up getting roles in both of Coppola's films and then in *A Nightmare on Elm Street*. Johnny Depp rounded out the cast of newcomers by playing the sweater-wearing good guy, Glen.

Craven had been trying to get the film made for a few years but hadn't been able to find anyone to back it. The upstart company New Line Cinema decided to take a chance on the movie, provided that Craven could keep the costs to a minimum. New Line ended up with a lucrative movie franchise that spawned seven sequels and untold millions in ancillary money.

The finished film is standard horror fare — with a few intellectual challenges courtesy of Craven. Like every effective horror film,

A Nightmare on Elm Street taps into a collective fear. Who hasn't had a nightmare? Who hasn't awoken with a start and had to shake off the chills? The name Freddy Krueger became instantly synonymous with that cold fear that comes to us in the form of nightmares.

One of the most spectacular sequences in *A Nightmare on Elm Street* involves Depp's character being sucked into a mattress and then spit violently up onto the ceiling in a grotesque geyser of blood. The sequence was designed by effects man Jim Doyle and was a very complex effect to get on film. It took Doyle a month to design the elaborate revolving set — it was 25' tall, 26' wide, and 30' long. A bedroom set measuring 19' x 15' x 13' and weighing about 10,000 pounds was built within the revolving structure. Crew members were bolted and strapped into their places, and some 500 gallons of fake blood were dumped out as the set revolved.

Craven had planned for the scene to be shot using a stunt double. But when the curious Depp saw the shot being set up, he asked if he could do it himself. "He kept telling me how wild the whole thing sounded," said Craven. "He was really disappointed when I told him that we would bring a stunt double in to actually do the gag. He begged me to allow him to do it himself, and finally I relented and let him go for it."

I spoke to Heather Langenkamp about working with Depp on the groundbreaking horror film. "I really had no idea Johnny Depp would go on to do the things he's done since *Nightmare*," she said, "but I do remember him being very serious about not pretending he knew what he was doing when he didn't and about listening, not just to Wes, but to everyone on the set. The process really seemed to interest him."

The huge international success of *A Nightmare on Elm Street* didn't have much of an impact on the fledgling career of Johnny Depp. Even though the film was very well reviewed — rare enough for a horror movie — the praise was mostly aimed at writer-director Craven's ingenuity and imagination. Depp wasn't disappointed because he never expected to be singled out in any of the reviews. "I played a kid who gets sucked into a bed and then spat out in a gush of blood," he said. "What are they going to write? 'Johnny Depp was great as the kid who died?'" Although his performance wasn't raved about, it wasn't panned either. It wasn't a bad performance at all, particularly in the context of the genre. His lines are spoken with conviction. We know who his character is and what his place is in the overall story. Depp need not be ashamed of this first performance.

Because Depp had made his debut in such a successful film, his agent, Tracey Jacobs, had a fairly easy time getting him interviews and auditions. She managed to get him cast in episodes of TV shows such as the prime-time soap opera *Hotel* and in a short-lived cop show called *Lady Blue*.

Johnny was soon cast in his second feature film, and this time it wouldn't make him proud. Shot in 1985, it was a film that falls into the time-honored genre of the "teen sex comedy." It was called *Private Resort*. Jacobs argued that taking the role was a logical step — it was only his second feature film, and already, at age 22, he was getting a costarring role. His agent was doing her job.

Starring opposite Depp in *Private Resort* was another up-and-coming young actor named Rob Morrow. At the time, he was a New York-based actor hoping for a serious career as a dramatic actor. Morrow would go on to bigger and better things when he costarred in the multi-award-winning television series *Northern Exposure*.

Private Resort was one of those instantly forgettable teen sex romps, with two young sex-obsessed guys who decide that the most likely place to score with chicks is a Florida resort, so they check in to one and try their luck. Jack (Depp) has his eyes on an attractive young rich girl and pretends to be a surgeon in order to seduce her. Ben (Morrow) is after one of the waitresses at the resort, but she is also being pursued by one of her bosses. Meanwhile, there is a house detective chasing them around and falling down a lot and a master thief who wants to rob the resort.

A lot of Internet chatter about this movie focuses on the fact that it contains the only nude scene that Johnny has so far consented to. It occurs about 15 minutes into the scant 82-minute running time of the movie, but it isn't something that should be remembered — it certainly isn't worth trying to find the movie for it.

When viewed now, *Private Resort* is a misogynist's dream — a dated sex comedy short on both sex and comedy. Depp doesn't like to talk about this movie, but at least it was an opportunity to learn and become more comfortable with acting. Besides, he wasn't really in any position at this point in his career to be choosy.

Private Resort became an embarrassment for all involved. The movie is embarrassing even to watch — for the sake of not just Johnny Depp but also Rob Morrow and the other serious actors who got caught up in the mess, such as Hector Elizondo, who plays the thief. It looks and sounds like a cheap porno movie without the hardcore sex. The photography is bad, the locations are bad, the costumes are bad, and, thanks to writer Gordon Mitchell, it contains some of the worst dialogue you'll ever hear.

Morrow has few good things to say about the movie, but he does recall having some fun at the time. "There was a test screening of the movie, and no one affiliated with it would go anywhere near the theater," he said. "Depp and I heard about it and wanted to see it. So we dressed up in the weirdest possible way. He had these dorky glasses on and a knit hat, and I put cotton in my mouth so my face puffed out. We walked in right past the executives who knew us." Both laughed hard at what they watched but were ultimately disappointed that they hadn't acted in something better.

Depp remembers the experience a bit more pragmatically. "Sure, it sucks bad," he said, "but it was a job, and I was again struck by the fact that I was being well paid to go to Florida and fuck around for a couple of months. I certainly wasn't complaining at the time."

Private Resort vanished from sight quickly, just as Johnny hoped it would. By this point, he was growing used to the weekly paychecks — this was his first experience of getting decent money on a regular basis. But after *Private Resort*, he started to become concerned about the quality of work he was doing. If he was going to continue this acting gig, then he'd have to seek out work that was more meaningful to him.

Johnny Depp was now a working actor, and he started hanging around with other actors on the rise. On the advice of his agent, he took some acting classes so he could become familiar with formal acting techniques, which he could then apply or discard as needed. Johnny was enthusiastic about the idea because he didn't think that he knew enough about some of the mechanics of acting. He signed up for classes at a place called the Loft Studio in Los Angeles, where he was able to interact with other young actors.

It was on the set of a student film there that he met a young actor named Sherilyn Fenn. She was a couple of years away from some memorable performances — as April in the dark and sexy movie *Two Moon Junction* and as Audrey Horne in David Lynch's darker and stranger TV series *Twin Peaks*. Sherilyn had dark, pretty, exotic looks, and Depp quickly became attracted to her. Within a few months, the two were engaged and living together.

Depp was next cast in a 1986 TV movie that aspired to being something cool but ended up being something average. It was a crime thriller called *Slow Burn*. It is notable mainly as evidence of the rapid decline in the acting career of the once-brilliant Eric Roberts rather than as an early indication that Johnny Depp was going to be one of the great actors of his generation.

Slow Burn was based on *Castles Burning*, a solid thriller by Arthur Lyons. Depp plays Donnie Fleischer, the son of a very rich man who is kidnapped and murdered in a most gruesome way. Roberts plays Jacob, a private investigator who uses his skills from a former career as an investigative reporter to try to solve the case. There are, of course, lots of twists and turns in the movie, and many of the characters aren't who they seem to be.

All in all, *Slow Burn* isn't that bad, but it just doesn't add up to much. Pay-per-view movies seem to have replaced the B-movies you could catch on the bottom half of double bills at your local drive-in — *Slow Burn* works best in that context.

Depp enjoyed working with Eric Roberts, an actor he greatly admired; "*The Pope of Greenwich Village* is one of my favorite movies of all time," Johnny has said. Roberts starred in his first film, *King of the Gypsies*, when he was just 22 and went on to do fabulous work in movies such as *The Pope of Greenwich Village*, *Star 80*, and *Runaway Train* before personal problems and battles with the IRS took the wind out of his career's sails. Roberts continues to work steadily in low-budget, direct-to-video movies and television series that don't seem to be around for long. He has never regained the sizable momentum that his career had in the early '80s. He is now known primarily as Julia Roberts's older brother.

Someone else whose name appears in the credits of *Slow Burn* would also go off on a spectacular Hollywood career ride — Joel

Schumacher. Schumacher is listed as the executive producer of *Slow Burn*, but he'd go on to direct some of the most stylish movies of the past 15 years — *St. Elmo's Fire*, *The Lost Boys*, *Flatliners*, *Falling Down*, *Batman Forever*, *Batman and Robin*, and *Tigerland*, to name just a few.

I asked Schumacher for his recollections of *Slow Burn* and the huge star in the making who was acting in it. "He [Depp] had that demeanor, like James Dean — now, I know how much of a cliché that is, but it happens to be true in some cases," said Schumacher. "He was a very cool guy without putting much effort into being cool. He seemed to have an attitude that he was applying himself but that an acting career really didn't matter to him all that much, yet you could see it in his face that he was well read, well prepared, and giving the job every due diligence. It comes as no surprise to me that all these A-list directors now want to work with him — I would love to work with him again."

The acting gig was starting to matter more and more to Depp with each job he completed. He was finding a form of expression that was new to him and quite exhilarating, and he was about to embark on a project that would be incredibly meaningful for everyone involved. It would give Johnny reason to believe that the effort to make films that spoke from the heart was worthwhile and essential to him if he was going to continue as a Hollywood-based actor. It would also teach him a thing or two about the stark realities of big-time Hollywood filmmaking.

Johnny Depp was about to go into the jungle with one of the few mavericks of contemporary cinema, Oliver Stone.

Chapter Three

Rumble in the Jungle

"Oliver Stone scared the shit out of me."

Johnny Depp

In late 1985, Johnny Depp was one of many young actors in town lining up to audition for a role in a film being written and directed by Oliver Stone. Stone had won an Oscar a few years earlier for writing *Midnight Express*; he'd also written the screenplay for the controversial

Johnny and fellow tabloid target
Charlie Sheen
RALPH DOMINGUEZ/GLOBE PHOTOS

Scarface for Brian DePalma. For years, Stone had wanted desperately to make a film about the Vietnam War that was a true reflection of what he'd seen during his time there. Unfortunately, he'd directed a film in 1981 called *The Hand,* starring Michael Caine, which had bombed both critically and at the box office, and it would be another five years before he was given a chance to direct again. But that effort, the incendiary *Salvador,* earned Oscar nominations for his lead actor, James Woods, and for him and cowriter Richard Boyle. It was

Hemdale, the British-based company that allowed him to make *Salvador*, that finally gave him the opportunity to make the war film he'd written ten years earlier, *Platoon*.

Stone was very hot at the time, and every young actor wanted in on this project, although Stone did his best to discourage prospective actors by telling them they'd be required to go through boot camp and combat training in the jungles of the Philippines. There would be no pampered-Hollywood-actor bullshit on this movie. This would be grunt work. It would be backbreaking and exhausting, both physically and emotionally. The actors who blanched at the harsh description were immediately crossed off the list; only those actors who were intrigued and enthusiastic passed through to the audition phase.

Depp was one of 30 actors chosen to make the trip to the jungles of Southeast Asia to make the movie. "Oliver Stone scared the shit out of me," said Depp. "He was so powerfully committed to making this movie his way that it was intimidating — but I wanted to be around that kind of determination, and I wanted to be a part of the telling of Oliver's story. I also wanted him to be happy that he chose me to help him tell his story. Looking back, it is easily the toughest fucking thing I have ever had to do, ever." It would be Depp's first taste of zen filmmaking and, strangely, would hand Johnny his first major disappointment as an actor.

The 30 actors Stone selected went through 13 days of combat training in the jungle just outside Manila. The training was run by Captain Dale Dye, a military man who turned his experiences into a lucrative career as a military consultant and supporting actor in films dealing with the army or war. Dye would also author the novelization of the *Platoon* screenplay for mass-market paperback release.

Dye was determined to run this Hollywood boot camp as much like the real thing as possible. The actors had nothing with them but what a soldier in combat would have: fatigues, boots, pack, weapons, et cetera. The actors were issued real rifles, dog tags, and red filters for their flashlights so they could see at night without being seen. They slept either in tents they had to put up themselves or in foxholes they dug themselves when they were on their mock patrols. They were lectured mercilessly on gun technology and maintenance. Every one of the recruits/actors got sick during the rigorous training.

Stone explained why he put his cast through this: "The idea was to fuck with their heads so we could get that dog-tired attitude, the anger, the irritation, the casual way of brutality, the casual approach to death. These are all the assets and liabilities of infantrymen. What I remember most about Vietnam and what a lot of guys remember is the tiredness . . . being so damned tired that I wished the Viet Cong would come up and shoot me just to get it over with." Stone's plan was to immerse his cast in the Vietnam infantryman's life, to indoctrinate them in the soldier's way of thinking, talking, and moving. Then, once these things were burned into the actor's subconscious and the shooting of the movie began, that don't-give-a-damn attitude would naturally emerge. "The only thing I could not teach the actors was the reality of sudden, violent death," said Stone.

Depp's role in *Platoon* is an interesting one. Johnny plays an idealistic young soldier named Lerner, an American who is fluent in Vietnamese and is called upon to act as an interpreter between Vietnamese villagers and the platoon's savage Sergeant Barnes (Tom Berenger). But we are left wondering how a young American could have become fluent in such a difficult Asian language. This fluency makes him intriguing, but it's also problematic, as Stone discovered in the editing room — Depp's character ended up being more interesting than the lead character, Taylor (played by Charlie Sheen, who inherited the role from his brother, Emilio Estevez, after scheduling problems got in the way). When Stone watched the footage, he thought that Depp was drawing attention away from his lead character, which would throw the whole story he was trying to tell out of whack. He made the tough decision to cut an important costarring role down to a few cameo appearances.

In the final cut, there are only 11 brief glimpses of Depp in the 120-minute film. We first see him exchanging a few words with Sergeant Elias (Willem Dafoe) in a field during a Charlie Sheen voice-over. Then, in a bunker scene, Depp can be seen wearing a red bandanna and playing a guitar; he takes a huge hit of weed, then blows the smoke into a gas mask worn by a fellow soldier. Later, in the background during the "Tracks of My Tears" dance scene, Depp can be seen again smoking pot — this time all his tattoos are in view. When one of the soldiers is killed, Depp is seen in a slow pan across the dismayed faces of the grunts. He is then on point when the platoon heads into the village — as he passes, we can see the name Sherilyn scrawled across his helmet.

In his only big speaking scene, Depp translates what a frightened villager is saying for the enraged Sergeant Barnes. Here we catch a good glimpse of his character — Lerner is shown to be sympathetic, trying to intercede on the villagers' behalf to prevent an impending slaughter. Later he is seen carrying a Vietnamese child away from her burning village.

In his next scene, he is shown on patrol during a driving rain. Shortly after that, during a jungle ambush, he is shot. Sheen's character, Taylor, tends to him, then carries him to the medics. Lerner mumbles that he doesn't want Taylor to leave his side, and Taylor tries to reassure him. Lerner, a bloody mess, is last seen being carried on a stretcher to a waiting evacuation helicopter.

It is interesting to compare what appeared on screen to what Stone wrote in his original screenplay. Although the screenplay went through many incarnations — including several that had the Dafoe character of Elias written as an American Indian — the character of Lerner was prominent in each of the drafts that I read.

One major scene that Stone decided to excise would have provided Depp with a nice chunk of dialogue. The scene involves the soldiers hanging around with Sergeant Elias talking about the girl-friends they left back home — it's easy to see why it was one of the first scenes to be disposed of, as it's really hokey, more like a John Wayne/Audie Murphy kind of scene than the tough, realistic scene that Stone wanted.

Later in the screenplay, Lerner is an active participant in the conversation Chris Taylor (Sheen) has with several of the grunts about Sergeant Barnes and Sergeant Elias. Lerner tells Taylor that Barnes is from "Tennessee someplace, hill country." He goes on to answer the same question about Elias: ". . . don't know. Done some time. Heard he worked in the oil wells in Oklahoma, made some break, and washed up in El Lay."

A page later, Lerner has a bit of dialogue that might have worked well in the movie had it been left in. He is talking to Taylor about a recent leave. "I was home on leave, y'know," he says, "and every-body's just worried about making money, everybody's out for themselves. They don't even want to talk about it, man, it's like the fucking *Twilight Zone* back there — you wouldn't even KNOW there's a war going on here. My sister says to me, why do you have to go there, like I started this."

When Depp went to see *Platoon*, he was shocked to see that his part in it had been cut back so radically. The movie was intense and brilliant, but his character no longer mattered much in the overall thrust of the story.

Platoon went on to break box-office records the world over and took home an armload of Oscars, including Best Picture and Best

Director for the vindicated Oliver Stone. It renewed national debate about the Vietnam War and those who fought in it. For several of the actors, including Charlie Sheen, Willem Dafoe, and the veteran Tom Berenger, the film meant critical acclaim, Oscar nominations, and several new career opportunities.

For Johnny Depp, it was an experience of grand proportions both physically and in terms of how he felt about his profession. He told me that several times during the making of the movie he stopped and looked around at his surroundings, wondering what he'd have done had he been of the age to be sent to fight in Vietnam. It brought home just how meaningful some movies can be, and he was now resolved to only do work that mattered to him.

But his resolve was about to be tested. He was about to be presented with an opportunity that was both too good to pass up and too hard to live through. Depp was about to go from actor to teen heartthrob — to say he was reluctant would be a great understatement.

Chapter Four

Might as Well Jump

"Sure it was [a fascist idea]. Cops in schools?"

Johnny Depp on 21 Jump Street

Johnny Depp, Holly Robinson, Dustin Nguyen, Peter DeLuise, and Steven Williams

J. RODRIGUEZ/GLOBE PHOTOS

Johnny Depp had just returned from the jungles of the Philippines and an extraordinary experience with Oliver Stone. Everything had changed. Stone had shown him that movie-making can be more than just a lark. And he came home to find that his relationship with Sherilyn Fenn was sputtering — he'd been away for a long time, and the two had grown apart.

Then Depp received an overwhelming opportunity — the chance to star in a television series about a group of young-looking undercover cops who infiltrate high schools to solve teen crime from the inside. The show was to be called *Jump Street Chapel*, but it became *21 Jump Street* when the producers realized audiences might mistake the cool cop show for something more religious. When presented with the offer, Depp reacted with indifference, which turned to downright hostility as he found out more about the show. He refused even to read the script for the pilot episode. His agent pressed him, but he insisted that either he would do work that mattered to him or he would do no work at all.

Creator Patrick Hasburgh and producer Steve Beers still needed to fulfill their commitment to FOX TV, so they went ahead and cast a young actor named Jeff Yagher in the role of Officer Tom Hanson. Three weeks into the shooting of the pilot, when it was nearly done, Hasburgh and Beers decided that Yagher just wasn't giving them what they needed. They decided to go back to Depp with a bigger offer.

Another of the show's producers, Joan Carson, remembers how Depp looked when he showed up for their first meeting: "He had a felt hat pulled down low with those deep-brown eyes peering out, with a coat that went right to the floor. He was cute as a bug's ear, but he looked like a waif. And I think that is part of his appeal — he can be waiflike, but his charisma comes through." The producers wanted that charisma.

This time around, with no other work in sight, Depp decided to read the script on the off chance that it might contain something positive, and he could then take the job without compromising his newfound professional principles. He found it. After reading the script and meeting with the producers, he decided that if the show was done right it could be a positive use of the medium and could send out good messages to the kids it was being aimed at.

Johnny signed the standard contract for young actors starting out on TV — it was for five seasons. Most actors who luck into a TV show hope that the show will run for five years or longer and then go into syndication, when it will pay off in a big way. Depp signed the contract with every confidence that *21 Jump Street* would be short-lived. "I thought the show would go one season, tops," he said. "I never thought it would turn into a long-term commitment or would be a big success." He signed for $45,000 per episode — not bad money for an actor who had yet to make a name for himself.

With Depp on board, the crew went back to work to shoot the season opener, which consisted of two one-hour shows. It aired first as a special two-hour movie of the week on 12 April 1987 and has subsequently been shown in reruns as a two-part episode. In this opening episode, we are introduced to young Officer Hanson (Depp) as he is assigned to the squad of young-looking cops. Their first case is a hunt for drug dealers. The characters are all introduced straight-forwardly; even though the show was hip and energetic for its day, it still contained a number of standard TV cop-show clichés. For example, Hanson is originally misunderstood and disliked by the other members of the squad, but through his actions and dedication he is quickly brought into the fold.

It is clear when watching the pilot episode that Depp was into the show at the start. The producers hoped that the popularity of the show would build up around Hanson, and they wanted him to have something more than typically one-dimensional TV-show characteristics. Depp delivers. He gives Hanson a lot of character, making him a great focal point. He also shows that he can play quiet, listening scenes better than anyone else on the show, which means we are always watching him whether or not he is speaking.

These early shows gave Depp the opportunity to work with the wonderful character actor Frederic Forrest, who played Captain Jenko in the show for the first six episodes. Depp and Forrest got along well; they enjoyed comparing Vietnam War movie experiences (Forrest played the tightly wound chef in Francis Ford Coppola's masterpiece *Apocalypse Now*). Ten years later, Depp would cast Forrest in a major role in his dirrectorial debut, *The Brave*.

In the third episode of the season ("America, What a Town," air date 19 April 1987), we see Depp's best friend from Florida, Sal Jenco, who plays Vinnie, a student in a shop class. Vinnie has no dialogue and never reappears.

Episode four was called "Don't Pet the Teacher" (26 April 1987), and it was a good illustration of how quickly a TV series can run out of gas. In this episode, Depp's character assists a woman whose car has broken down. He is attracted to her and she to him — as were millions of young women between 18 and 34 years of age, according to the already high ratings. Hanson asks her out on a date, and she accepts. Of course, she ends up being the teacher who is receiving threatening messages — and the victim in the case that he's been assigned to go undercover and solve.

In the seventh show of the first season, Frederic Forrest has been replaced by actor Steven Williams, who heads up the squad as Captain Fuller — to explain Forrest's departure, his character is killed by a drunk driver in the story line. In this episode, a gang takes hostages, including Hanson. The producers were trying to vary the Hanson character to keep their main draw interesting, so Depp was required to play a wider array of emotions — grief, anger, fear — in this episode than he had so far.

Episode nine of that first season clearly demonstrated just how much control over the show Depp could exercise, using as leverage his general indifference to the show versus its huge popularity with fans. The episode is called "Blindsided," and it concerns the daughter of a policeman who accuses her father of sexually abusing her. In desperation, she tries to hire a hitman — undercover cop Hanson — to kill him. The girl, Diane Nelson, is played by Depp's real-life fiancée at the time, Sherilyn Fenn. This episode, which aired on 31 May 1987, also marked the introduction of a new character named Sal Banducci, called Blowfish because of a funny thing he could do with his face. He is played by Depp's best friend, Sal Jenco, now ready to be more than an extra.

The final show of that first season, "Mean Streets and Pastel Houses," is a curiosity — in it, Johnny seems to be just goofing around. He plays an infiltrator to a white supremacist punk band called KKK (Klean Kut Kids). The episode was actually shot earlier in the season but held back to be used as the season finale, even though the departure of Forrest necessitated some new shooting. Also of note in this episode is a very young-looking Vancouver actor playing the role of Tober — Jason Priestley.

After the first season and the astounding success of the show, Depp was still toeing the party line, but the cracks were starting to show. "I'm not trapped," he told TV Guide. "I mean, it's good. The best thing about the show is that kids learn from it, they can see the things that are going on in their schools and see them objectively. It teaches kids about safe sex and drugs. The worst thing is that some of the scripts we do are not important, they're purely for television."

It was the attention, the fame, that caught him by surprise. He told US magazine that "It got a bit strange, I'm not used to it. I don't hate it; I don't mind it; it's not an ugly thing."

Because Sal Jenco has been Johnny's friend for so long, he has a perspective on Depp that can be trusted. "There is no bullshit involved with him," said Jenco. "He's a completely straight guy. He took the onset of celebrity pretty much the same way he would have taken a four-dollar-an-hour job pumping gas."

One of the common misperceptions about Depp is that he always shuns interviews and is something of a press hermit. If anything, the opposite is true. In fact, early in his career, he spoke openly — and maybe naïvely — to the press about even the most personal areas of his life. It wasn't until much later, when the media turned on him, that his relationship with the press changed.

In some early interviews Johnny gave, for instance, he spoke frankly about his first experience with drugs at age 11 and his first sexual experience at 13. "I decided to be open about that stuff from the start," said Depp. "Hopefully, kids can learn from it or at least find some comfort in it. Kids can say, 'Jesus, he went through the same thing I am going through now — maybe I'm not a bad kid like everybody says.'"

The second season of *21 Jump Street* began on 20 September 1987 with a show called "In the Custody of a Clown," which is about a young man being used as a bargaining chip between his callous parents. To escape the pressure, he sets up a fake kidnapping with the help of his grandfather. In this episode, Depp wears a dress and a wig for one of his costumes — a foreshadowing of his role in *Ed Wood* and his cameo in Julian Schnabel's *Before Night Falls*.

It was about this time that I had lunch with Depp one afternoon on the set of *21 Jump Street*. His frustration with being in the series was starting to show. He was, and still is, very polite and well spoken, but there were things he hated about where his life had taken him. The pressure was starting to build. He prefaced many sentences with, "I know I shouldn't complain, but . . ." and throw in the odd "I know I sound like an asshole whining about this stuff, but. . . ." He talked about being away from his family and friends and Sherilyn — their relationship was now in tatters because he was living in Vancouver to shoot the show. He imported his best friend to Vancouver and got him on the show, and he talked his mother into moving there too so she could be nearby. He felt trapped by the series and very uncomfortable with the constant adulation from teenage girls: "You should see some of the fucking stuff I get in the mail, man," he said. He saw the success of the show as an iron gate that was swinging shut on his career as a serious actor. This wasn't just posturing on the part of a spoiled young actor; he was genuinely dispirited. I told Johnny that I hadn't watched a single episode of *21 Jump Street* and couldn't really comment on its quality. "That's good," he answered. "I don't want to talk about the fucking show anyway."

We spoke at length about the making of *Platoon* and about "wild man" Oliver Stone. Depp spoke enthusiastically about his desire to work with Stone again — "provided I ever get off this fucking show." Stone had mentioned a movie that he wanted to make about the life of Jim Morrison, the front man for the Doors, and Johnny badly wanted to be a part of the project.

As lunch continued, we spoke about his music. A year earlier, he'd joined a band called the Rock City Angels, hoping to play gigs with them between acting jobs, but mere weeks later he'd joined the *21 Jump Street* cast. He'd had to give up the band. Then I asked him what he'd do if the show went all five seasons. "Oh, it'll never get to that," he answered. "I won't make it that long, man." He still wanted to get back to his first love, music.

When the assistant director called him back to the set, he stood and politely shook my hand. He lit a cigarette and smiled. When I told him I was going to hang around and watch the shoot for a while, he replied, "Don't bother, man, you've got to have something better to do." As a matter of fact, I didn't, so I watched the shoot and how Johnny worked. He applied himself fully, but he certainly didn't make it easy. He questioned every line and made sure his views on the story line were known, including how he thought it could be improved.

Depp now found himself, quite suddenly, a huge star on the small screen. When he was interviewed by *TV Guide* profiler Elaine Warren, she described him like this: "Depp has acquired a taste for $80-a-shot cognac and is a fan magazine star, routinely mobbed by teenage girls. . . . How cool is Johnny Depp? He's so cool that he orders a $75 bottle of wine without blinking as he sits down and says 'hi' at his favorite Vancouver Italian restaurant."

In the third episode of the second season, called "Besieged," Depp and Jenco have a few long scenes together, during which their years of friendship show through clearly. But it was now clear that Depp was just going through the motions and having as much fun as he could with a difficult situation. At this point, he was still showing up on time and working professionally, but he'd lost whatever interest he'd had in the show.

"Honor Bound," which aired on 8 November 1987, is interesting in that it took another stab at a tough issue and allowed Depp some space to do some real acting. The story line concerns a military academy where some of the cadets are thought to be involved in hate crimes, specifically the killing of homosexuals. Depp and costar Peter DeLuise — son of funny man Dom DeLuise and Johnny's closest ally on the show — go undercover at the academy to investigate. DeLuise plays an effeminate gay cadet, while Hanson plays a redneck cadet with a cocky attitude and a southern accent.

Two shows later, Depp's character was given a girlfriend, played by Dorothy Parke. The producers were trying everything they could to keep the Hanson character vital and compelling. They were also trying to keep Depp interested in the show.

The following episode, called "Christmas in Saigon," is also intriguing in that it involves the Asian Jump Street cop Ioki and his escape from Saigon. What gives the show some depth is that much of it is based on the real-life experiences of *21 Jump Street* costar Dustin Nguyen.

Episode 12 of the second season has Depp's character thinking about leaving the force. He goes AWOL, leaving town instead of going to a special course at the police academy. Hanson starts to show a rebellious side in this episode — definitely a reflection of the sentiments of the actor playing him. The producers were now seeing real evidence that their young pinup was starting to feel seriously unhappy about the show and his role in it. It seemed to them that, the more popular the show and Depp got, the more unhappy he seemed to become. By this point in the series, Johnny was receiving 10,000 letters a week from adoring fans. All the producers could do was try to make Depp happy by giving him what they thought he needed to make his work meaningful.

Episode 13 of the second season was written by the show's creator, Patrick Hasburgh. Called "A Big Disease with a Little Name," it deals with a hard-hitting subject, something Depp was always requesting. In it, Hanson is assigned to protect a student with AIDS who is being harassed at school.

Strangely, just as Depp was growing more and more combative, he delivered what is probably his best performance of the whole experience. It is in the episode called "I'm Okay — You Need Work," which aired on 21 February 1988. A kid Hanson arrests on drug charges ends up in a privately run rehab clinic; after learning of charges of patient abuse in the clinic, Hanson checks himself in to investigate and finds himself trapped inside. The show is something of a sequel to the two-part episode that kicked off the series. It contains a lot of sharp dialogue and some genuine tension; also, look for a young-looking Christina Applegate in a small role.

In the next episode, Depp's character blames himself for the death of his girlfriend, who is shot during the robbery of a variety store. The show is a typical revenge story line, but it seemed to answer fans who liked handsome Hanson better without a sexy girl-friend. It appeared that the character's relationship had clouded the fantasies of the millions of young girls who were wallpapering their rooms with Johnny Depp photos.

Episode 18 of the second season, called "Brother Hanson and the Miracle of Renner's Pond," is notable because it was the first show shot around Depp's new policy of refusing to participate in scenes in which Hanson had to do something that Johnny deemed morally reprehensible. This episode was sloppily written, with awful dialogue. Officer Hanson is sent to a small-town school where a teacher refuses to teach the theory of evolution because his son survived a near-death experience, and the teacher believes it was the hand of God that revived him. This friction in the school causes some students to start burning books in protest. Depp, a voracious reader and book lover, demanded that he have nothing to do with any scene involving an orgy of burning books.

The problem of the show's poor quality was compounded by Depp's resentment about having no control over the way his image was being hustled and hyped. At one point, FOX TV made a series of commercials plugging the show that featured images of Johnny with a deep voice intoning "Depp, Depp, Depp" over and over again. "I would have put the kibosh on it early," said Depp. "But when you are starting out and they have a product to sell, they shove you down America's throat."

It got bad enough that Depp resorted to trying to sabotage the show, or at least his part in it, so the producers would consider releasing him from his contract. "I offered to do a year of the show for free if they would just let me out of the remaining years of the contract," said Depp. "They were trying to turn me into the New Kids on the Block or Menudo. I just couldn't play that game. I would rather shrink back into everyday life than get stuck being that."

But there were positive experiences too. The show airing on 1 May 1988, called "The Best Years of Your Life," was a good example of how television can be used to convey a constructive message. This show dealt with teen suicide. Hanson and his partner arrest a young boy who then commits suicide the next day. The event plunges them into a deep, soul-searching depression. Besides being one of the

CHRIS HELCERMANAS-BENGE/SHOOTING STAR

better shows in the five-year run of *21 Jump Street*, it is memorable for an early appearance by future superstar and fellow tabloid target Brad Pitt.

The final show of the second season has a bit of silliness at the end that has to be seen to be believed. The cast, including a very bemused-looking Johnny Depp and Sal Jenco, all sing "See You in September" at the close of the show, after a story about a student suspected of blowing up toilets. The episode features a young actor named Max Perlich, who'd become one of Johnny's friends and a cast member of *The Brave*.

Depp was now begging to get off the show. He was drawing a ridiculous amount of attention, both positive and negative, and it was leading to all sorts of jealousy and back-stabbing among the cast. Newspaper gossip columns started to regularly feature items about Depp, usually about his bad behavior. Some of the stuff was warranted, but most of it wasn't. There were pieces about Depp throwing temper tantrums on the set and making outrageous demands — he responded to them by saying, "I have a couple of ideas where these stories came from. There are a couple of people who don't like the fact that I am outspoken about certain things. But as far as temper tantrums and throwing punches at producers, it is such bullshit, it is hilarious." One of the show's producers, Joan Carson, concurs. "All the fights on the set were show-related," she said. "There was little truth to the description of him turning into a prima donna."

One of the more gossipy items to appear in print involved the breakup of Johnny Depp and Sherilyn Fenn. The story said that the split was the result of Fenn's appearance in an erotic film called *Two Moon Junction*. The film did feature some racy sequences, but they were hardly what ended the relationship. Depp and Fenn were two passionate people who, because of work, spent no time at all together,

and finally they just drifted completely apart. In any case, before the ink dried on that story, Depp was being linked with another up-and-coming actress, Jennifer Grey.

One gossip column item that was true, however, was about Depp being arrested for assault after an altercation in a downtown Vancouver hotel. Depp had gone to the hotel, where he'd lived during the first season of the show, late one night to visit friends. He was prevented from going up to the guest floors of the hotel by an overzealous security guard who claimed that he couldn't roam around the halls of the guest area unless he was a guest. Depp explained that he used to live in the hotel and was just visiting friends who were expecting him. The guard told him that he knew who Depp was and didn't care. Here the story gets a bit dicey: either the security guard put his hands on Depp to physically move him out, or Depp tried to bulldoze his way past the guard. Either way, a wrestling match and a few punches followed. "That guy had a real boner for me," said Depp. "He had a wild hair up his ass, and he got real mouthy with me. I ended up spitting in his face. I shouldn't have done that, but he shouldn't have put his hands on me." The police were called, and Johnny was hauled away. After being fingerprinted and photographed for mug shots, he spent the night in jail. Charges were later dropped because there was really nothing to the case, but the incident did put Depp in the papers and label him a "hellraiser."

At the end of the second season of *21 Jump Street*, a press junket was organized in Chicago. The main cast members were to greet fans and talk to the press; FOX TV thought that taking the cast on the road to cause a ruckus and get on the local news would make the show even more successful. This gave the already gravely discontented Depp the opportunity to throw his weight around even more. Cast members Peter DeLuise, Holly Robinson, Dustin Nguyen, and Steven Williams all agreed to do the tour and were extremely cooperative.

But Depp — the cast member teenagers most wanted to see — announced that he wasn't sure if he was interested in participating in the event.

At 9:30 AM on the day of the Chicago event, the cast members were in a government office schmoozing with the press and hanging out with Mayor Eugene Sawyer. No Depp. By 10:30, over 7,000 people had gathered in Daley Plaza. It was still not known if Depp would attend the event; the best the organizers had been able to get out of him was, "I don't know if I'll be there or not."

Then there was a flurry of activity and crackling voices over the walkie-talkies. The elevator doors opened, and out walked Johnny Depp, his arm around his new girlfriend, Jennifer Grey. He was dressed in a ripped white T-shirt, a tattered red plaid shirt, and a leather jacket. It seems that he'd decided the night before that going to Chicago to do this thing "might be fun," so he and Jennifer had jumped on the last available flight out of Vancouver.

But his indecision was not as casual as his behavior suggests. He saw a chance to fuck with the producers. He wanted to tell them that they'd never be able to comfortably count on him.

The crowd in Daley Plaza was getting frenzied. A local FOX TV personality named Robin Brantley was hosting the event, and she was doing her best to incite a teenage-hormone riot. Legions of girls were screaming "Johnny! Johnny! Johnny!" in a constant chant. Brantley was egging them on by yelling back "Johnny who?"

Finally, the cast of *21 Jump Street* took the stage and were thanked for attending the Windy City's annual Be Good, Go to School, Say No to Drugs Youth Festival. Depp sheepishly stepped up to the microphone. The applause and screaming were deafening. "Hello, I'm Johnny Depp." More screaming. "My basic message is simple. Protect your mind. Protect your heart. And take care of yourself." His hands scratched through his hair. He waved to the crowd and backed away from the microphone. More screaming.

To his credit, Depp mostly toed the line while in Chicago. He'd pulled his little mind-fuck on the producers, but once he'd committed himself to the event he was there. When asked by a reporter about his feelings toward his audience, he replied, "I really do appreciate the audience. Our show deals with important themes like drugs, suicide, life, and death. The most important thing is to tell the kids to stay away from drugs. Drugs are the worst. I just tell people to stay far away from them. I would also like to tell people to stay in school. That's equally important."

Compare this to what he told *Playboy* contributing editor Kevin Cook in the January 1996 issue of the magazine. "Sure it was [a fascist idea]. Cops in schools? I mean, bad things happen in schools but this show was even worse than having cops in schools. It was preachy, pointing the finger. And it was hypocritical because the people running that show, the very highest of the higher-ups, were getting high. They were getting loaded. And then to say, 'Now kiddies, don't do this,' was horseshit. I was miserable living that lie for three years. Mortified. I was getting loaded too. Am I really the one to say 'don't get high?'"

There were more screaming crowds awaiting the cast later that day. The actors were to assemble by a Marshall Field's department store on State Street for a 2 PM autograph session. The event was being held in an open space that links the store with a subway station; by noon, 5,000 girls had mobbed the scene, causing disruptions in subway service. The crowd spilled up and onto the street above, completely blocking the subway entrance. While all this was going on, Depp was in another part of the city having lunch with Grey. He missed the first 45 minutes of the autograph session, but when he finally did arrive he enjoyed the crowd and complied with every request for photographs and autographs. When it was time to leave, a FOX TV reporter tried to corner him for an impromptu interview. When she pointed her microphone in his direction, he leaned over and bit the end of it, saying, "I don't think this thing is working." Then he strolled off with Grey.

The idea that this event would be fun wore thin very quickly. Depp backed out of a scheduled lunch with some lucky fans who'd won a lunch date with the *21 Jump Street* cast. And he was nowhere to be seen during a press conference for the national press.

Another of the show's producers, Bill Nuss, tried to spin the whole thing by saying, "You have to understand what it's like for thousands of people to be screaming your name. Think about it for a minute. I think it scares him sometimes. But I think he senses a responsibility to people. He doesn't want to appear irresponsible."

Depp's unhappiness wasn't a secret. Nuss did his best to hide it and to make Depp's role in the development of the show seem to be greater than it was, telling reporters, "Johnny had a lot to do with the suicide episode we ran last year." Depp then told a reporter, "I just want to make it very clear that I'm not out there saving someone's life just because I'm Johnny Depp. That's not how it goes in real life. In real life I won't be solving the problems of the world. People forget that this is a show and I am just an actor. So instead of me being the cure I wanted people to learn how to handle their own problems."

The third season of *21 Jump Street* began on 6 November 1988. The season opener was called "Fun with Animals" and introduced a character named Booker, played by Richard Grieco. The new officer is assigned as Hanson's partner, and the two don't get along. The addition of Booker was a clear indication that the producers had begun to accept that Depp's days on the show were numbered and that they could no longer force Johnny to stick with it. As his behavior became more unpredictable and his complaints about the scripts grew, they started to think that keeping him on board was no longer worthwhile.

In a number of third-season episodes, many of Hanson's lines were shuffled off to other characters or written out completely. When Depp did appear, he pretty much phoned in the performance. He refused to learn his lines anymore; he would simply give them a once-over before shooting and then deliver them as ineffectively as possible. The fourth episode of that season, called "Coach of the Year," contains one of the most lackluster performances of Depp's entire acting career. By show number seven, called "Dragon and the Angel," it is obvious that Depp was no longer interested in expending even minimal effort. In this show, he simply clowns around on screen with his friend Peter DeLuise — Depp often says that if it weren't for his friendship with DeLuise he would have gone insane. The following episode, "Blu Flu," also features Depp giving a walk-through performance, but it is hardly noticeable because he has almost nothing to do.

But then, just when Depp was about to be written off as a spoiled brat who was trying to sabotage the show, he surprised everyone.

In the ninth show of that season ("Swallowed Alive," which aired on 5 February 1989), Depp showed up to work. The story line was good, and the quality of the writing was well above what it had been. In it, Officer Hanson becomes an inmate in a juvenile detention center to investigate the murder of one of the inmates. This is one of the best shows of the whole series and one of Depp's strongest performances.

In the 11th show of the season, Depp is again given some meaty dialogue and some interesting scenes involving a journalist friend who screws Hanson around, causing him to be suspended from the force. This episode features Depp cutting loose with some of the only passionate outbursts he ever filmed for the series.

Things then took a turn for the worse.

By show number 17, Depp was refusing to do nearly everything he was told, so his part was whittled down almost to a cameo appearance. This episode, called "Blinded by the Thousand Points of Light," is about the investigation of a predator who has been targeting homeless teens. Up-and-coming actress Bridget Fonda does some nice work in this show, but Depp is only in it for about four minutes and only in scenes that have no bearing on the story.

The path that *21 Jump Street* would take was written all over the next episode. Richard Grieco was being primed as the focal point of the series in this episode about dealing with street gangs. It includes a hilarious sequence that features Officer Hanson flatly refusing to get a tattoo.

As the fourth season debuted, it did so without Grieco — he'd graduated to his own show, called *Booker*, based on his *21 Jump Street* character. The producers decided to try shifting the focus of the show back to the reluctant Depp. For the show leading up to Halloween 1989 ("Old Haunts in a New Age"), publicity posters showed a large photo of Johnny Depp with a small Peter DeLuise over his right shoulder. The caption read "Spend Halloween on the Street," and there were photos of the two actors in Halloween costumes. DeLuise was Dracula, and Depp was done up as a Mohawk-haired Travis Bickle from *Taxi Driver*.

Show eight of the fourth season focuses on a tough subject, which is handled, for the most part, in a responsible fashion. A female officer is raped and turns to Hanson for comfort. Depp walks through the show but still manages to be fairly effective.

Show 11 deals with child pornography and abuse. Depp refused to portray someone who enjoys indulging in pornography.

In episode 15, the fact that Depp wanted out was worked in as a joke. "Back from the Future" involves a cop in the future who is trying to reconfigure the Jump Street program. He interviews the long-retired members of the original squad — Hanson, however, isn't one of them. He's still on the force, working out of the same office all these years later. This in-joke episode was directed by Peter DeLuise.

Shows 18 and 19 were shot in Florida and amounted to not much more than a paid vacation for Depp and his old Florida pal Sal Jenco. The plot has Hanson and Penhall (DeLuise) following a bomber to Florida on spring break. It ends up with the two traveling to El Salvador to look for Penhall's wife, only to discover that she was killed during the civil strife there. The show features a terrific Mexican actress named Elpidia Carrillo, who'd also end up being cast by Depp in his directorial debut.

The last bit of interesting work Depp did on *21 Jump Street* was in an episode called "The Senator," in which each cast member tells a similar story in a *Rashomon*-like way, but each story is presented through a different movie genre. Depp's story is a black-and-white silent film and is very interesting to watch.

By this time, the writing was on the wall — Depp wouldn't be coming back to *21 Jump Street.* The producers decided to let him go without a fuss; if he was only going to be half there, he might as well not be there at all. On 16 July 1990, Officer Tom Hanson made his final appearance on *21 Jump Street* in an episode that contains nothing else of note.

Depp now had to make some decisions. He was at last free to do work that meant something to him, but he first had to find that work. He was determined to avoid playing any of the myriad Hanson-like characters he was being offered. He wanted to strike out in as opposite a direction as he could. And, with the help of an eccentric Baltimore-based filmmaker named John Waters, he was about to do just that.

Waters is a writer-director known for making films that the term "tasteless" was invented to describe. He was making gross-out comedies long before that subgenre officially existed. He had his own little repertory company of misfits — one of his favorite actors was an obese transvestite named Divine, who appeared in *Polyester* and *Pink Flamingos* — and he'd gained some notoriety as a cult shock-meister (although he can't be that bad since Baltimore declared 7 February 1985 "John Waters Day").

In 1988, Waters was trying to get off the ground a film that would be as close to the mainstream as he likes to go. It was called *Cry-Baby*, and it was a musical comedy homage to teen movies of the '50s. It was to be his biggest movie to date, and he'd make it with the comfort of a Universal Pictures distribution deal backing him up. This meant, for the first time in his career, that one of his movies had the potential to be seen by a lot of people the world over. The pressure was on Waters to deliver a movie that people might actually want to see — unlike some of his previous nausea-inducing films.

Since Waters wrote the script, including the lyrics for the musical numbers, and would direct the film and have a hand in producing it, casting was crucial to him. Not surprisingly, the cast he put together was an eccentric one, including notorious underage porn star Traci Lords, ex-heiress/kidnap victim/bank robber/political terrorist-turned-actress and author Patty Hearst, future talk show host Ricki Lake, and musician Iggy Pop. "More than anything," said Waters, "I need actors who can take a step back and laugh at themselves good-naturedly."

As for the lead role, Waters admitted he had no idea which actor he wanted as the leather-jacketed, tattooed, juvenile delinquent who has a distinctly sensitive side and is often shown openly crying. This actor would also have to perform in several musical numbers that come up during the movie, much like in films such as Elvis Presley's *Jailhouse Rock.*

Waters knew what type of actor he wanted, but he was at a loss where to begin his search. "I literally went down to a newsstand and picked up every teen magazine there," he said. "I felt like some kind of pedophile. Every single one of these magazines either featured a large photo or a small photo or a star with 'See Johnny Inside' written in it. Depp was in every one of them."

At the time, Depp was hoping for exactly the kind of role Waters was trying to fill. "I was looking for a role that was the diametric opposite of the bullshit way I was being thought of." Depp was being offered a lot of characters to play, but most of them frightened him because they were only slight variations on Hanson. He was starting to worry that the *21 Jump Street* experience had screwed up his career permanently. Then he was contacted about reading *Cry-Baby.* He read it and loved it, then went out and found out a bit about John Waters and loved that too — then he set up a meeting.

"When Johnny told me how much he hated the teen-idol image," said Waters, "I told him to stick with us — we'll kill that, we'll get rid of that in a second, because we're going to make fun of your teen-idol status from first frame to last."

Apart from the creative attractions that *Cry-Baby* held for Depp, the fact that he was being offered $1 million to play the lead character sweetened the pot. He had the chance not only to make a low-budget, independent-in-feel movie but also to earn a huge salary for doing it.

But the "yes" from Depp came only after a period of consultation and consideration. As much as everything was pointing to a Depp–Waters collaboration, some in Depp's camp weren't so sure it was the right move for Johnny. Often when a young actor becomes a big star, those advising him or her tend to favor the biggest offer rather than the best offer simply because it translates into bigger commissions for them. Even some of Johnny's friends weren't sure that doing a self-parody at such a young age was the wisest move. But Depp, to his credit, was unshakable. "I've always admired people like John Waters, who has never compromised, who has been through the ringer because he has stuck to his guns," said Depp. "The easy way is boring to me."

Waters commented that he thought "it was really brave of Johnny to take a movie that was just a mockery of the images created around him. Especially since the first thing he told me when we met was that *Cry-Baby* was the strangest script he had ever read."

Cry-Baby is essentially a larger-scale retelling of the story Waters told in an earlier film called *Hairspray*. Depp plays Cry-Baby, a juvenile delinquent who runs with a bad crowd, rides a motorcycle, and is covered in tattoos. But he has a sensitive side, evident in the opening sequence when he is getting an immunization shot in his high school gymnasium — when the needle is applied, Cry-Baby sheds a tear.

Like the hero in every other teens-in-leather-jackets epic, the hero of *Cry-Baby* falls for a girl from the right side of town and tries to win her over by showing her his strengths as a person, hoping she will see beyond the tattoos and wild friends.

The movie was shot in Baltimore, the hometown of Waters and the place where he prefers to set and shoot all his films. By all accounts, the experience was a positive one for both Depp and Waters. Johnny referred to Baltimore as "the strangest place I have ever been in," but he also said, "I would become part of the John Waters repertory company in a second."

Waters already had a film in mind that he hoped to work with Depp on after *Cry-Baby*, but the project never came to fruition.

Waters had this to say about his star: "He's everything a star should be, the very opposite of a flash in the pan. Working with him was almost as exciting as it must have been working with Johnny Hallyday in France in the beginning."

Depp was often asked about his relationship with the openly gay Waters. There was some gossip at the time that had Depp accompanying Waters to gay bars and being repulsed by a gay man who asked if he could kiss Johnny on the cheek. Depp denies this completely. "I've had men come on to me," said Depp, "but I'm not one of those guys who get pissed off and go, 'Oh, Jesus Christ, I'm a straight man!'" Was Depp aware of the sexual orientation of Waters during the filming of *Cry-Baby*? "I never thought of him in such labeled terms," Depp said. "I'd notice the fact that I was working with a Swedish director much more than if someone was gay." Waters mentioned that "Johnny is the least homophobic hetero boy I have ever met. He wasn't the least bit uptight about it."

Cry-Baby didn't perform all that well in North America. It did develop something of a cult following in parts of Europe and Australia, making Depp a huge movie star in those parts of the world. Yet the film was still a success. Waters told me, "Johnny and I were both looking to do things that would take us in a different direction. I was looking to expand the size and reach of my films, and Johnny was trying to shake an image. I think we both succeeded and were allowed to proceed as we wanted to."

In the end, Waters's propensity for wacky behavior seemed to rub off on Depp. After working together, Depp decided to do something special for his director. So he had him ordained. "I sent away to the Universal Life Church and had John ordained by mail," said Depp. "He is now and forever Reverend John Waters because of me."

While Waters was editing *Cry-Baby*, another young director

called and asked if he might see some footage of Depp. He was thinking of casting Johnny in his next film but had never seen any of his work. The director was Tim Burton, and his visit to Waters would initiate another huge turning point in Depp's life.

Chapter Five

Depp and Burton, Burton and Depp: Part 1

RALPH DOMINGUEZ/
GLOBE PHOTOS

"He is him and that's all he is."

Johnny Depp on Tim Burton, from his introduction to Burton on Burton

Director Tim Burton is an eccentric filmmaker in the best sense of the term. A former animator who made early films with Pee-Wee Herman and a movie about a pieced-together dog called *Frankenweenie*, Burton, surprisingly, was offered a chance to work within the studio system and grabbed it. Warner Brothers backed his first big hit, *Beetlejuice*, starring Michael Keaton, Alec Baldwin, Geena Davis, and a very young Winona Ryder. And, based on audiences' love of that film, Warner Brothers turned to Burton to make the big-screen, live-action *Batman*. Burton had comic-book enthusiasts foaming at the mouth when he announced he was casting Michael Keaton as the Caped Crusader; Burton shrugged off the outcry, saying that he planned on taking the Batman legend in a new direction and that Keaton was perfect for what he wanted to do. He was right, and the comic-heads had to agree. The movie was dark and fabulous. Keaton was great as Batman, and Jack Nicholson chewed the scenery with every on-screen appearance as the Joker. The movie broke box-office records and has inspired three smash-hit sequels.

Given such enormous success, the studio immediately pressured Burton to develop a sequel. He wasn't averse to considering it, but he didn't want it to be the next project that he did. He was eager to make a movie based on a character that he'd been carrying around with him since his animation days — a young man named Edward who has long, sharp scissors at the ends of his arms instead of hands. The huge success of *Batman* led Burton to believe that he could get anything at all made, so he took his cherished idea to Warner Brothers, the studio where he'd made three hugely successful movies. However, "Warner Brothers didn't get it," said Burton, "which was good because I knew they really didn't want to do it. I try to work with people who want to do what I want to do."

Burton turned to a young novelist named Caroline Thompson to write the screenplay with him. He'd met her through an agent while he was in preproduction on *Beetlejuice*; now he asked Thompson if she'd be interested in fleshing out a screenplay based on ideas and sketches he had about a young man with scissors for hands. "I had read Caroline's novel called *First Born*, which was about an abortion that came back to life," said Burton. "It was good. It had sociological things that were thematic, but it also had a fantastical element to it, which was nice. That combination was close to the feeling I wanted for *Edward Scissorhands*."

Thompson was enthusiastic about the idea, even though Burton, as he readily admits, isn't the most communicative of people, especially when his ideas are based on feelings. "I was really lucky to meet Caroline," said Burton. "She was very in tune with my ideas, which was good because these had been inside me a long time — it was symbolic and not something I wanted to pick apart and analyze. I needed someone who understood what the basic thing was about, so there wouldn't be a lot of grade-school psychology going on in terms of discussing the project. I could be fairly cryptic, and it still came across to her." Burton paid Thompson a small fee to write the screenplay before there was anyone else attached to the project.

Undeterred by Warner Brothers' lack of interest, Burton took Thompson's screenplay and shopped it around town. He proceeded with confidence — this was the first project he would shepherd through the process completely on his own, and he believed in it entirely. He packaged up the screenplay and sent it out to the studios, saying that this was the movie he wanted to make. He told prospective producers that they had exactly two weeks to respond to the project either way, after which time the script would be taken off the table. "It was a route that I was determined to take," said Burton. "That way, no one could force changes on me."

The script found favor with Joe Roth, who was running Twentieth Century Fox at the time. He found the idea too interesting to pass up and decided that he might want to develop a long-term relationship with Burton. Roth gave him the green light to make *Edward Scissorhands* provided the costs be kept in check.

Once the deal was struck at Twentieth Century Fox, it was time to cast the film. The studio had a wish list of actors whom it thought would ensure box-office returns — "The studios are always saying, 'Here is a list of five people who are box office,' and three of them are Tom Cruise," said Burton. Michael Jackson and Tom Hanks were briefly considered, and Burton met with Cruise about playing Edward. Of Cruise, Burton said, "He certainly wasn't my ideal, but I wanted to talk to him. He was interesting, but I think things worked out for the best. A lot of questions came up — I don't really remember the specifics — but at the end of the meeting I did feel like [saying], and probably even said this, to him: "It's nice to have a lot of questions about the character, but you either want to do it or you don't.'"

One of the major concerns Cruise allegedly had was about the scars that cover Edward's face, the result of years of Edward inadvertently nicking himself. The prosthetic scars would take hours to apply each morning, and Cruise was worried, not out of vanity, as was reported, but simply because they'd be distracting. It was also reported in the *Los Angeles Times* that the character's "lack of virility" was one of his reasons for deciding against doing the movie.

Johnny Depp's agent had a copy of the screenplay, and she let Depp read it. He was blown away by the story, the character, and the imagination behind it all. He was dying to meet with Burton and to throw his name into the mix. A meeting was set up, but Burton was only doing it as a courtesy and because he was forced to start widening his net. All he'd heard of Depp was the odd mention of him as a teen idol.

That first meeting between Depp and Burton lacked drama and barely hinted at the long and symbiotic relationship the two would develop. It was a simple get-together over coffee in the lounge of the Bel Age Hotel between them and producer Denise Di Novi. Depp was very nervous — this movie was something he really wanted to do. "I realized that it was something that was only going to come around once," said Depp. "I knew that I would never see this opportunity again. I felt so attached to the character and the story; then the reality set in. I was TV boy. No director in his right mind would hire me to play this character. I had done no work otherwise to show that I could handle this kind of role." Depp had prepared by watching everything Burton had done, which made him even more anxious to be a part of the project.

Both showed up at the meeting looking disheveled, and then

both talked in half-sentences and used a lot of word association. After a cordial conversation, they parted with a handshake. Depp was fired up; he felt an immediate connection with Burton. Burton was oddly impressed with Depp as well. But, as Johnny recalled, "My chances were slim at best. Better-known people than me were not only being considered for the role but were battling, kicking, and screaming for it."

Then Burton visited John Waters's editing suite to see how Depp looked in action as *Cry-Baby* was being cut together. Burton went in liking the Depp he'd met but still unsure that he could pull off the movie he had in mind. After spending a couple of hours looking at the footage, Burton was satisfied that he'd found his Edward.

A few days later, Depp received a phone call from Burton — "You are Edward Scissorhands" was the entirety of the conversation. Burton was happy about his choice and, looking back, said, "I'm glad Johnny did it. I can't really think of anyone else who would have done it for me that way."

Because Burton hadn't seen Depp's work or really heard of Johnny, he started asking around before their meeting — what he found made his choice even clearer. "In America at the time, Johnny was very well known as a teen idol, and he was perceived as difficult and aloof," said Burton. "All sorts of things are written about him in the press that are simply not true. I mean, in person he is very funny, a warm guy. He's a normal guy — at least in my interpretation of what is normal. But he is described as being dark and difficult and weird, and he is judged by his looks. That is thematically what *Edward Scissorhands* is about, so he could really relate to these things in a way that I think is unique to him."

Burton was also excited about being able to include one of his heroes, aging actor and chef Vincent Price, in the *Edward Scissorhands* cast. Burton had made an animated film about Price and was working on a documentary of him. Depp was also immediately taken with this genteel old man who carried himself with such dignity. And when Price saw all the attention Depp was getting, he sat the young actor down to discuss the ups and downs of success in Hollywood. Price gave him a piece of advice: "Buy art." Depp has done so — probably not the kind of art Price had in mind, but he has heeded his wisdom.

In fact, one of the first pieces of art Depp acquired caused him a few more public-relations headaches. He bought a ghoulish-looking clown's face painted by none other than the notorious John Wayne Gacy while he was awaiting execution for the sexual torture and murder of 33 young men. Depp immediately got rid of the painting when he discovered that the proceeds of the sale had not gone to the families of the victims, as he'd been led to believe. Depp was asked about the incident by a *Rolling Stone* contributor in 1991: "The paintings are really weird and scary and great," Depp answered, "but I didn't want to contribute to anything as evil as that." Subsequently, he has invested in more recognizable artworks, including pieces by Jean-Michel Basquiat, which prompted Depp to contribute the foreword to a biography of the modern artist.

Johnny Depp's personal life was about to take another wild twist — a new young woman was about to enter his life. His engagement to Jennifer Grey had ended peacefully after eight months. Grey had been looking for a stable relationship, and Depp had started to spin off out of control. They'd decided to go their separate ways.

Johnny then dated around a bit. On a fairly unbelievable note, an "actress" named Tally Chanel claims that she was engaged to Depp for a while. When she met him, she says, she was working as a hostess at the premiere for *Die Hard 2*, and she opened the door of Depp's limo when it arrived. "Our eyes locked, and he asked me to

marry him" is how her story goes. She told tabloids that they'd had a relationship that lasted for a year and consisted of quiet nights at his home ordering Chinese food.

Once again, Depp's private life was about to become tabloid fodder.

Depp and Burton hung around together during the planning of *Edward Scissorhands*. One night, Burton suggested that they go to the premiere of a movie called *Great Balls of Fire!*, a film biography of Jerry Lee Lewis starring Dennis Quaid and *Beetlejuice* star Winona Ryder. In the lobby of the theater, Ryder and Depp noticed one another. Ryder recalled that initial moment: "I was getting a Coke. It was the classic glance, like the zoom stuff in *West Side Story*, and everything gets foggy. It wasn't a long moment, but it was suspended."

They didn't formally meet that night. Their first meeting came a few weeks later when a friend dragged Winona to Depp's suite at the Chateau Marmont hotel on Sunset Boulevard. Ryder was a bit hesitant because of what she'd read and heard about Depp. "I thought maybe he would be a jerk," she said. "I didn't know. But he turned out to be really, really shy." That first meeting wasn't much more than a couple of drinks and some conversation.

It was another few weeks before they went on their first official date, at a party at the Hollywood Hills home of LSD guru Timothy Leary. According to Depp, "When I met Winona, we fell in love. It was absolutely like nothing before — ever. We just slid into it. We started hanging out and just continued to hang out."

Ryder had never had a "boyfriend" before. She'd gone out with actor Robert Sean Leonard (*Dead Poets Society*, *The Last Days of Disco*, *Driven*), but their relationship was more platonic. When Ryder met Depp, she was 17 and he was 26. Early on, they found that they had several quirky things in common that endeared them to one another: a fondness for J.D. Salinger's *Catcher in the Rye*, the

Johnny and Winona – Hollywood couple
DAN GOLDEN/SHOOTING STAR

writings of Jack Kerouac, and Ennio Morricone's soundtrack from the film *The Mission* among them.

Winona Ryder was born Winona Horowitz on 29 October 1971 in Winona, Minnesota. Shortly thereafter, her parents moved to California, where they became seriously committed hippies. In fact, Winona's godfather was none other than the late Timothy Leary. Her father, Michael, knew Leary and the Beat poet Allen Ginsberg — another reason Johnny found her absolutely cool — from his work as a rare-book dealer and archivist.

Winona began her acting career at 12. While performing on stage at a community playhouse, she was spotted by famed casting agent Deborah Lucchesi, who asked her if she'd do a screen test for a film she was casting called *Desert Bloom*. Winona did the test but did not get the role in the film — it went to Annabeth Gish — but it did lead to her being cast in her first film, *Lucas*.

During the shoot for *Lucas*, the producers asked Winona how she wished to be written up in the credits. Winona and her parents first thought of the name Winona Huxley but quickly ruled it out. She then assumed the last name Ryder "because my dad was probably listening to a song by Mitch Ryder at the time."

After making her debut in *Lucas* in 1986, Ryder quickly became one of the kid actors to watch. She earned excellent notices in films such as *Heathers* and *Beetlejuice*, then won the hotly competed role opposite Dennis Quaid's Jerry Lee Lewis in *Great Balls of Fire!*.

Johnny and Winona quickly fell in love. When Depp flew to Boston in October 1989 to spend time with Winona, who was shooting *Mermaids* there, costar Cher watched the pair. She says she knew early on that this was a hot romance — it was all Winona would talk about when they were not exchanging lines. Cher also remembers that Winona was wary of getting mixed up in Johnny's "scene," a life that included screaming, adoring teenage girls and fan clubs.

In January 1990, they were crowned the new "it couple" in Hollywood in a strange ceremony in Las Vegas. Depp and Ryder were both in Las Vegas to attend the annual ShoWest convention, a splashy unveiling of new Hollywood products to distributors and theater owners that includes a parade of stars and awards. Depp was named "Male Star of the Future," and, conveniently, Ryder was named "Female Star of the Future." A month later, on 26 February 1990, the *Los Angeles Times* reported that Depp, 27, and Ryder, 18, were officially engaged.

Depp was fairly open to the press about his relationship with Ryder, but he'd come to bitterly regret his candor. He said early in their relationship that, despite having gone through one divorce and two failed engagements already, he had every intention of getting engaged to Ryder as soon as possible. Depp then suffered the embarrassment of having a company print bumper stickers that read "Honk if you haven't been engaged to Johnny Depp!" He took comfort in the fact that Ryder was a magazine cover girl and the topic of gossip column items as well. "Winona is a big help to me," he said at the time. "She knows exactly what I am going through, because she is going through the same thing."

They were so smitten with one another that they ended up in a Los Angeles tattoo parlor one day. They decided to immortalize their love by each getting a tattoo of the other's name. At the last minute, though, Winona decided against it; Depp had "Winona Forever" burned into his arm. "I'd never seen anyone get a tattoo before," said Ryder. "I was pretty squeamish about it." After the fact, Depp recalled, "She kept taking the bandage off and looking at it."

Ryder reciprocated with a nice gesture of her own. She bought Depp a star — a real star in the sky. She bought it so she could officially name it after him. The star is located in a northern constellation called Cepheus and can only be seen with a fairly powerful telescope.

Depp and Ryder often spent their weekends at her parents' home in Petaluma, California. "My parents loved him a lot," said Ryder. Depp was pleased at their affection. "It could have been very easy for them not to like me; other people might have just seen the tattoos," he remarked.

Around this time, director Francis Ford Coppola was about to start production on the long-awaited third installment of his epic. *The Godfather: Part III* had already gone through a difficult gestation. The original screenplay began with the 70th-birthday celebration of Corleone consigliere Tom Hagen (Robert Duvall), but negotiations with Duvall broke down when Paramount Pictures balked at giving him fee parity with Al Pacino and Diane Keaton. Duvall resolutely decided, later to his regret, that he wouldn't be a part of the third installment of the series. The script had to be completely rewritten, and by the time shooting began the script was about the final days of the Corleone empire, with side plots involving Vatican corruption and the illicit relationship between Sonny Corleone's illegitimate son Vincent Mancini (played by Andy Garcia) and Michael Corleone's daughter Mary. Coppola wanted Ryder to play Mary. Winona was naturally ecstatic about being in a film of such profile and lineage, and she was eager to work with a director of Coppola's stature.

But Ryder had been working nonstop for a long time, and she was starting to wear down. She had made *Great Balls of Fire!, Welcome Home, Roxy Carmichael,* and *Mermaids* with virtually no time off between them. She was now about to start her fourth film in a row, and it promised to have another long, physically draining shooting schedule.

Ryder reported to Rome to begin work on *The Godfather: Part III* and fell ill almost immediately upon checking in to her hotel. Doctors were quickly summoned to her suite. They determined that she was suffering from exhaustion exacerbated by a severe upper respiratory infection. Depp dutifully dropped everything and flew to Rome to be with her.

Further examination showed that Ryder would need a lot more time to recover than the schedule for the film's production would allow. The decision was made to replace her. Coppola had gone down this road before while making *Apocalypse Now;* the original star, Harvey Keitel, wasn't interpreting the role in a way that Coppola found acceptable, so Keitel was replaced by Martin Sheen after several weeks of expensive location shooting. Coppola then had to face the possibility of replacing Sheen when the actor suffered a massive heart attack while on location in the Philippines. The decision to replace Ryder was disheartening to all involved, but it was made swiftly for the good of the production.

Coppola then made the bewildering decision to cast his young daughter, Sofia Coppola, as Mary. Sofia was a neophyte actor and was completely overwhelmed by the task. She has since gone on to become a pretty good writer-director herself with a promising 1999 debut, *The Virgin Suicides*, but on the set of *The Godfather: Part III* she suffered because of the difficult position she'd been placed in.

As if things weren't bad enough, rumors began to circulate in the entertainment press that Depp was involved in Ryder's decision to "back out" of *The Godfather: Part III*. Depp was about to start shooting *Edward Scissorhands*, and he wanted Ryder to costar with him. A theory was advanced that the reported illness was, if not completely invented, then certainly embellished for the sake of avoiding what might have been a huge breech-of-contract lawsuit against Ryder. Nothing could have been further from the truth, but it made for interesting "news" on *Entertainment Tonight*. Further supporting the real story, it was clear that Coppola held no ill will toward the young actress when he eagerly cast her in *Bram Stoker's Dracula* soon after. Rather than being bitter about the press reaction to her illness, Ryder was bewildered: "I never could figure out why no one would believe the truth. The stuff about Johnny coming all the way to Rome just to have me pack up and leave with him was just stupid."

This incident is another example of the suspicious way we view public people — anything they do is naturally assumed to be more nefarious than it first seems. It's hard to fathom how difficult it would be to endure this scrutiny, to have every detail — true or imagined — of your private life written up in the newspapers. "I remember us desperately hating being hounded all the time," said

Ryder. "It was horrible, and it certainly took a toll on our relationship. Every day we heard or read that we were breaking up or that we were cheating on each other, but we weren't. It was like mosquitoes constantly buzzing around us."

The fact that Ryder ended up being cast in *Edward Scissorhands* had more to do with Burton than Depp. Burton had worked successfully with Ryder in the past and knew she was more than good enough for the role. "I like her very much," said Burton. "She is one of my favorites. Also, she responds to this kind of dark material, and I thought the idea of her, as a cheerleader, wearing a blonde wig, was very funny. I think she might say that it's probably the most difficult thing that she has ever done because she did not relate to her character."

Of Winona and Johnny's romance, Burton added, "I don't think their relationship affected the movie in a negative way. Perhaps it might have if it was a different kind of movie, something that was tapping more into the positive and negative sides of their relationship. But this was such a fantasy . . . they were really professional and didn't bring any weird stuff to the set."

Edward Scissorhands tells the story of a young man who was created by a lonely old inventor (Vincent Price) in the laboratory of a huge castle on a hill overlooking a pastel-hued suburb. When the inventor dies suddenly, he leaves his creation, Edward, unfinished — he has scissors for hands. Edward lives alone in the castle until a local Avon lady (Dianne Wiest) finds him and takes him home to care for him. Adventure ensues as Edward's newfound family tries to introduce him to society. Edward, of course, becomes a curiosity as he struggles to fit in, discovering along the way the joy and pain of love and encountering human duplicity.

Edward Scissorhands was shot in a Florida setting that didn't have to be changed much. Members of the small community chosen allowed the film company to repaint their houses in pastel colors and embraced Hollywood's visit by making the location shooting an event to plan picnics around.

Depp was known for his hard work on the set. His costume — he always wore a black leather bodysuit and his scissorhands rig — was extremely uncomfortable in the Florida heat, which often climbed above 100°F. He dramatically curbed his coffee intake because he knew that going to the bathroom would be time consuming and uncomfortable. He even learned how to gingerly hold a cigarette between his scissors. "I just had to deal with it" is how Depp described the situation.

One particularly amusing thing happened during the shooting that played on one of Depp's childhood fears. Johnny had grown up with an irrational fear of singer and TV personality John Davidson — "I think it had something to do with how perfect his hair was," he explained. Burton perversely sought out Davidson and cast him in the small role of a TV talk show host who interviews Edward. Another of Depp's weird recurring dreams has Johnny stuck on Gilligan's Island with the Skipper furiously chasing him around; Burton, however, couldn't work that one into the film.

Edward Scissorhands was well received, taking in $56 million at the domestic box office, and it garnered positive reviews almost across the board. Depp was singled out in some of the reviews, and he earned a Golden Globe nomination for Best Performance by an Actor in a Motion Picture: Comedy/Musical.

Depp had this to say about his character: "He's the character that I deeply understood. Still now, I miss Edward. I can remember the last time in makeup, I really had the feeling that I was leaving somebody — somebody who was very close to me." And, about his first venture with Burton, Depp said, "We have a sort of understanding of language. It took maybe three-quarters of the way through *Edward*

Scissorhands for me to get it. It's kind of . . . Tim and I stutter a lot when we work together, and there is a lot of maniacal gesturing."

What is most impressive about Depp's performance as Edward is the beautifully projected poignancy of innocence. Depp's future *Fear and Loathing in Las Vegas* director Terry Gilliam said, "I saw *Edward Scissorhands*, and [Depp] first appears with a terrible-fright wig on, and he's got pasty makeup, and you think, 'Oh, this is a joke. This is never going to work.' And within 10, 15 minutes I totally believed the character. Now that's an extraordinary talent."

Standout performances are also turned in by Dianne Wiest, veteran character actor Alan Arkin, and Winona Ryder. What kept the film from being more broadly accepted was probably Burton's odd blend of the nice and the pastel with the dark and the weird.

What *Edward Scissorhands* did for Depp was give his career some legs. He was now considered an actor to watch. He'd managed, with only two features, to distance himself from his reputation as TV heartthrob. And he was about to go into a different place, both professionally and personally.

Chapter Six

The Low Road

"If the reader prefers, this book may be regarded as fiction. But there is always the chance that such a book of fiction may throw some light on what has been written as fact."

Ernest Hemingway
A Moveable Feast

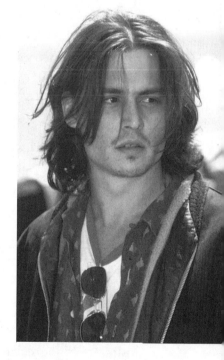

S. FINN/GLOBE PHOTOS

As the '90s gathered steam, Johnny Depp stayed true to his word that he would not do anything that didn't truly fascinate him. He'd be offered some of the biggest films made in Hollywood — films that turned the actors who accepted the roles into huge stars — but refuse them if they weren't intriguing enough.

Depp turned down a movie, for instance, about a bomb on a speeding bus; *Speed* made the middle-of-the-road Keanu Reeves into a major-league A-lister. Depp also turned down two films that eventually went to Brad Pitt and helped to consolidate his superstar status: *Legends of the Fall* and *Interview with the Vampire.* Regardless, the films that Depp did choose, especially in the early '90s, would solidify his reputation as one of the most interesting and unpredictable actors of his or any generation.

But Depp wasn't turning into a complete art snob. Evidence of this can be seen in his 1991 cameo appearance in New Line Cinema's *Freddy's Dead: The Final Nightmare.* The film even had 3-D sequences. It was directed by Depp's friend Rachel Talalay and written by a young screenwriter named Michael DeLuca, now the president of production at New Line Cinema. Depp appears only briefly as a young guy on a television screen. If you look for his name in the credits, you won't find it — he's listed as Oprah Noodlemantra.

Depp's next film would be one of the strangest and most misunderstood movies of his career. Johnny accepted a role in the film that ended up being called *Arizona Dream* because he was eager for the opportunity to work with master European filmmaker Emir Kusturica. The experience turned out to be everything he'd hoped it would be.

Kusturica began his career in his native Yugoslavia before that country was broken into pieces by war and civil strife. He worked in Serbian TV and was no stranger to controversy even in the earliest days of his career. He was interested in capturing the struggles and the history of his homeland on film, but his real dream was to make a big movie about the mythical "American dream," particularly as it is seen through the eyes of an Eastern European. "The American dream," he said, "is the dream of everyone in Western civilization. To have a car, some money, and a house. But when I was living in America for a couple of years, I found that America itself was very different. People are unhappy and a lot poorer than I expected. There is a problem, then, because by destroying the illusion of the American dream you are destroying part of your youth, a childhood spent watching movies."

This, then, is the subject matter of *Arizona Dream* — an exploration of the mythology of the American dream. To accomplish this, Kusturica assembled a cast that included some quintessentially American actors: Johnny Depp, Jerry Lewis, and Faye Dunaway.

Depp plays a soul-searching young man living in New York who is tricked into running his uncle's Cadillac dealership in Douglas, Arizona. Once there, he succumbs to the eccentric charms of an older woman, played by Dunaway. The two share a strange and sometimes moving love story.

Although Kusturica has made only a handful of films, nearly all of them have received prestigious awards at film festivals around the world. He's been a particular favorite at the Cannes Film Festival, where he has won the coveted Palme d'Or twice — in 1989 for *Time of the Gypsies* and in 1995 for the epic *Underground* — and has been named Best Director for a third film, 1984's *When Father Was Away on Business*. All three films focus on life and death in Yugoslavia.

Because his films have received such tremendous international acclaim, we might think that Hollywood would offer up one of those golden invitations to the promised land. That didn't happen. But something even better was offered to Kusturica — a teaching position at the film school of Columbia University in New York City. The opportunity to live in America was the most appealing part of the offer, and it was the reason for his immediate acceptance. He'd finally be living in the place that he'd been fascinated with for so long. The position would also give him the chance to write and develop his next movie, his long-considered film about the American dream.

The kernel of the idea for the script would ultimately come not from Kusturica himself but from one of his students. Kusturica took that kernel and expanded it into a long screenplay, first called *The Arrowtooth Waltz*, then *American Dream*, and finally *Arizona Dream*.

He showed the script to a few people he knew, and none knew what to make of it. He had no real connections to the filmmaking community in Hollywood and was on the fringe of the New York scene despite his success. Since he was much better known in Europe, he realized that Europe was where the money to finance the movie would have to come from. French producers Claude Ossad and Yves Marmen came up with the fairly sizable (at least for a European art movie) budget of $17 million. Kusturica was finally going to make his dream film.

He appealed to Depp for a number of reasons. Johnny was off the beaten path, and he committed himself only to movies that had deep personal meaning for him. Depp said, "I was thrilled at the prospect of making a film with Kusturica because when I saw *Time of the Gypsies* I was completely blown away by it — it was by far the greatest thing I had ever seen."

Often referred to as a quirky "little" film, *Arizona Dream* was actually a substantial and complicated undertaking, shot on location in Alaska, Arizona, and New York. The pressure of making what was essentially an American movie with American movie stars quickly took a toll on the sensitive European director. Adding to the pressure was the fact that much of the movie was shot at night, making the cast and crew a lot more tired and cranky than they otherwise would have been. Kusturica quickly lost control of his cast (or so he thought) and his budget (or so he was told). Already a deeply neurotic man, he succumbed to a nervous breakdown while shooting.

Kusturica laid the blame for his nervous collapse squarely at the feet of the money men, who were constantly hounding him about his budget. He left the Alaskan set and returned to his home in New York, vowing not to return to complete the film unless the pressures on him were reduced.

When the producers threatened to replace Kusturica, the ploy met a wall of resistance from the united cast, led by Depp. The cast informed the producers that they wouldn't complete the movie with anyone other than Kusturica directing it. It was Kusturica and his vision that had caused them to sign up for the project in the first place, and it was with him that they would finish the film. The problem was that he was emotionally frazzled, and no one knew if he could complete the film.

Even though the producers of the movie were French, this was being treated as an American project. Having Depp in the lead role even gave the producers hope that the film would be picked up for worldwide distribution. "I am European, not an American," explained Kusturica. "I just wasn't ready for what they were throwing at me. They didn't want imagination — they wanted a beginning, a middle, and a nice neat end where everything turns out happy."

To his credit, Kusturica did shoulder some of the blame for the chaos. "I don't know what's the matter with me," he said. "Perhaps I'm just crazy, but I have the vision, and I just have to see it through no matter what the cost. I would hate to be my producer. With both *Arizona Dream* and . . . *Underground*, I thought I was going to die at least twice. It was too much of a strain."

During this unscheduled break in the production, Depp made his first visit to Paris. He was instantly enchanted with the city. He even slept in the bed where Oscar Wilde died. "Paris is a great city," he said. "I felt an almost immediate affinity to the place, not just the fact that it was Paris, but there is an attitude and pace that suits me." Ever since he read Hemingway's *A Moveable Feast*, about days as a struggling young writer in Paris, Depp had thought of the city as a magical place.

Because Depp and Kusturica have similar sensibilities, they quickly reestablished their bond when shooting continued. Depp is always eager to learn and is like a sponge when it comes to working with talented directors or actors. Kusturica's influence is clearly evident in

Depp's *The Brave*. Kusturica uses expression and movement in place of dialogue in his films, so it's very important to him that his actors be good enough to pull off performances that have few words. *The Brave* has a similar style.

Fellow *Arizona Dream* cast member Vincent Gallo could barely contain his envy when talking about making this film with Depp. "At the time, Johnny was completely reinventing himself," Gallo said. "He was trying to get away from the TV star image that he hated so much. He was dating Winona. They were buying thrift shop clothes. He was tattooed and earringed — I hated him." Gallo also talked about the close relationship that quickly developed between Depp and his director: "Johnny has this need to be heavily involved with the director. It is almost a love affair. Emir and Johnny carried around Dostoevsky and Kerouac books and wore black from head to toe. They had never worn black in their lives. They kept everyone in the cast and crew awake all night because they were blasting music and getting drunk."

To be fair to the obviously envious Vincent Gallo, at least one other cast member — namely, Oscar winner Faye Dunaway — also had some problems with how much time Kusturica spent with Depp. But in her autobiography, she praises *Arizona Dream* as "an innovative and quirky film. Emir has woven into the film surrealistic elements that are not unlike the magical realism envisioned by writers like Gabriel García Marquez, where neither the story nor the characters are what they seem. It is unfortunate that the studio [Warner Brothers] failed to see what a wonderful director Emir is and what a beautiful film *Arizona Dream* is."

"Quirky" seems to be the catchword when describing *Arizona Dream* — it also applies to the reception of the film. Kusturica's cut was released in Paris in 1994, long after it was shot; it was instantly hailed as a work of genius and became a smash hit in the city, playing for weeks on end to full houses. But Warner Brothers didn't like the film because it didn't fall into any describable category. The studio was sure that in North America the movie would be savaged by critics and ignored by audiences if released as it was. So the studio brought in its own editors to hack up the footage and reshape it into something that could salvage a bit of revenue. But the movie never got a theatrical release in North America — Warner Brothers decided that it would be more economical to release it directly into the video market.

Despite the difficulties involved in making *Arizona Dream*, Depp and Kusturica immediately started talking about making another film together. Kusturica suggested a modern-day retelling of Dostoevsky's *Crime and Punishment* set in New York City. A script was written, and Italian-based financiers were in place. Then, as often happens in independent moviemaking, the Italian money evaporated, and the project died. Strangely enough, another film called *Crime and Punishment in New York* was released on video by MGM in early 2001, but Kusturica had nothing to do with this project.

After his trying but rewarding experience in *Arizona Dream*, Depp opted for yet another off-center character. *Benny & Joon* was another troubled project, but Depp badly wanted to be a part of it. In fact, the movie was so plagued by problems that it barely got made at all. It was only through the perseverance of the young Hollywood producers that the project rose above the smoke.

The movie focuses on Benny, a lonely man who runs an auto-repair shop in Seattle with his sister, Joon, a young woman with complicated emotional and mental problems. Benny's loyalty to his sister is unwavering, even though it comes at the expense of his own life. An odd young man named Sam comes into their lives, and he falls hard for Joon, with whom he alone can communicate effortlessly.

Sam, played by Depp, is a clown at heart, and Benny is deeply suspicious of him, but Sam eventually wins him over with humor.

Actor Woody Harrelson was originally chosen to play Benny, and Laura Dern expressed a strong interest in playing Joon. Dern decided against the project in the end. Harrelson formally committed to the project on paper, but he dropped out at the last minute to accept what he correctly considered to be a much higher-profile project for Paramount Pictures — *Indecent Proposal,* with Demi Moore and Robert Redford. (From the "six degrees of separation" file: one of the young women whom director Adrian Lyne talked to about the role ultimately played by Moore was a French singer-actress named Vanessa Paradis — now Johnny's love and mother to his child.)

At the time that *Benny & Joon* was coming together, Depp had made only a few movies, but already he had direct control over his career, and his reputation as a movie actor was developing in a satisfactory way. He was starting to be known as an actor attracted to playing outcasts and fringe dwellers. When asked about his penchant for seeking out these subterranean characters, he responded, "I gravitate towards someone who is different, who is judged by his appearance instead of his heart, who is looked upon as a freak. I guess you could say that freaks are my heroes."

Producers Susan Arnold and Donna Roth were Hollywood veterans who were getting ready to strike out on their own and become full producers. They were looking around for a debut project that would be a terrific movie without being too expensive or complicated.

In 1989, they happened upon a screenplay called *Benny & Joon* by an unknown writer named Barry Berman. "The first time Donna and I read the screenplay," said Arnold, "we could both see that it was filled with little jewels — simultaneously funny, romantic, and poignant. Both of us felt equally passionate about the project to fight hard for it." Berman is a graduate of the Ringling Bros. and Barnum & Bailey Clown College in Venice, Florida, and had spent several years crisscrossing the country in oversized shoes and a big red nose. He'd also read everything he could get his hands on about Charlie Chaplin and Buster Keaton and committed their screen performances to memory. After quitting the circus, he teamed up with Lesley McNeil; they decided to write a screenplay about dreamers and families and one strange guy in the middle who is a real-life incarnation of Buster Keaton.

Arnold gravitated toward the characters in *Benny & Joon* in a more personal way. She'd worked for several years with the Immigration Workshop, a California-based arts program that works with underprivileged and disenfranchised people and psychiatric patients. "My experiences with the workshop certainly piqued my interest to make a movie about someone who has had a bit harder time going through life than most of us," she said.

The novice producers sought out a director who'd connect with the material on the same level that they did. From early on, they talked to Canadian-born Jeremiah S. Chechik, who'd directed several award-winning TV commercials and the well-received comedy sequel *National Lampoon's Christmas Vacation*. It was a good match. "Jeremiah passionately loved the script, and more importantly he loved the characters," said Donna Roth. "Not only could he see the heart of the story, but he understood the humorous side as well."

"In the most simple way, *Benny & Joon* is a romance between two oddities who fall in love," said Chechik. "The story is universal because every human heart contains that potential for both pleasure and pain. The story had a fablelike quality to it, but it was still very believable."

Chechik knew that he had to cast the movie very carefully. A recent movie he'd admired was *Edward Scissorhands*, and he wanted to talk to Depp because his performance as Edward had really moved him. "He is so emotionally expressive, doing what seems to be so little," maintained Chechik. "It was clear to me all along that he would bring a thoroughly original and exciting energy to the role of Sam." Depp and Chechik met to talk about the movie, and Depp connected with Chechik's vision immediately. He could see the possibilities of this character, who lacked a back story and a developed character arch but had an incredible ethereal quality. Chechik went away from the meeting convinced that Depp would be brilliant.

Producer Donna Roth concurred, offering an enthusiastic endorsement of the actor. "There is something magical about Johnny, there is no doubt about it," she said. "The first time we met him, it was like meeting a blind date at the front door and discovering, 'My God, he is so wonderful.'" Roth went on to say that in the end everyone involved in the project thought that Depp's performance exceeded their already high expectations by a considerable margin.

Depp had always been a fan of Charlie Chaplin and especially Buster Keaton, and he saw this role as a chance to try out some of their physical comedy. "I had such a great time getting reacquainted with Harold Lloyd and Buster Keaton and Charlie Chaplin," he said. "Comedy, especially physical comedy, is extremely demanding. I developed even greater respect for those guys as I began to try to do what they did in such a seemingly effortless way."

Once the casting controversy was over, Aidan Quinn had been cast as Benny, and Mary Stuart Masterson had won the role of Joon. Harrelson narrowly escaped a massive lawsuit due to some back-room deal-making between MGM and Paramount. When Depp was asked about the musical chairs, he said, "Laura Dern is great, and Woody Harrelson . . . well, I've never seen anything he's done, but he is probably very good. But Aidan Quinn is my idea of what a perfect man is. And Mary Stuart Masterson has a knowledge and a wisdom beyond her years. We'll be fine."

Quinn also responded to the script very strongly, saying, "I thought the material was particularly interesting because it was such a multilayered story. It's a love story, a story about a family and the difficulties they face when one of them suffers from a mental illness."

Two other actors who have since come into their own were also featured in *Benny & Joon.* Julianne Moore played a potential love interest for Benny, and Oliver Platt played one of his coworkers and friends. Moore has gone on to take over the Oscar-grabbing Clarice Starling role that Jodie Foster vacated in *Hannibal,* and Platt recently starred opposite Warren Beatty in *Bulworth.*

Depp threw himself into the role of Sam with enthusiasm and vigor. He watched silent comedy after silent comedy, studying Keaton and Lloyd and Chaplin until he knew their every move by rote. He was still unsure of himself when it came to performing the physical comedy, so he hired a mime named Dan Kamin to act as his coach and choreographer. Kamin had written a book called *Charlie Chaplin's One-Man Show* and was a consultant on Richard Attenborough's film biography of the star, *Chaplin.* Coincidentally, Attenborough had offered Depp the role of Chaplin, but Johnny had turned him down because he'd found the task overwhelming.

Kamin first taught Depp the magic touches and sleights of hand, and then they worked up to pratfalls, like those that Keaton used to do. Kamin remarked, "Keaton's subtle movements are the hardest to capture, but Johnny got it, he did a marvelous job. But it wasn't a fluke — he was really committed to it and worked really hard on everything from the smallest moves on up."

Mary Stuart Masterson threw herself into her role with equal dedication. Many of the paintings we see in Joon's house were painted by Masterson herself. She has fond memories of working with Depp even though she had a difficult time during the shoot. "The first day on *Benny & Joon*, my husband and I had just split up, and I was in the hysterical funk you get in when you're trying to pull it together," she said. "But when Johnny walked in, the energy of the room changed. There is really something amazing about him, his generosity of spirit."

Aidan Quinn is not a guy given to gushing, but he had only positive things to say about the movie. "I thought it [*Benny & Joon*] turned out pretty much the way we hoped that it would," he said. "I thought Johnny Depp's performance was terrific, still do. At the time we made the movie, he was a question mark in a lot of ways as an actor — would he go this way? would he go that way? — but you watch him in that movie, and you try to forget all that tabloid junk for a minute, and you'll see an actor who is deeply committed to being the best actor he can be."

Chechik and producers Roth and Arnold decided to shoot the movie in Spokane, Washington. The wonderful Riverfront Park was used as an outdoor location, and an abandoned warehouse was converted into a soundstage for all the interior sets.

The publicity for *Benny & Joon* was unusual. The American promotional poster featured Depp sitting on a stool with his head thrown back — and splattered with so much paint he looks like a Jackson Pollock canvas.

Depp is very good as the likable but mysterious Sam, but ultimately the movie was just too odd for large audiences to warm up to. Depp tried his best to help the film succeed, willingly giving interviews. In one, he resisted attempts to slot the movie into a category. When the interviewer referred to it as a "date movie," Depp responded with a quizzical "Date movie? I've never heard that phrase before, is it a new phenomenon?" He went on to register his main complaint about Hollywood studios, an opinion that has been refined over the years but has never changed in spirit: "People don't want to just see tits and screwing and shootings and decapitations. I think movie executives have badly underestimated the moviegoing public."

On 21 June 1993, it was announced that the engagement of Johnny Depp and Winona Ryder was officially off. As an explanation for why the two had gone their separate ways, the report stated, "They're young and they grew apart."

Ryder was combative about the breakup. Depp was heartbroken. He altered his "Winona Forever" tattoo to read "Wino Forever," and he went into a downward spiral that only intensified as the next few months brought more disturbing events.

Early in their relationship, when Ryder was asked to comment about her life with Johnny, she spat back, "I don't like discussing my relationship with Johnny with the press. It's nobody's business. How do you explain a relationship anyway? Nobody knows anything about it, nobody. Not even friends know what my relationship is like. I don't even know. You try to figure out your own feelings and interpret them for yourself, and you have these really incredible, powerful feelings — and then some writer who doesn't know the first thing about it is writing about what it's like."

Years later, long after her relationship with Depp had ended and Ryder was involved with Soul Asylum singer Dave Pirner, she was still constantly being asked about her relationship with Depp. To her credit, she has never publicly uttered an unkind word about him, although she admitted to not following his career and not going to see the movies he made directly after their breakup.

In August 1993, Johnny Depp went into business. Depp, along with Chuck E. Weiss, the subject of the Rickie Lee Jones song "Chuck E's in Love," bought a nightclub on Sunset Boulevard. (For the past several

The Viper Room
CHRISTOPHER HEARD

years, the club has been run by Depp's pal Sal Jenco.) The entrance is on a side street, Larabee, and it is fairly nondescript. It is a small club, with a capacity of 200, that is painted black with a few glimpses of dark green, and they named it the Viper Room. Since opening, however, it has been the site of a couple of newsworthy incidents, and is referred to as "the notorious Viper Room" whenever it's mentioned in the press.

What Depp envisioned when he bought the club was a cool little hangout where he and his pals could listen to Chet Baker, Frank Sinatra, and Billie Holiday. He could invite bands to play or get up on stage himself and play when he felt like it without the pressures of touring and the other things that get in the way of musicians enjoying their music. "I liked the idea of a sense of nostalgia for the

'20s," said Depp. "So when we built the Viper Room, I built it in that style — an old speakeasy with viper music. When I thought of the club, the music of Fats Waller and Cab Calloway was playing in my head. Nobody plays that stuff anymore."

But the word *infamous* seems to have followed this club throughout its history. When it was called the Central, it was owned by the murderous thug Charles "Lucky" Luciano and was a known hangout for Benjamin "Bugsy" Siegel.

Despite Depp's intentions, the Viper Room kept up the trend, earning its own "infamous" moniker on Halloween night in 1993, when a tragedy unfolded there — a tragedy that has dogged Depp and the club ever since. On that night, one of Hollywood's finest young actors dropped by after a long day of shooting. He had a guitar under one arm and his girlfriend, pretty actress Samantha Mathis, on the other. Not long afterward, River Phoenix wound up in a convulsing heap on the sidewalk in front of the club, his brother Leaf (later known as Joaquin) frantically calling 911 for help. River died of a drug overdose in the hospital shortly thereafter. He was 23 years old.

What really happened that night, and why has Depp been tarred for life by the incident?

The day began early for Phoenix, who was taken to the set of his latest film, *Dark Blood*, a vampire movie by Dutch filmmaker George Sluizer. Shooting wrapped just after 7 PM. River was driven back to his hotel, the Nikko, in West Hollywood. His brother Leaf and his sister Rain Phoenix were in town to visit their brother and to audition for director John Boorman for a movie called *Safe Passage*, to which River had already committed. He'd also signed to play the role of the interviewer in the high-profile film version of Anne Rice's *Interview with the Vampire* with Tom Cruise and Brad Pitt.

At the hotel, the party — and, reportedly, the drug use — began. River called down for some vegetarian snacks from room service.

Before heading out to the Viper Room, where the Red Hot Chili Peppers were going to be playing an impromptu set (bassist Flea and John Frusciante, who'd recently rejoined the band, were friends of River's). River checked his schedule for the next day, then headed out to Depp's club with his brother and sister. He passed his director, George Sluizer, on their way out of the hotel. Sluizer wished them well and told them to have a good time.

River and his party arrived at the Viper Room at about midnight. River was seen talking to Flea and Frusciante near a private room that Depp keeps at the club, set apart from the main area by a two-way mirror for his privacy. Phoenix was then shown to a table near the back of the club. The place was packed with people, many of whom were wearing Halloween costumes, and there was a lot of noise. From here on, the facts get a bit dodgy.

There have been published reports, including a lengthy account in a book on River Phoenix called *Lost in Hollywood* by John Glatt, that suggest Phoenix was approached by a few drug peddlers looking to sell drugs to a rich movie star. Depp hotly denied this story; he argued, quite reasonably, that if he allowed drug dealers to openly sell drugs in his club then in all likelihood it would be closed down. According to Glatt, a "musician friend" of River's approached Phoenix with some Peruvian Brown, telling the young actor that it would make him feel wonderful. Phoenix supposedly accepted it and went into the men's room to take it. Immediately after snorting the substance, he started to shake and feel weird. He was then violently ill. Other patrons in the men's room came to his aid and splashed cold water on his face. "Someone" then supposedly gave him some Valium to help him calm down.

At about 1 AM, Phoenix was seen staggering through the club to his table in the corner. At this time, Depp went on stage to play music with Flea, Gibby Haynes from the Butthole Surfers, and Al

Jourgensen from the industrial metal band Ministry. It was a loud jam session, and the four were having, by all reports, a great time.

Phoenix was now having trouble breathing and had fainted a couple of times. His body was battling a number of powerful drugs. He asked his girlfriend to take him outside, and they headed out the back door of the club onto Sunset Boulevard. River collapsed as soon as he hit L.A.'s version of fresh air. He was slipping into and out of wild convulsions. By now, Leaf, Rain, and Samantha were beginning to panic. But they were unsure whether to call for medical attention, knowing that they were well-known people and that illegal drugs were involved.

Two photographers happened onto the scene. They were cruising the clubs looking for shots of celebrities out celebrating Halloween. One of them described seeing Phoenix "flopping around on the pavement" in a terrible seizure, his head bouncing off the pavement and his arms flailing about. They rushed over to try to help him. Neither of the paparazzi attempted to take photos of what was happening. One rushed to a nearby liquor store to summon help; Leaf Phoenix had already made the decision to get to a phone and was frantically calling 911.

Actress Christina Applegate came out of the club and witnessed what was happening — she immediately burst into tears and ran back around the corner.

When the ambulance arrived, Phoenix was in deep trouble. He'd gone into cardiac arrest and had no blood pressure. By this time, word had spread to people inside the club. Flea rushed out to help his friend. He got outside just as River was being loaded into the ambulance. He begged to accompany him to the hospital and was allowed to do so provided he rode up front with the driver.

By 1:45 AM, River Phoenix was pronounced dead.

Depp responded to the tragedy by closing down the club for two weeks — mostly out of respect for Phoenix but also out of concern that the club would turn into a ghoulish stop on the tourist bus trips through Hollywood.

Johnny doesn't like to talk about that night, but he did open up about it to *Playboy* in 1996. "When River passed away, it happened to be at my club. Now, that's very tragic, very sad, but they made a fiasco of lies to sell fucking magazines. They said he was doing drugs in my club, that I allow people to do drugs in my club. What a ridiculous fucking thought! 'Hey I'm going to spend a lot of money on this nightclub so everybody can come in here and do drugs. I think that's a good idea, don't you? We'll never get found out. It's not like this place is high profile or anything, right?' That lie was ridiculous and disrespectful to River. But aside from River, and his family trying to deal with their loss, what about the people who work at the club? They have moms and dads in, like, Oklahoma, reading about the place where their daughter tends bar and thinking, 'Jesus, she's out in Hollywood swimming around with these awful creatures.'"

It wasn't generally known at the time just how deeply the whole situation affected Johnny. On top of his own grief, he was very concerned about his young nieces and nephews and how they'd react to everything that was being written about their uncle and his nightclub. And as the media frenzy got more intense, Depp's anger grew. For a while, Johnny refused to comment on the tragedy, but he finally decided to issue a statement to the press: "Fuck you. I will not be disrespectful to River's memory. I will not participate in your fucking circus."

The Viper Room was never meant to be an "in" place, at least not in the way that it has become one. It is now a tourist attraction. There are always long lines of fresh-faced young people from all over the world who are hoping to get in and hang with the seriously cool people they've been reading about. And, despite its reputation, it remains a legitimate club to launch hot new bands or have eccentric author readings or, in one case, host the victory celebration for the newly elected mayor of West Hollywood.

Over the years, the Viper Room has played host to several eclectic acts. Timothy Leary once held court on tuning in, turning on, and dropping out. The Go-Go's reunited there. Members of The Sex Pistols play there, as does Johnny Cash. When Depp closed the club for remodeling, he opened it again in grand style with Courtney Love and her band Hole playing the first show. Brad Pitt was in the audience, as was Tom Hanks.

The Viper Room also became the home of the band P — the members include Gibby Haynes, guitarist Bill Carter, ex–Sex Pistol Steve Jones, Red Hot Chili Pepper Flea, Sal Jenco, and Johnny Depp. The band recorded an album, also called *P*, that was released by Capitol in the summer of 1996. The cover featured an abstract drawing in the manner of Jean-Michel Basquiat, a face with large teeth and two skinny arms throwing a pair of dice. The album includes songs with titles such as "I Save Cigarette Butts," "Mr. Officer," "White Man Sings the Blues," and "Michael Stipe." The music isn't bad, but it does sound like a bunch of guys goofing around in a recording studio.

Depp often has big tough guys looking after the club for him, sometimes acting as unofficial bodyguards. "I get some real psychos hanging around the place sometimes — I've even gotten death threats," he said. "There was this guy who was going around saying he was me. He would phone up the studio heads and say, 'This is Johnny Depp; hey, I never got paid for *Edward Scissorhands.*'" Another regular stalker is a transvestite who claims that he was legally married to Johnny in a private ceremony several years ago and wants Depp to acknowledge him.

Depp's next film, *What's Eating Gilbert Grape*, is one that Johnny has difficulty speaking about, partly because he has yet to see it. But it also represents one of the darkest times in his life away from the screen.

At the time, the ostensible reason for his depression was the breakup with Winona Ryder, but that was only part of the story. "It has more to do with me," Depp explained, "with the difficulty of being inside my skin. I was doing what I could to numb that feeling, doing some in-depth poisoning." It was during this period, he admitted, that he drank more than he ever had before. "I was soused, really doing myself in," he recalled. "When it gets constant, when you're going to sleep drunk, waking up, and starting to drink again, it will start killing you quick." Depp spiraled downward until he found himself living on booze, coffee, and cigarettes — no food and no sleep.

His lifestyle soon caught up with him. "I was sitting around with some pals when my heart started running at 200 beats a minute," he recounted. "That's very scary. You mentally try to slow down your heart, but you can't. When my heart started racing, I . . . hoped it was just an anxiety attack, but when it went on for 45 minutes I knew it wasn't anxiety, it was all the shit I had done to my body. My friends got me to the hospital, where I got a shot of something — BOOM! — a shot that basically stops your heart for a second. I could feel myself curling up, going fetal. Then it was over. I went home." It was an experience that Depp described as "scaring" him "into shape."

Kevin Sessums profiled Depp at the time for *Vanity Fair* and asked him if heroin was a part of his problem. "Oh, let's not talk about that," he quickly answered. "It was a very scary, sad time for me. I have never seen *Gilbert Grape*, I can't watch it."

Depp has even suggested that his dark times might have been self-induced: "I don't know if I subconsciously made myself miserable for a little bit because I knew that's what this particular character needed."

What's Eating Gilbert Grape is based on a novel by Peter Hedges. When asked about the casting of Depp in the title role, Hedges said, "I think it is absolutely perfect casting, I couldn't have asked for better." Asked to elaborate, he added, "He has an almost burning desire to make ugly choices. He comes to a movie with a physical beauty that's just astonishing, and at the same time he has no interest in being that. When I first met him, he had really long hair and was very quiet and shy."

What's Eating Gilbert Grape is about the struggles of a family in a tiny town called Endora, Texas. Gilbert Grape (Depp) works in a grocery store that is hanging on by a thread because a huge supermarket has just sprung up on the outskirts of town. Gilbert has been the man of the house since his father's tragic suicide. He looks after his two sisters (played by Laura Harrington and Mary Kate Schellhardt), his mentally challenged teenage brother, Arnie (astonishingly well portrayed by Leonardo DiCaprio), and the family's mother, a woman (valiantly acted by Darlene Cates) so obese that she has been unable to leave the house for years. Life in Endora just goes on and on — nothing much ever happens there — and frustrations are starting to set in for Gilbert and his sisters. He has an affair with the wife of a local insurance agent, but he knows it's the wrong thing to do. The most exciting event on the horizon is the upcoming 18th birthday of Arnie, a near medical miracle. Then a mother and daughter traveling across the country drive into town. Their mobile home breaks down, and they end up staying until spare parts arrive from another town. Gilbert is instantly infatuated with the young woman (Juliette Lewis), and he starts to consider, for the first time, a life outside Endora. His dilemma really resonated with Depp. "That mixed-up family and Gilbert having to be responsible, those issues really clung to me," he said.

Because Johnny was having a tough time during the shoot, he

Johnny with *Gilbert Grape* co-star,
Leonardo DiCaprio

once again attached himself to his director, Swedish filmmaker Lasse Hallström. Hallström was best known then for making the wonderful, Oscar-nominated movie *My Life as a Dog* and was later nominated for another Oscar for making an emotional film from John Irving's novel *The Cider House Rules.* Hallström said of Depp, "Johnny likes to hide behind the eccentrics he plays. He has real ambitions, but he is deeply afraid of appearing pretentious." Depp hung around a lot with Hallström trying to get him to teach him phrases in Swedish. Hallström complied, but all the phrases he taught Depp were nonsensical (e.g., *"Jag har en liten rotta I huset mitt,"* which means "I have rats in my house").

The pacing of the film is languid, but it makes for an oddly compelling piece of work — mostly because of the fascinating performance by Leonardo DiCaprio, who blows everyone else off the screen. That is not to say that the other actors aren't good, because they are all very solid; it's more of a testament to just how good DiCaprio is. In fact, *What's Eating Gilbert Grape* showed for the first time what a serious, talented young actor he is. At the time, many who were unfamiliar with DiCaprio assumed that Hallström had

cast a real mentally handicapped boy. Years later, after he'd made *The Beach* for a reported $20 million, I spoke with DiCaprio. He said of *What's Eating Gilbert Grape*, "It is the kind of role you take if you want to do this work seriously. You can either be a vain *movie star*, or you can try to shed some light on different aspects of the human condition. I was interested in stretching myself to the furthest limits I could." DiCaprio was just a teenager when he made this movie. When I asked him about working with Depp, he smiled broadly. "He's cool," he said. "I was just a kid, and I wanted to hang around with him and be accepted by him — he played a lot of good-natured jokes on me. He's a great actor, and I was really proud to be working alongside him."

Some of those good-natured practical jokes involved Depp paying young Leo to smell the most disgusting things he could find — rotten eggs, pickled sausages, a decayed honeycomb — because his animated reactions to the odors amused Depp. "I think I ended up making about 500 bucks off Johnny," recalled DiCaprio.

In an interview, Hallström told me that the Arnie role was "the toughest role to cast because I was looking for someone who wasn't that physically attractive, which doesn't describe DiCaprio. I had to look beyond what I was seeing. Leonardo was very in tune with what I was thinking about for Arnie; that was how he ended up in the movie." In fact, DiCaprio was so in tune with the role that his work in *What's Eating Gilbert Grape* earned him an Academy Award nomination.

The movie brought together a very diverse and interesting cast, including one standout, Darlene Cates, who played the obese mother. Although Depp doesn't like to speak about his experience on the movie, the one thing he does discuss is the way Cates inspired him. She was spotted by author Peter Hedges when she made an appearance on *Sally Jesse Raphaël* to speak about not leaving her house for five years. She courageously agreed to put herself on display in the film. "One of the things I hoped for *What's Eating Gilbert Grape* was that it would change some people's attitudes and make them more tolerant," she said. Depp was profoundly impressed with Cates. "The first time I met Darlene," he recalled, "I looked beyond her size, and I saw this sweet face and those soulful eyes, and I thought she was so beautiful. I found her very brave to unravel her emotional life in front of the whole world — this is someone who had never acted before in her life."

Depp's relationship to the character of Gilbert Grape was odd in that it cut close to home on a number of levels. "There are things that happened in my life that directly parallel things in Gilbert's life," he said. Yet there are also several departures that allowed for a fascinating characterization from Depp. Gilbert is not a showy role, and this is no over-the-top performance; instead, it is reserved, measured acting. There were physical differences too. Part of his commitment to the role involved going to a dentist to have his teeth bonded and chipped. Depp also dyed his long, unruly hair a particularly unattractive shade of red.

As with all of his roles, Depp thought Gilbert through carefully: "Gilbert Grape would seem like a pretty normal kind of a guy, but I was interested in what was going on under the surface — the hostility and the rage and that he is only able to show it a couple of times during the film. I understand that feeling of being stuck in a place, whether it is geographical or emotional. I can understand the rage of wanting to completely escape from it, from everybody and everything you know, and start a new life."

Depp further described his character as having "at some point or another allowed himself to die inside, slowly kind of killing or martyring himself for his family, becoming a surrogate father — even to his mother. That kind of loyalty may start out as pure love, but it can work against you, with love and devotion turning into resentment and guilt and losing yourself, which is the worst thing that anyone can do, because then you hate others because of what you've done to yourself."

Depp's personal problems were not helped by having to live during the shoot near Austin, Texas, "a place," he said, "that seems to me what all of America was like during the 1950s." The shoot was long and tough, and the cast and crew weren't happy about spending three months in a place called Manor, Texas. Because Lasse Hallström was a Swedish filmmaker making a movie in America about Americans, he was very precise about his locations and the way his characters presented themselves. He liked to shoot a number of takes of each scene. Depp didn't respond well to that method: "Whether he shoots five or 50 takes of the same scene, only the first two or three will contain anything worthwhile."

The film was released in 1995 with very little fanfare, and it disappeared from sight quickly. It received some respectful reviews but also some negative ones, mostly from critics who complain about action movies and sequels cluttering cinemas only to dump on a movie that represents the kind of remedy they say they want. Depp took the brunt of the shit because his role was perceived as just another quirky outsider, the kind of character he was being criticized for playing too frequently. Watching the film today, it's hard to see past the brilliance of DiCaprio and the performance of Cates, but watch Depp's performance carefully and you'll see a wonderful bit of acting.

Speaking of quirky characters, Johnny Depp was about to team up with Tim Burton again and to give his most ebullient and enjoyable performance to date. He was also about to fall in love all over again.

Depp and Burton, Burton and Depp – Part 2

"I owe him a tremendous debt and respect him more than I can ever express on paper."

Johnny Depp on Tim Burton

The second collaboration in the Johnny Depp–Tim Burton symbiosis was a truly bizarre but ultimately sweet and uplifting movie called *Ed Wood*. The movie tells the story of real-life '50s and early '60s filmmaker and author Edward D. Wood Jr., who

Johnny with Martin Landau and Tim Burton at the Cannes Film Festival, 1995
BENITO GELY/GLOBE PHOTOS

made such films as *Glen or Glenda?*, *Bride of the Monster*, and *Plan 9 from Outer Space*, the movie that he is now most remembered for.

Wood probably would have been a mere footnote in movie lore were it not for *The Golden Turkey Awards*, a book written by the self-righteous, pompous critic Michael Medved and his brother Harry. This book labeled Wood the "Worst Director of All Time" and *Plan 9 from Outer Space* the "Worst Movie of All Time" — neither of which can really be true given the highly subjective nature of film viewing.

This cheap mudslinging, written about five years after Wood died, stuck, and he became legendary for being the "worst" director in the history of movies.

Wood was one of those dreamers/losers whom both Depp and Burton find wildly attractive. Wood spent his whole life trying very hard to make it big in Hollywood, but it never quite happened. He was spirited and fought hard for his dream. He was known for his fondness for angora sweaters; he was a known transvestite who hung around with the weirdest of the weird. In 1978, Wood passed away at the age of 54 in a seedy part of L.A. — he didn't live to see the bizarre acceptance and reverence that his work attained. To learn more about this fascinating, truly Hollywood story, read Rudolph Grey's excellent history of the filmmaker called *Nightmare of Ecstasy: The Life and Art of Edward D. Wood Jr.* (1992, Feral House).

How Burton and Depp got together to collaborate on *Ed Wood* is another of those classic moviemaking stories of near misses and almosts, but eventually the perfect combination of elements emerged.

Ed Wood began life in the heads of two USC film school graduates. Scott Alexander and Larry Karaszewski had toyed with the idea of writing a movie about Wood during their days at USC, but they went on to bigger things upon graduation — the team wrote the extremely successful albeit truly awful *Problem Child* movies. Fearing that Hollywood producers would pigeonhole them as writers of sophomoric comedy, the pair revived their idea of doing a black comedy about Wood and the Hollywood dream factory. They constructed a 10-page treatment and took it to a young director whom they went to USC with, Michael Lehmann. Lehmann had made a very dark film called *Heathers* that attracted a lot of notice (he'd also make a movie that would be put down onto many lists of all-time-worst movies, *Hudson Hawk*). Lehmann loved the idea and discussed it with *Heathers* producer Denise Di Novi, who was now partnered with Tim Burton. All were in favor of making the film. It would be written by Karaszewski and Alexander, directed by Lehmann, and produced by Di Novi and Burton. Burton had no interest in directing it because, at the time, he was very busy with a movie for Columbia Pictures called *Mary Reilly*.

Mary Reilly was a retelling of the classic Dr. Jekyll and Mr. Hyde story, told from the perspective of the housekeeper. Burton was all set to make the movie with Winona Ryder in the lead role. But then the studio started exerting pressure, telling Burton that he had to speed up the process. When he balked, he was informed that there were five directors lined up just waiting for the chance to make the movie if he didn't want to. This approach turned Burton off the project completely. Then the studio decided that it needed the star power of Julia Roberts in the lead role. Burton backed out. He was replaced by British helmer Stephen Frears. In the end, the film was well made, but the story was pointless, and the movie was a dismal failure at the box office.

Having dropped out of *Mary Reilly*, Burton turned his attention fully to *Ed Wood*. But now he didn't just want to produce it — he'd been developing *Mary Reilly* for a long time only to see it come to nothing, and he didn't want to waste another year not directing a film. He told Karaszewski and Alexander that he was now interested in directing *Ed Wood*, but he wanted it done soon. Six weeks later, they placed a 147-page screenplay on his desk.

Burton quickly set the project up with Columbia Pictures. They got under way, and everything was going smoothly until Burton decided that the movie should be shot in black and white. Columbia honcho Mark Canton wasn't thrilled and said he'd go along with it only if the studio could reserve the right to demand color if executives weren't happy with black and white after the first few sets of rushes. Burton balked again — he wanted total control over the film. Canton decided to cancel the movie, but fortunately the script sparked interest from just about every other studio in town. Burton decided to go with Disney because he'd had a terrific working relationship with the studio on *A Nightmare before Christmas* and because Disney promised him the control over the project that he sought. It then took only a month to get *Ed Wood* under way again.

When it came time to cast the role of Ed Wood, Burton's first thought was of his friend, Johnny Depp. "Johnny liked the material," said Burton. "He responded to it. That is why I feel so close to Johnny, because I think that somewhere inside we respond to very similar things. . . . It was interesting for me, after working with Johnny before, to explore a more open kind of thing. He really did a great job and found just the tone that I wanted."

Depp was sitting around at home when the call came. Burton asked him how long it would take him to get to the Formosa Café, a famous Hollywood watering hole. Hard as he tried, Depp couldn't pry out of Burton what this meeting was about. Depp nonetheless agreed to meet him, and they hung up around 8 PM. Depp was sitting in the Formosa Café at 8:20 and, over a beer, listened to Burton explain his next project. "By 8:25 PM, I was completely committed to the project," said Depp. "I was already familiar with some of Wood's movies. I knew that no one could tell his story as well as Tim could. Tim's passion became my passion." Depp's engagement with the material really comes across — Johnny gives one of the most broadly sketched performances of his career in *Ed Wood*. In the end, the film is a lot more fiction than fact, but it perfectly captures Wood's spirit.

Depp has been a voracious reader for most of his adult life. He began his research into Wood by reading everything available about him. But that proved to be of little help, partly because no two things written about Wood agree on anything and partly because Burton was not trying to make a rigidly biographical film.

Johnny wanted to take the research as far as he could, and that included the transvestitism. He went around the house wearing women's shoes and Wood's favorite women's angora sweaters. "I'm telling you, being a woman is hard," declared Depp. "You've got all the makeup and the bras and stuff — it's a lot of hard work. You can never fully understand what it is like to be a woman until you have to wear those clothes. And playing a transvestite is even harder. You have to make a real commitment to it. You have to hide stuff and tuck it away, and it's really painful. I'm telling you, I have a lot of respect for transvestites."

Ed Wood is one of those movies that is completely wacky without being silly. The performances by Burton regulars Johnny Depp and Jeffrey Jones are wonderful. Also of note are Bill Murray playing the attempted transsexual Bunny Breckenridge and Martin Landau as Hungarian bogeyman Bela Lugosi (a role that would earn him an Oscar for a wickedly funny, although quite embellished, performance).

Burton's decision to use black-and-white film was completely appropriate because it gives the movie the atmosphere of the era in which it is set. The writing is first-rate and was published in screenplay form by Faber & Faber. The two screenwriters later continued their success by writing two more high-profile film biographies: *The People vs. Larry Flynt* and *Man on the Moon*, both for director Milos Forman. But *Ed Wood* isn't biographically accurate — Karaszewski and Alexander throw in hilarious fictional episodes to advance the story and deepen the audience's sense of who Wood was and why his petty dreams were so important to him. For example, one scene has Wood storming off the set of *Plan 9 from Outer Space* in a frustrated huff while in full drag. He goes into a dark bar for a drink, and sitting there is his hero, Orson Welles.

Welles, played by Vincent D'Onofrio (with another actor's deeper voice dubbed over), shares his Hollywood frustrations with the starstruck Wood. Wood complains about the squeeze that the money men are putting on his latest film, and Welles replies, "Tell me about it. I'm supposed to do a thriller at Universal, and they want Charlton Heston to play a Mexican!"

The wonderful thing about *Ed Wood* is that it never makes fun of a guy who has already received more than his fair share of ridicule. Instead, the writers, Burton, and Depp treat their subject with kindness and respect. The movie focuses on the time Wood spent making just three of the 30 movies that he finished — *Glen or Glenda?*, *Bride of the Monster*, and *Plan 9 from Outer Space*. It ends with a triumphant premiere for *Plan 9 from Outer Space* — something that never really happened, but it allows an opportunity for the grinning Wood/Depp to utter the lines "This is the one. This is the one I'll be remembered for."

Martin Landau has been a terrific actor for decades but has only recently come into broad popular acceptance, largely a result of his work on *Ed Wood*. He has some interesting things to say about working with Johnny Depp; although it seems that one new actor a month is called "the next James Dean," Landau thinks that Depp is the only credible heir. "Back in New York in the '50s, James Dean was one of my best friends," recalled Landau. "It's very hard to compare the younger actors of today with Dean, yet I can honestly say I don't know of anyone who comes closer to Jimmy than Johnny. They share a similar subtlety in their work. But Jimmy's was a fragile talent — not as developed as Johnny's is."

But Depp was no rebel without a cause; in fact, his charitable side showed through when his involvement with the Make-a-Wish Foundation brought a little girl to the *Ed Wood* set for an all-day visit. The seriously ill girl was a huge Depp fan whose wish was to meet him. Depp spent the entire day with her, being as attentive as humanly possible. Her questions were answered, and she was made to feel that she was Depp's good friend.

Depp got so far into his characterization of the peppy, wildly optimistic Wood that he'd often take Wood home with him after shooting. Maverick filmmaker Jim Jarmusch tells a story about staying at Johnny's house for a while during the shooting of *Ed Wood*. "Sometimes I would go and pick him up at the set so we could go out for dinner. It would take him three hours to stop being Ed Wood. I would have to slap him to get that stupid smile off his face. We'd be in a Thai restaurant, and Johnny is going, 'Isn't this Pad Thai fabulous?' like Wood."

Depp's involvement with the character cemented his symbiotic relationship with Burton. It was with this second film that Depp and Burton really found their rhythm in working together. There were no rehearsals. "We had a walk-through the day we started shooting," said Depp. "It consisted of him saying, 'You know, it'd be good if you stood here.' Then he would let me get the feeling of what I would be doing and saying on that spot. Then we would move onto the next spot. We just walked, we didn't do any dialogue. But he had, I imagined, a vague idea. He would then say 'Action!' and you'd do it, and then there would be silence. And then, in your head, you'd be going, 'Okay, I fucked it up bad'; then he would tell you that it was exactly what he wanted."

If Depp thought the problems he had with the press during his relationship with Winona Ryder were bad, he was about to find out that they could get a whole lot worse. His next serious relationship would be a tumultuous four-year romance with British supermodel Kate Moss.

Moss was born in Addiscombe, Surrey, near London. When she

was very young, her family moved to another London suburb, Croydon. Just like Depp, Moss inadvertently stumbled into her career; she had no idea she'd be involved in modeling, never mind ending up a supermodel. In 1988, or so the story goes, Moss was discovered by Sarah Doukas of Britain's Storm Agency as the two passed one another in a waiting area at New York's Kennedy Airport. Less than a year later, Moss was featured in her first film, a quasi-soft-porn movie called *Inferno*. It was followed by her first taste of major exposure when she was featured on the cover of the British pop culture magazine *The Face*. The issue contained the photo layout that would give rise to the controversial "waif" look. Because of that shoot, Moss is credited — or blamed, depending on your point of view — for the widespread popularity of that look in the late '80s and early '90s. Millions of young women strove for the emaciated look, and Moss came under fire because it had such a devastating effect on their self-image. Depp was defensive of Moss. "Kate eats like a champ," he said. "She eats more than I do. She is thin, so what? She is being criticized because her metabolism is more active than most people's."

In 1993, Moss hit the big time, a contract with Calvin Klein in excess of $1 million. Her rake-thin body in Klein ads drew a lot of attention; one of the most famous features Moss — completely naked — stretched out on a worn sofa on her stomach.

When asked about his reaction to seeing these ads on 100-foot billboards, Depp said, "I think she's beautiful. Calvin Klein is lucky to have her. If we are apart and I see these ads, it makes me miss her, not just because of the billboard but because she is on my mind all the time anyway."

Depp first met Moss at Café Tabac in New York City. It was January of 1994. Kate was once asked by a journalist if it had been love at first sight (a stupid question but one that entertainment jour-

Johnny with Kate Moss
RON DAVID/SHOOTING STAR

nalists feel compelled to ask). She replied, "No, not the first moment I saw him, but after we talked for a while I just knew we'd be together. That has never happened before." A couple of weeks later, they turned up at a club in Los Angeles called Smashbox — it was the first time they were photo-graphed as a couple. It was mid-February, and the occasion was the unveiling of a short anti-drug film that Depp had made to benefit the organization D.A.R.E. (Drug Abuse Resistance Education). At the end of the film, the name Kate Moss can be seen in the credits, thanked for helping the filmmaker get it made.

Before this party, the New York tabloids had already begun their scrutiny of the relationship, claiming that the couple were holed up in the Royalton Hotel in New York City waiting out a severe snow-storm.

A month after the Smashbox party, Kate and Johnny were photographed on a beach on the Caribbean island of St. Barts. Pictures of the couple kissing and cuddling on the beach were taken by another tourist who happened to recognize one or both of them — and then felt duty-bound to sell the photos to tabloid publications all over the world.

The pair were back in New York on April 5th for the premiere of

John Waters's new movie, *Serial Mom*, and they stayed there for a while. While in New York, they caught a show by the Man in Black, Johnny Cash, at the Fez Club. Depp and Cash had met earlier when Cash played at the Viper Room — an evening that Depp still refers to as one of the special nights in his life. Kate then agreed to appear in Cash's video for "Delilah's Dead."

In May, Depp got to see Kate work for the first time. A special fashion event was staged in L.A. by Isaac Mizrahi to benefit the AIDS Project. Johnny watched Kate on the Mann's Chinese Theater catwalk and then joined her at the party afterward. The pair left early with model Linda Evangelista and headed to another party at the Viper Room.

Soon the couple were on the move again, this time to London to attend a launch at the Tramp Club for model Naomi Campbell's book *Swan*. Johnny had to return to New York to fulfill his media-relations duties before the release of *Ed Wood*. That weekend in September 1994 is one of the most notorious of Depp's public life — it was the weekend of the "Mark Hotel incident." It was reported that the couple had had an enormous fight involving fisticuffs and furniture being thrown around in their hotel suite . . . but more on that later.

On September 11th, a reception was held at the James Danziger Gallery in New York City in celebration of *The Kate Moss Book*. Pictures from the book adorned the walls of the gallery. As reporters and photographers surrounded Moss and Depp, all calling out questions, Johnny felt increasingly uneasy. When one reporter asked him if he took photographs, he replied, "Yeah, I take Polaroids of my dog." He was asked if he ever took any pictures of Kate: "No, just the dog." The dog was a black-and-white pit bull mix named Moo — a gift from Kate.

At the same party, Depp became something of a public activist. When photographers aimed their cameras at him, he held up a poster opposing French nuclear testing in the South Pacific. Depp later made a short film about his opposition to the testing, and he and Moss allowed themselves to be photographed for antitesting posters seen all over London. It was said at the time that this issue was brought to Depp's attention by a new acquaintance, Marlon Brando, with whom Johnny was getting ready to work.

Moss and Depp were seen together after that fall. He took her to the premiere of *Ed Wood* during the New York Film Festival. The following day, they participated in an event for the Pediatric AIDS Foundation, and they were both seen playing with the children and having a great time. Later the same evening, at Metronome in New York, Johnny threw a birthday party for his friend Mickey Rourke.

When the Christmas holiday rolled around, the couple decided to spend it in Aspen, Colorado. A terrific photo was taken of the pair as they window-shopped. Kate is dressed in furry boots and a bright down-filled jacket; Johnny is dressed in black from head to toe, with sunglasses and a wool cap, a cigarette is dangling from his mouth, and he is giving the photographer the finger. Kate reported to *Elle* magazine that she did some skiing and found it quite enjoyable — no word on whether Johnny was on the slopes.

When Kate's birthday rolled around in 1995, Johnny threw her a surprise birthday party at the Viper Room. He'd told Kate to put on a nice dress because he was taking her out to dinner. At the Viper Room, she was surprised to see that her parents had flown in from England, and designer John Galliano had come from Paris for the party. Moss recalled, "I couldn't believe it. I just started shaking. I had to rush into the office for a few minutes to compose myself." When she emerged, it was to a soulful rendition of "Happy Birthday" by Thelma Houston and Gloria Gaynor.

They also attended the Golden Globe Awards together in January 1995. Depp was nominated in the Best Performance by an Actor in a

Comedy or Musical category for his work in *Ed Wood*. They sat at a table with fellow nominee and costar Martin Landau and director Tim Burton.

Every other day, there were stories about the couple in the tabloids. Coverage became more and more ridiculous as shows such as *Entertainment Tonight* started reporting daily that Depp and Moss were getting married or splitting up. They did split up briefly a few times — "It was always my fault," maintains Depp — but they always found their way back to one another. On December 17th, Depp agreed to participate in an AOL on-line chat. The first question was whether or not he and Kate were on speaking terms; "As of about three minutes ago, yes," Depp answered. When Kate was asked by the moronic television show *Entertainment Tonight* whether she and Johnny were soon to be married, she wearily said, "He's my boyfriend. That's all. We're not getting married."

The couple went back to Aspen for Christmas 1995 to celebrate the holidays with Kate's brother Nick — this time Kate had someone to ski with.

Moss has a friend named Meg Matthews, who was married to Oasis founding member Noel Gallagher. At one point, the two couples found themselves vacationing on the same Caribbean island, Mustique. Johnny and Kate went to Mustique many times during their relationship, usually staying at a villa called Stargroves (owned by Mick Jagger and Jerry Hall). When Depp and Gallagher found themselves there at the same time, they spent hours together talking about music. During one of these conversations, Gallagher mentioned that he had written a song for the new Oasis album that required some slide guitar music, but slide guitar isn't one of the many instruments that he plays. Johnny mentioned that he'd played a bit of slide guitar, and Gallagher invited him to join the band to record the song.

Depp and Burton, Burton and Depp — Part 2

Johnny with one of his idols, Iggy Pop
ROSE HARTMAN/GLOBE PHOTOS

Depp was very hesitant at first — although he'd recorded with his own bands before, this was Oasis, and their album would sell millions of copies. He finally agreed to do the gig, but his schedule made it difficult. The song was being recorded in London, but even when Depp was there at the same time as the band it was difficult to pin him down. In fact, he ended up playing his slide guitar portion of the track on a portable tape recorder in a hotel room. When we hear the song "Fade in/Out" on the *Be Here Now* album, the some-what hollow sound in the slide guitar portion is the result of using that tape recorder. When the drums come back up, we return to the music recorded in the studio. Depp also appeared in the video for the song; he is seen behind a bar in a split screen shared with footage of the band playing on stage.

I once asked Gallagher about Depp's playing on the album, and he told me that "Johnny plays down the fact that he is a fucking good musician, because he doesn't think he is. Well, let me tell you, he is.

I tried for a long time to replicate his slide guitar stuff so I could play it on stage during concerts, and I never really got it."

Depp would appear with the band once again when "Oasis and Friends" contributed a song to a CD called *Help*. The proceeds of the album went to the victims of the senseless violence in Kosovo.

Depp was now one of the most well-known young movie stars on the scene. He was dating one of the most famous supermodels in the world, and he was playing music on an album with one of the world's biggest bands. He was becoming a pop culture icon, and Depp would begin to question where he was and where he wanted to go — both professionally and personally.

Chapter Eight

1410

"Did Beethoven get thrown in jail for it?"

Johnny Depp, after being told by a reporter that Ludwig van Beethoven had once thrown a chair out the window of his Vienna hotel suite

Bad boy. Hellraiser. Brat. Johnny Depp's been called them all, mostly because of one extremely overpublicized event early one September morning at the Mark Hotel at 77th and Madison in New York City.

That Depp has had problems with authority figures over the years is without question, but much of the time he's been reacting to the perception that he's being picked on specifically because he is "Johnny Depp." Back in 1993, he told Canadian entertainment journalist Johanna Schneller about an episode that happened when he pulled his pickup truck over to the side of the road to light up a cigarette. A security guard immediately ran up to the truck and told him that he'd have to move it right away, that he wasn't allowed to stop there.

Depp meets the NYPD
WALTER WEISSMAN/
GLOBE PHOTOS

Depp, about to move on anyway, made a wisecrack: "Yeah, yeah, officer, we're just looking at the angle of light across the dashboard here. It's important to see it from just this angle." The guard wasn't amused and told him sternly that he wasn't to remain parked there. "Yeah, okay, right, hmmm" was Depp's response. Johnny then proceeded to sit there without moving. When the guard said he was going to call the police, Depp finally moved off with a smirk.

Not long after this incident, Depp was arrested in Beverly Hills for . . . jaywalking. I have strolled around Beverly Hills a lot, and I have jaywalked on numerous occasions, but now that I know it is such a serious matter there I will govern my actions accordingly. "The cop was one of those guys who puts on a uniform, and suddenly he feels his penis begin to grow," Depp explained. "He's all bent out of shape and hard as nails, a real idiot." As the officer was writing out the jaywalking citation, he demanded that Depp put out his cigarette. Johnny asked why that was necessary and said that he really didn't want to. The officer grabbed his arm and twisted his wrist until the cigarette dropped to the ground. He then stomped it out with his heel. Depp proceeded to light up another cigarette immediately. So, Depp continued, "He and his partner grabbed me and put me in handcuffs. They then took me to a holding cell, where they kept me for a few hours." Depp explained that "I'm not scared of these people; they just make me angry. You get the feeling that there is nothing you can do, but there is something you can do. Don't take shit from them."

Spoiled-brat behavior from movie stars and rock stars is usually worn as a badge of honor. In the '60s and '70s, rock stars who didn't trash hotel rooms were written about with wonder. Bands such as The Who (Roger Daltrey, Keith Moon, John Entwhistle, and Pete Townshend) seemed to make destroying hotel rooms part of their daily life on the road. In fact, the members of The Who are under a lifetime ban from all Holiday Inns because of something that happened in Michigan after a concert. Apparently, drummer Keith Moon didn't like being told that he couldn't have an extravagant room-service order filled at 2 AM and ran amok: television sets were thrown through windows, and furniture was destroyed. For the grand finale, The Who drove a Rolls-Royce into the hotel swimming pool.

Johnny Depp was staying at the Mark Hotel, Suite 1410, because there was no room at his favorite New York hotel, the Carlyle. On the September night in question, he returned to his room after a frustrating day, and he was tired. He took some of his frustrations out on the elegant furnishings. He smashed a picture frame and damaged an antique table. He set the broken picture frame out in the hallway.

He made enough noise to wake up the guest staying in the suite next door, so this guest called down to the front desk to complain. Security man Jim Keegan was dispatched to investigate. When he arrived at Suite 1410, he immediately noticed the broken picture frame in the hall. There was a loud commotion inside the room. Reports stated that Depp was having a huge fight with Kate Moss, but he has repeatedly denied this.

Keegan rang the doorbell and then banged on the door. Depp answered. He wasn't in the best shape. He wasn't drunk or blasted on dope — he'd simply had a very bad day and had lost control. In the process of venting, he'd knocked some furniture around. Keegan told Depp that he'd have to leave the hotel immediately or the police would be called. Johnny apologized for the ruckus and said he'd immediately pay for any damage incurred. Keegan was adamant that he go. Depp argued that there was no legitimate reason why he should be forced to leave the hotel at 5 AM. Keegan made good on his promise and called the police. At 5:30 AM, Johnny was escorted from the Mark Hotel by three police officers from the 19th Division of the New York City Police Department. The policemen at the scene reported that Depp was in "a possible state of intoxication." Kate Moss was also in the suite, wearing bright pink pants and a pink shirt. She was uninjured and calm. When the handcuffs came out, Depp said, "Ah, c'mon guys, you aren't going to lock me up for this, are you?" He was taken to the precinct and put into a holding cell. Moss wasn't arrested. Depp told the cops, "She's probably really mad at me now." In fact, she left the Mark Hotel and checked into the Royalton Hotel — supposedly the site of another huge public fight between Depp and Moss. Johnny has denied this rumor, however, saying that the Royalton is a known hangout for journalists, so why would he make a scene there?

Depp was then transported to another cell at Central Booking, and from there he was taken to the infamous Tombs, located in the back of the New York City Police headquarters. With a few exceptions, he was treated like every other prisoner brought through the system — although few other detainees are asked for an autograph by every female officer they encounter. And before you think that Depp is one of those guys who just dislikes the police, his comments on the treatment he received need to be considered: "The New York City cops that I dealt with were all really nice guys, and they treated me with every courtesy that I could have expected. They were just doing their job, man."

When the Mark suite was assessed by Keegan, it was alleged that Depp had damaged 10 different items, but two of the things on the list were cigarette burns to a rug and a velvet chair. The entire dollar value Depp was responsible for came to about $9,000 — the damage to the furnishings added up to only about $2,000, and the rest was the regular bill for his stay in the $1,200-a-night suite.

When Depp appeared before a judge the next day, the charges

against him were dropped in less than one minute. The judge added the condition that Depp stay out of trouble for six months or the incident would be revisited.

"It wasn't a great night for me," recalled Depp. "I'm not trying to excuse what I did or anything like that, because it is someone else's property, and you gotta respect that. But I got into a headspace, and I'm human."

Speaking of respect: Depp took Marlon Brando's recently published memoirs, *Songs My Mother Taught Me*, to read in his cell. When the book was returned to him, he found that it had been defaced — cordial messages such as "Depp is an Asshole," "Fuck you, Depp!," and other such pleasantries had been scrawled across the pages of the book.

The most ironic thing about this entire minor mess was the identity of the neighbor who phoned in the complaint — it was none other than Roger Daltrey, former professional hotel trasher from The Who.

This incident, of course, appears in every profile of Depp. The most quoted account of the events was written by David Blum for *Esquire* magazine. It carefully details the events, but it does so in the snidest fashion imaginable. It's one of the most remarkably slanted, malicious bits of journalism perpetrated against a celebrity. I'm not attempting to defend Depp across the board on this, but it seems to me that the embarrassment of having a picture of him being taken away in handcuffs qualifies as sufficient punishment for the severity of his crime. But Blum felt the need to extend Depp's sentence of humiliation. In his article, Blum reiterates something Depp told him and then translates it into his own sarcastic version. For instance, when Depp commented that, at the time, he spent more time living in hotels than in a home of his own, Blum writes, "He pauses, as if to allow a nation of home-dwellers to consider that remarkable fact."

Blum also refers to Depp landing on the cover of *People* magazine after the arrest — he mentions that Depp's "only complaint about it was the poor choice of photo." But Depp's real response was "*People* did a piece on me like I was some sort of hellion on the road to ruin. And they went and found a picture of me that made me look the most unhealthy and disheveled and put that on the cover. Such disgusting pigs."

Blum's article is one-sided. "He [Depp] cruises around Los Angeles in his black Porsche Carerra, parking wherever he feels like paying the tickets," Blum writes, ignoring the fact that Depp has been known to cruise around poorer neighborhoods in Los Angeles to pass out $20 and $50 bills to the needy.

Depp's response to the *Esquire* piece was telling. "There was this cretin at *Esquire* . . . and they were cunts, man, this guy had a hard-on for me in the worst way. It was so apparent, he wore it all over his face and his clothing — it was all over him," Depp said. "When I showed up for the photo shoot, they had built an entire hotel room on a stage. And this fucking weak, pathetic photographer — glorified paparazzi — was going along with the obvious idea. And I said, 'What's this for?' and he said, 'Well, we thought, or the magazine thought, you might enjoy taking the piss out of the incident and just beating the shit out of our hotel room here and just fucking destroying it.' I said, 'Wow, this must have cost you a lot of money, building this.' 'Yeah, it really did,' he said. And I said, 'I'm not fucking touching it.'"

Is it necessary to constantly point out the negative behavior of celebrities? Shouldn't the positive things they do be mentioned to counter the less favorable press? Are stars rewarded enough without being celebrated for a few acts of charity? Is it sycophantic to defend a celebrity when you know that his or her media representation is less than accurate? Celebrities are public people by choice; a lot of them mourn their loss of privacy while having a full-time publicist on staff to make sure their names stay in the limelight. It has to be difficult to have your every move scrutinized. Movie stars are human beings too, and that must be taken into consideration. I am an admirer of Johnny Depp and his work. I think he's an interesting individual, but he can certainly act like a goof at times. Then again, so can I, and so can you.

The Mark Hotel freakout was bad enough, but one night later Depp was back in the news with another assault rumor. Johnny and a couple of friends, including tattoo artist Jonathan Shaw, were in a New York bar called Babyland when the fracas supposedly began. There was a headline splashed across page 6 of the *New York Post* the next day that read "Depp, Pals in East Village Brawl." The item included such pithy comments as "It didn't take long for Johnny Depplorable to show his wild side again following his hotel hijinks the other night. Depp allegedly sparked a fight. . . ." The victim in this incident said that Depp "slammed" into him and screamed "Fuck you!" Supposedly, a couple of people who were with Depp then roughed this fellow up. When Depp was asked about it, he shrugged it off, making a joke out of it. "This guy walked past me in the bar. He then pulled out what resembled a penis — but I have a sneaking suspicion that it might have been a thimble — then this fucking guy says something like 'Suck my dick.' I had just gotten out of jail, and it was on the condition that I stay out of trouble for six months. My first instinct was that same animal instinct that we all have inside of us — it was to go for this guy's throat. But nothing happened. Hey, I let it go, man, who wants to go back to jail for something like that?"

I find this tale interesting because I had a run-in with Depp a few months after this incident. It happened in a hotel hallway in Los

Angeles. A guy was standing in the hallway with his back to me talking to a couple of women. I started walking down the hall toward the elevators when the guy stepped back into my path. I tried to step around him but ran out of space and bumped solidly into him. He turned around, and it was none other than Johnny Depp. He said, "Hey, man, I'm sorry. I didn't see you there." I told him it was all right, there was no harm done. He persisted in his apology, saying, "I wasn't being an asshole, I didn't hear you, man." Now what looks better on page 6: "Johnny Depp swore at me and had me beaten up for running into him" or "When I ran into Johnny Depp, he was apologetic and polite"?

Reports of such misbehavior seemed to breed other tales of alleged barroom violence. Take the "Globe Incident" as an example. This story involved a man named Jonathan Walpole, a member of the British aristocracy (a direct descendant of Sir Robert Walpole), and an evening in a London club called the Globe. Walpole claimed that he was standing at the bar and moved to retrieve his drink — which turned out to be not his glass but Johnny Depp's. Depp reacted to this egregious affront by turning to young master Walpole and, well, let's hear it from the aristocrat himself: "He pulled both my ears — very hard." Indeed. Could a claim be any sillier? Walpole said he then explained to Depp that that simply wasn't the way people greet one another in England. He said Depp answered by "jumping on my back, grabbing me around the neck, and trying to force my head to the ground." Nothing ever came of this allegation either.

There have been more serious assertions — or at least they look serious when they hit the papers and quote some loudmouthed lawyer. In the early '90s, Depp was sued by a woman who claimed she'd been showered with glass from a broken window in New York's Lone Star Roadhouse on 52nd Street. The incident allegedly took place after a drinking binge by Johnny Depp and Iggy Pop.

There have been other incidents — including some that I will cover later — but the question here is whether a few incidents spread out over years of public life justify labeling Depp a crazy hell-raiser, especially when we compare him with the likes of Roger Daltrey.

Chapter Nine

The Icon of Cool

"Johnny Depp has moved from massive clean-cut success on the US teen TV show *21 Jump Street* to become a freak befriender and ultra-cool icon for the '90s."

New Music Express

Johnny Depp's next movie, one of his most delightful, connected Depp with one of his idols, a man who'd become very close to him and a help to him in a time of creative upheaval — Marlon Brando. *Don Juan DeMarco* is about a young man in present-day New York who believes he is Don Juan, the world's greatest lover, but is, nevertheless, suicidal. He seduces one last beautiful woman, then decides to end his life, only to be rescued by a psychiatrist who is within days of retirement. During his evaluation of the young man, the psychiatrist finds that aspects of his own life that have atrophied are being reawakened. Depp plays Don Juan, Brando plays Dr. Mickler, and

HENRY MCGEE/
GLOBE PHOTOS

the cast is rounded out with nice performances by Faye Dunaway as Mickler's wife and Bob Dishy as his cynical colleague.

The movie was born in the imagination of writer, director, and ex-psychologist Jeremy Leven. His original screenplay was called *Don Juan DeMarco and the Centerfold* in reference to the nude model who touches off Don Juan's delusional episode. On its title page, Leven gives credit to his inspiration, stating that the script is "Based in part on *Don Juan* by Lord Byron." Leven's revised draft, dated 20 December 1993, is a good read, although it is a bit darker than the film turned out to be. Leven leaned more heavily on the psychoanalytical aspects of the story. There is also a lot more ink given to the rekindled relationship between Dr. Jack and his wife, Marilyn, including a slow-motion lovemaking scene that, if it was shot at all, was excised from the final version of the film.

Leven is interesting in that he is so completely un-Hollywood in his background and his aspirations. He is from Connecticut, and before he turned to writing movies he served as everything from an off-Broadway theater director to a Harvard University faculty member. He has even written two novels, *Creator* and *Satan: His Psychology and Cure, by the Unfortunate Dr. Kassler, JSPS*. Leven turned to moviemaking in 1985 when *Creator* was adapted into a movie that starred Peter O'Toole. The following year, he wrote a teen comedy called *Playing for Keeps* that was made by Bob and Harvey Weinstein, soon to be the moguls behind Miramax.

When Leven finished writing *Don Juan DeMarco*, his backers, New Line Cinema, got a copy of the script to Depp. He was struck by the story and what he described as its wonderfully poetic and fluid dialogue. He told New Line that he'd certainly commit to the project, but he had one condition — he'd sign on only if the company could persuade Marlon Brando to play the role of Dr. Jack Luchsinger (changed to Jack Mickler when the film was about to go into production). At the time, New Line saw this request as a cruel joke. Leven recalled, "I really thought the movie was dead at that point. It had been reported in the entertainment press that Johnny Depp was interested in doing the movie, and he was absolutely perfect for the role. To lose him would have meant that the momentum that the project had would have deflated considerably." Leven went through the motions of getting the script to Brando and was utterly astonished when he expressed interest in discussing it further.

Depp was also surprised by Brando's interest and then by his commitment to the project. Depp had made the suggestion not to be a smart-ass but because he idolized Brando. His fantasy was to make this wonderfully written movie with the person he considered the greatest actor ever. As it turned out, Depp wouldn't have been in the movie were it not for the participation of Brando, and Brando wouldn't have agreed to do the film were it not for Depp signing on.

The initial meeting between Depp and his hero took place at Brando's Mullholland Drive estate. Depp recalled, "I was really nervous on the way to the house. I kept thinking about who I was going to meet and the things he had done in his career. But that vanished almost instantly when I got there. Marlon said 'Hello' and invited me into his house, and he was no longer this towering icon for me. He was just this great, wonderful guy that I was lucky to be working with."

Oscar winner Faye Dunaway had worked with both Brando and Depp before, although she hadn't seen Brando in almost 30 years. She describes making *Don Juan DeMarco* in her autobiography, *Looking for Gatsby*: "The first day we were doing a table reading of the script, in comes this big man with a dog, which put us all immediately at ease, and we started reading the script. . . . He [Brando] wasn't letting himself be bullied by the demands of the script. He just found a way to swim around these words, and search and fish and improvise."

Dunaway tells a wonderful story about the relationship between Depp and Brando on the set. "Marlon made it clear to everyone just how approachable he intended to be the very first day we started shooting," writes Dunaway. "Taped to the door of his trailer was a sign he had made. In black block letters it read 'Don't knock, the door is open, come on in.' One day Johnny got there before him, and took the hundreds of scarves that were used in the harem scene and hung them throughout Marlon's trailer. You couldn't move in that trailer without either brushing past a scarf or ending up with one clinging to you, but Marlon was quite taken with the bordello Johnny had created for him."

The harem sequence was a surreal experience for Depp. It's a fantasy sequence in which Don Juan stumbles into a large room with a huge swimming pool. In the room are no fewer than 250 gorgeous naked women. During the shooting of this scene, Depp was gentlemanly almost to a fault. He spoke to as many of the women as he could, asking them if they felt all right about the scene and if they were comfortable with the nudity. After the shot wrapped, Depp commented, "It was really strange. The first thing I felt was uncomfortable. When you walk into a room with 250 naked women . . . it's impossible to focus on it. There were so many girls, and they were all so nude, it would have almost been more intense if there had been three nudes. It would have been more shocking. I just wasn't able to take it all in."

Depp was overwhelmed to be working with his idol. Like most young actors, he'd watched a number of Brando's films several times over, trying to absorb technique, but he was initially hesitant to ask Brando about acting. "We eventually did talk about it," said Johnny. "I think he felt compelled to tell me about his experiences, to offer advice. He said I should play *Hamlet*, for one thing." Depp said that the scenes he played with Brando in *Don Juan DeMarco* were among the most memorable moments of his career. "There are times when you are trying to get somewhere inside, but there is so much stuff going on around you — the guy with the slate marker, the grip over there drinking coffee, the director going 'Action!' when you aren't ready. Marlon was there for me then. He helps create an atmosphere that makes those moments easier. Even if it's just by laughing and looking at you. Marlon helped make the scenes between us totally private."

For his wonderful characterization of Don Juan DeMarco, Depp used the influence of a few other famous people; there is a bit of Errol Flynn in there, along with a pinch of Ricardo Montalban and Fernando Lamas.

Because Johnny was having so much fun making this film — he was enjoying the material and was still in awe of the fact that he was working with Brando — he was relaxed and in the best of spirits. His makeup person, Patty York (who has worked with Depp for several years), described his demeanor during the shoot: "He was so generous and happy that he would give you the shirt right off his back. And I do mean that; he came into the makeup trailer for his daily regimen, and I commented to him that I liked his shirt. He took it off and gave it to me." Nor was it uncommon for Depp to treat the crew members to champagne at the end of a long shooting day.

Depp's wardrobe person on *Don Juan DeMarco*, Kenn Smiley, said, "Johnny is so totally different from most actors. He really likes who he is, and he is really secure in that. He treats people the way he wants to be treated. That's why we all stay with him."

Don Juan DeMarco was released to almost universally positive reviews and brisk initial business — it would make a fairly solid $23 million during its initial domestic release. But the movie was ultimately too eccentric to catch on the way *Sleepless in Seattle* did. That said, it remains a movie often cited as one of the most enjoyable of Depp's career.

Johnny Depp doesn't go out of his way to appear on TV chat shows or awards shows, but he doesn't necessarily turn them down either. He is free with his time when he is promoting a film and when he is asked to present an award; if it is for something or someone meaningful to him, he will do it. He won't look like the most natural presenter in the world, but he'll do it. He agreed to be a presenter at the 1994 Academy Awards — his first time on stage at the Big Show. When host Whoopi Goldberg introduced him, Depp sauntered onto the stage in a tuxedo with long hair and a mustache. "Tonight we also honor the people who supply music for films. This song is a perfect example of their art. To sing his own composition 'Philadelphia,' ladies and gentlemen, Neil Young." Depp's opinion of the appearance? "I haven't seen it, but people tell me that it went okay. My face was probably frozen with fear, because there is this weird artificiality about those things. Backstage, all I could think of was how do I get out of this? I absolutely almost fled. I had a few options swimming around in my brain. Just collapse, fall over unconscious, that was one. Projectile vomiting, that was another."

During this period, Johnny Depp and Kate Moss were still a serious item. Whenever he spoke of Kate, it was always with sweet affection; he'd say things such as, "She is a wonderful girl, and I can't stand being away from her." He made television appearances — which he usually does only when promoting a movie — with Kate. He agreed to participate in certain projects just because she asked him to.

Depp was described in the 22 October 1994 edition of the British music magazine *New Music Express* as having "moved from massive

The Icon of Cool

Johnny Depp on Channel 4's "Big Breakfast,"
with Kate Moss, Amber, Lorraine, Lidija, and
Naomi Campbell
RICHARD CHAMBURY/GLOBE PHOTOS

clean-cut success on the U.S. teen TV show *21 Jump Street* to become a freak befriender and ultra-cool icon for the '90s." This isn't a very generous way of describing his friends, but it's not entirely inaccurate either. For instance, Depp has been known to hang around ex-Pogues member Shane McGowan (who recently made news when Irish pop star Sinead O'Connor tried desperately and unsuccessfully to get him off dope). In 1994, McGowan and his new band The Popes were scheduled to perform on the long-running British music program *Top of the Pops*. As an added treat, Depp was invited to go to England to surprise his friend and introduce the band. He flew in from L.A. shortly before the show, and he was still suffering from jet lag when the show's host, Claire Steyes, introduced him as Johnny "Edward Scissorhands" Depp. Depp sheepishly introduced the band and left the stage. He has explained that he did the show for two reasons: because Shane McGowan is a friend of his and because Kate Moss convinced him it would be a cool thing to do.

McGowan and The Popes had been the attraction on opening night for the Viper Room in 1993, and Depp later directed and starred in the music video for their song called "That Woman's Got Me Drinking," in which Depp plays a falling-down drunk to McGowan's bartender.

Notable among Depp's TV appearances was his participation in a PBS special called *The United States of Poetry*. The program featured Depp in shadowy black and white reciting the words of his hero, Jack Kerouac. Colorful scenes of American vistas, both urban and rural, are intercut with shots of Depp reading "America, I've given you all, and now I'm nothing. Everything is perfect, it's not happening, man. . . . Got up and dressed up, went out and got laid, then died and got buried in a coffin in a grave."

Depp has even been known to appear in print ads for clothing. As hard as that may be to believe, he has joined a large roster of American A-listers who accept ridiculous sums of money to appear in ads with the strict provision that they run only in the countries in which they were made. Everyone from Harrison Ford to Mickey Rourke has appeared in ads displayed only in Japan. Depp appeared in print ads for the European department store Hermes, as did bug-eyed actor Steve Buscemi. Depp wears an open blue button-down shirt over a white T-shirt and khaki pants. He looks upward and away from the camera.

Later in 1995, Depp was receiving myriad lucrative offers from major studios to star in every movie that was simultaneously being offered to the likes of Brad Pitt and Tom Cruise, including a film that would go on to make a rather large splash — *Titanic*. Depp decided to accept an offer to work with a filmmaker he'd always admired: Jim Jarmusch. Jarmusch wanted him to star in his black-and-white revisionist western called *Dead Man*, and he was only too eager to comply.

Depp has made an entire career out of playing eccentric characters in interesting movies. He can always be counted on to deliver something off the beaten path, but he will never be confused with Tom Cruise in terms of box-office clout. *Dead Man* defies categorization; it is a black-and-white psychological drama/western with some comedy thrown in, and it's unlikely to make even half as much money as *Mission Impossible*.

Jarmusch has epitomized the term "independent filmmaker" since his 1981 debut, *Permanent Vacation*, which he wrote, produced, directed, and edited. He followed it with the film that put him on the map, *Stranger than Paradise*, then really hit his stride a couple of years later with *Down by Law*, which featured a then-unknown Italian actor named Roberto Benigni. These films got Jarmusch respect and awards all over the world, but they didn't get his name anywhere near the top of that all-important weekend-grosses chart.

With both Depp and Jarmusch involved in *Dead Man*, it ended up being one big celebration of independence — they had license to do whatever they wanted. There is, for instance, a character named Sally, a frontier transvestite, played by none other than Iggy Pop (looking like a 70-year-old grandmother). In the credits, Sally is listed as Salvatore "Sally" Jenco. In another in-joke, as Depp's character, William Blake, strolls down the muddy streets of the town called Machine, he sees a prostitute giving vigorous oral sex to a client beside a saloon. The client notices Blake staring and casually pulls out a pistol, aiming it at him to indicate that he should be on his way. The client is played by Depp's friend and Viper Room regular Gibby Haynes of the Butthole Surfers.

Dead Man is a lush, beautifully shot western, but it's as eccentric as they come. William Blake is an accountant from Cincinnati on his way out west to take a position in a mining operation. When he arrives in the vile, two-mule town where the job is, he is met by a giggling, greasy-haired English office manager who informs him that there is no job — the letter he received offering it to him is dated three months earlier, and, since they'd heard nothing from him in the interim, they assumed he wasn't coming and gave the position to someone else. Blake is devastated because he has spent everything he had on the trip west. He demands to see the firm's owner, who turns out to be a senile, shotgun-toting brute who hasn't a shred of sympathy for Blake.

Blake meets a sympathetic local girl who invites him into her bed to be consoled. The pair are interrupted by her boyfriend, a known gunslinger. A gunfight erupts, and the girl is fatally shot in the chest. Blake is able to grab a gun and shoot the gunslinger several times, killing him, before noticing that he is badly injured himself. A bullet has traveled through the girl and lodged in his shoulder. Although he is seriously wounded, he is forced to flee town — the gunslinger happened to be the son of the mine owner.

Blake ends up in the middle of nowhere and passes out. He is revived by a Native American who goes by the name of Nobody (Gary Farmer), who nurses him back to health. When Nobody first learns Blake's name, he jumps to his feet and scurries off, startled. It seems that Nobody believes Blake is the reincarnation of the great English poet William Blake, whose words the young Nobody learned when he was forced to attend the "white man's school." Nobody decides that he must become Blake's loyal protector. A posse of killers hired by Mitchum's character is after Blake, so he and Nobody go on the run.

As oddball as it sounds, *Dead Man* is a very good movie. Gary Farmer describes it as "a road movie, with a horse." Movies that are strange for the sake of being noticeably cool end up being little more than contrived and self-indulgent. But this isn't the case with *Dead Man*. Jarmusch is an eccentric thinker; this is what a western looks like to him, and as it unfolds it just gets more and more interesting, especially in the interaction between Depp and Farmer.

Gary Farmer is Cayuga of the Wolf Clan, Ongwehon:we, from Ontario, Canada. He makes Nobody a delightfully and completely unpredictable character that we cannot take our eyes off; his deadpan delivery as he recites the poetry of William Blake is hilarious. Depp's performance inspired him. "Johnny goes through most of this movie pretty much half dead," said Farmer. "It takes a lot of patience to be half dead and play down your energy, especially for someone like Johnny."

Also part of the wonderfully diverse cast of *Dead Man* was a great Hollywood personality in his final screen performance: Robert Mitchum, who plays the mine owner. A glance at the long and successful career of Mitchum reveals many parallels with the career of Depp. Mitchum wanted, more than anything, to do good work and would go to great lengths to achieve it. Like Depp, he was interested in working with diverse and interesting filmmakers from whom he could learn. His personal life was frequently the subject of newspaper stories, and he too had his share of run-ins with the law. Depp was initially intimidated by the cinematic icon. "He was about seven feet tall and in great shape," recalled Depp. "He was a real tough guy, but a tough guy who had an enormous heart."

Jarmusch didn't arbitrarily select William Blake as his hero's name. "William Blake was a visionary poet, painter, printer, and inventor. His work was revolutionary, and he was imprisoned for his ideas," explained Jarmusch. "I was reading books by Native Americans on Native American thought, and it struck me that many of Blake's ideas and writings sounded as though they could have come from the soul of a Native American."

Dead Man was a tough shoot. It was filmed in Sedona, Arizona, and Virginia City, Nevada; the days were often very hot, and the conditions were less than ideal for living, let alone making a movie. There were dust storms and high winds. "Visibility was all but nil," recalled Depp. "You couldn't see the camera, and you couldn't see the other actors . . . which was kind of nice when you come to think of it."

Always one for a little adventure, Depp stayed in a manor house called the McKay Mansion while living in Nevada; the house was supposedly haunted by the ghost of a little girl in a pink dress. Depp told a journalist that that was precisely what he liked about the place: "I *wanted* to see some spirits there."

Jarmusch and Depp had been friends for several years before they found the time and the material to work on together, and their working relationship was unique and exciting. "He [Depp] is one of the most precise and focused people I have ever worked with," said Jarmusch. In fact, Jarmusch wrote the part of Blake with Johnny in mind. "What I love about him as an actor is his subtlety and interesting physicality, which is underplayed," said Jarmusch. "He has amazing eyes, which he uses to great effect. I didn't really appreciate his precision until I worked with him; he never makes a false move."

By the end of the making of *Dead Man*, Depp was starting to grow a little tired of playing outcasts and weirdos. "I hope this is the last of these innocents that I play," he said at that time. "This is a naïve young guy who is trying to get his life together. What is different about this piece is that he is trying really hard to make his life work but ends up slowly, literally, dying. And he knows he is dying. It's a beautiful story."

Dead Man was unveiled at the 1995 Cannes Film Festival; despite Jarmusch's usually lofty stature there, the movie was not well received. Some of the French journalists openly turned on Jarmusch, standing up at the end of the screening and yelling toward where he was sitting, "Jim, this is a piece of shit."

Oddly, Depp would play another innocent of sorts in his next film, but this time he was an innocent who could come up with the goods when the situation required it. It was a big-studio film, and Depp was criticized for even agreeing to make it. It was widely reported that the usually staunchly independent actor had taken the role as a deliberate stab at widespread commercial success.

Nick of Time was a gimmicky thriller made by commercially oriented director John Badham (*Saturday Night Fever, Blue Thunder*). It was gimmicky because the story on the screen was supposed to unfold in the real-time 90 minutes that it took to watch the movie. It didn't really come off that way, but that's how it was sold. The movie is essentially a remake of one that Alfred Hitchcock made in 1934 and then remade with James Stewart in 1956: *The Man Who Knew Too Much.*

In *Nick of Time*, Depp plays an accountant with a small daughter. Recently widowed, he is going into Los Angeles by train with his little girl for a job interview. He is met at the station by a couple of unsavory strangers (played by Christopher Walken and Roma Maffia) named Mr. Smith and Ms. Jones. They are conspirators in a plot to assassinate a candidate for national office; their plan is to grab someone who has no possible motive to commit the crime and force him to do it by holding a loved one hostage.

Despite reports to the contrary, Depp didn't look at *Nick of Time* as the movie that would propel him into the upper echelons and get him the scripts usually reserved for Keanu Reeves or Tom Cruise. He liked the story. And even though he had no children of his own at the time, he said, "I have some nieces and nephews that I absolutely worship, and if anything happened to them I would go crazy and do anything at all to save them."

Depp was asked by *Playboy* magazine about doing "the Keanu thing" and the criticism he received for it. His initial response was

"Who cares?" But he went on to elaborate: "I'm interested in story and character and doing things that haven't been done a zillion times before. When I read *Nick of Time* I could see the guy mowing the grass, watering the lawn, putting on the Water Wiggle in the backyard for his kid, and I liked the challenge of playing him," said Depp. He also expressed an interest in working with *Saturday Night Fever* director John Badham. The $4–$4.5-million paycheck couldn't have hurt either.

When I spoke to Badham about *Nick of Time*, he remarked that even he initially had reservations about casting Depp. "I knew he was a great actor because I had seen him in enough interesting roles to see his diversity," Badham said, "but he had never played a guy who wears a suit and tie and has a nine-to-five mentality."

Another big reason Depp signed on to do *Nick of Time* was the opportunity to act alongside another actor whom he deeply admired: Christopher Walken. Walken is clearly one of the finest actors ever; he has an incredible versatility and range, having done everything from Shakespeare to song-and-dance musical theater to his Oscar-winning role in *The Deer Hunter*. In *Nick of Time*, Walken plays one of his stock villains — a guy who is ruthless but not particularly bright, a volatile combination.

Nick of Time began principal photography on 2 April 1995, with almost all of the location shooting being done at the Westin Bonaventure Hotel right in the middle of downtown Los Angeles.

John Badham had scored with a couple of big-budget films (e.g., *Blue Thunder* and *Dracula*), but this movie presented him with the opportunity to try something a bit different — he shot the film in a style usually reserved for documentaries. Also, the story and the gimmick behind it meant that the film had to be shot in mostly chronological order. So some of the scenes were shot on the fly — in Ed Wood style — without any time to go back and redo them if they weren't perfect. This would normally freak a director out, but Badham was delighted because it gave the film that cinema verité look he wanted.

I sat down with Badham in the Four Seasons Hotel in Toronto just after he'd made *Nick of Time*, and I asked him about working with Depp. I wanted to know whether the Depp whom he knew by reputation was the Depp who showed up to work with him on the film. "That's interesting," said Badham. "Because I am not unlike anyone else out there — I read magazines, and I watch television, so the stuff I knew about Johnny Depp from those sources painted him as someone that I would more than likely have a hard time with. So when his name came up for *Nick of Time*, I was a bit cautious." To assuage his uneasiness, he started to ask around about Depp, talking to people who'd worked with him before. "The information I was getting back was fascinating because, of all the people I asked who had worked with him, to a person they all reported that he was shy and quiet and dedicated and hard-working." And, as it turned out, they were right. "He was all the things the people who had worked with him had said he would be," Badham continued. "What was even more interesting to me was that he had already read the script over a few times and connected on the points that I was hoping to steer him towards."

I asked Badham how he'd describe Depp to a colleague wondering about the experience he had working with Johnny. Badham chuckled a bit before saying, "He was wonderful to work with, really. I mean, there were days, several days actually, when Johnny would show up — on time, mind you — for his very early call, and one look at him told me that he had not been to bed yet from the night before. But he was prepared to shoot what needed to be shot, and he handled what was expected of him."

Nick of Time didn't really work, not because it was poorly acted or made, but because it became predictable very quickly. It started off with an interesting premise, but holes that developed early on couldn't be filled. And the fact that it was sold as a gimmick project, a real-time thriller, didn't help because it didn't feel like it was unfolding in real time. Nor did it really need that gimmick to be interesting. When I read the Ebbe Roe Smith and Patrick Duncan screenplay of *Nick of Time* (dated 27 January 1995), it was interesting as a political thriller, but it lacked the intricacies that make covert assassination plots compelling to an audience. The story as laid out by Smith and Duncan was poorly thought out and never had a realistic hope of succeeding.

As for Depp's performance as an accountant named Gene Watson, it does take a while to get used to seeing Johnny play an everyman in a suit and tie. But he does well in the role of a frustrated father pushed to extraordinary measures to protect his daughter. The criticism leveled against him for selling out to the lucrative action movie scene was silly because *Nick of Time* isn't an action movie, nor did it have a particularly large budget. At the end, *Nick of Time* brought in a disappointing $9 million during its domestic release.

Johnny Depp's friendship with Marlon Brando had deepened since their initial meeting on *Don Juan DeMarco*. After finishing *Nick of Time*, Depp was given a chance to work with Brando again in a project that would end up demonstrating just how precarious creating a movie can be, no matter how big the names involved in it. In fact, the events surrounding the making and the unmaking of *Divine Rapture* make one wonder why this kind of thing doesn't happen a lot more often in the huckster-driven world of filmmaking.

Divine Rapture is set in Ireland and was supposed to have been shot there. It is something of a satirical look at miracles and the Catholic Church. The wife of a fisherman (Debra Winger) dies and comes back to life with the help of a local priest (Marlon Brando)

who has been linked to miracles in the past. An American reporter (Johnny Depp) goes to Ireland to investigate/debunk the story and raise questions about the woman's fate and the nature of miracles.

All reports indicated that Brando was really excited about the project and loved Ireland from the start. He rented a large house in Shanagarry — at a cost of $7,500 per week to the production — and hired several local people to work for him as assistants. Depp stayed in a house in nearby Ballymaloe.

Kate Moss planned to join Johnny in Ireland for some of the shoot once her modeling obligations in Paris let up. In the meantime, Depp was rattling around in a small Irish town with nothing to do. He happened to run into fellow actor Val Kilmer, who was in Ireland recovering from a nasty breakup with his wife, Joanne Whalley. Depp and Kilmer were often seen drinking together.

The director of *Divine Rapture*, Thom Eberhardt, was feeling a lot of heat even before shooting. Because this was to be a fairly low-budget independent movie, both time and money were very tight. Brando was paid $1 million up front as a nonrefundable bonus for signing his name to a contract, but Depp lowered his price considerably for the opportunity to work with his friend and teacher once again.

The shooting schedule was a tight eight weeks, and as the start date loomed the shooting locations couldn't be used because arrangements hadn't been properly made. Saying that "Churches are divine and sacred places, they are not film sets," the bishop of Cloyne put the kibosh on plans to use a local church for the central location. The director had nowhere to set up his cameras.

Weather became Eberhardt's next enemy. The skies in Ireland had been ideal for weeks on end during preproduction, but as soon as the cameras were ready to roll the weather quickly turned ugly and unpredictable.

Filming got under way in early July 1995, and Depp's work amounted to only a few days of shots that didn't require any acting or characterization — "I jumped over a fence in one of the shots," he said — before production was forced to halt on July 16th. The money had dried up. Eberhardt assured everyone that the break in production was only temporary, that everything would be straightened out by July 21st.

Depp was told he could leave Ireland if he wished, so he headed to Paris to spend some time with Moss. He would never return to the Irish location.

When July 24th rolled around and there was still no sign of more money, it was announced that *Divine Rapture* had been cancelled.

Depp now found himself without a project to work on and in a position to relax and mull over what to do next.

Others involved were less fortunate. One of the producers, Barry Navidi, had invested over $2 million of his own money in the production, and it was lost forever. But he didn't seem to be all that upset — any producer knows that investing in films is as risky as drilling for oil. You can drill 1,000 holes looking for oil and come up with sand, but sometimes when you drill the next hole you hit a gusher that erases all the previous disappointments. Navidi was more upset at the loss of a potentially interesting movie; he was saddened that he'd never get to see the film he'd worked so hard to create.

When I asked Depp for his take on the whole *Divine Rapture* debacle, he said, "You want my experience of it? I had gotten the script from Marlon. He said, 'Hey, man, come over here and join me in Ireland. We'll do this thing. It'll be fun.' I said, 'Sure.' I went over. We started shooting, and we were having a great time. Everything was really good. Next thing we knew, they were saying, 'It's over.' And that was that. It was like being in the middle of good sex and then having the lights come on, and your mother is standing in the room."

The Icon of Cool

There were a few offers that Depp could now think seriously about. He was interested in making a film called *The Cull* before that project was torpedoed by financing woes. He was also being pursued to star in a live-action film version of the popular cartoon *Speed Racer*. But perhaps the most interesting offer was a literary work being developed into a film — Depp's favorite book, *On the Road*.

For a number of years, director Francis Ford Coppola had been talking about making a film from the classic Jack Kerouac novel, which has inspired so many other young writers and artists. He'd even made it to the screenplay stage. Every young actor in Hollywood would kill to have the chance to work with Coppola and to act in the film version of *On the Road*, and, since Depp had a special relationship with the book, the project would have meant even more to him. The film, however, simply hasn't been made — perhaps for the best.

When I was speaking with Depp about his adaptation of another renowned piece of American literature, *Fear and Loathing in Las Vegas* (more on that later), we touched on the subject of the movie version of the Kerouac book. "I was excited as hell to talk about *On the Road* as a movie, but at the same time the idea made me queasy," said Depp. "The idea that I would be embodying that character . . . I wanted badly to do it, but I wasn't sure I wanted to do it, if that makes any sense. If I did it, there would be a finality to it, rather than just thinking, 'I would love to make a movie from *On the Road*.'"

What Depp decided to do next was something that he'd wanted to do for years but thought he needed to grow into. He would direct his first feature film. He would cowrite the script with his brother and star in the film — which would ultimately be an exhilarating, challenging, and heartbreaking experience.

Chapter Ten

The Brave

"They live in a country
and communities where it
is not customary to look
forward into the future, for
they live without incurring
the expenses of life, which
are absolutely necessary
and unavoidable in the
enlightened world; and of
course their inclinations
and faculties are solely
directed to the enjoyment of the present day, without sober
reflections on the past or apprehension on the future."

YORAM KAHANA/SHOOTING STAR

George Catlin, North American Indians, 1832

Of all the things that Johnny Depp has done, *The Brave* is one of the
most fascinating; it is also the most revealing of the way he feels
about his profession and the way he is misunderstood by the public.
It is a movie that hardly anyone has seen, yet when Depp is profiled
it is always mentioned as being a colossal vanity project that died a
thudding death — not a fair representation.

Having watched *The Brave* a few times, and knowing what Depp invested in the project emotionally, physically, and financially, I'd argue that it is probably the most intriguing film he has ever done. It is certainly worthy of close examination.

At the time of writing, *The Brave* isn't available for general consumption. It has never been released in any form in North America. It played at the 1997 Cannes Film Festival and was so soundly savaged by the press that it was unable to find distribution for either broad theatrical or video release.

Sometimes the story behind the making of a film is so compelling that it overshadows the film itself. The struggle to get the legendary sequel to Robert Towne's *Chinatown* made is incredible if you are interested in the vagaries of the film world (the film was finally made by director-actor Jack Nicholson, with disappointing results). German director Werner Herzog's Sisyphian struggle to make *Fitzcarraldo* resulted in one of the finest "making of" documentaries ever made, Les Blank's *Burden of Dreams*. Johnny Depp's *The Brave* is one of those projects. The story of the production of this film sounds more like the legacy of an Egyptian curse than the making of a movie.

The Brave had been kicking around Hollywood for a number of years. The story was first told in a novel, *Raphael, Final Days*, by Gregory MacDonald. A young writer at the usc film school named Aziz Ghazal thought the novel was cool and obscure. He adapted it into a screenplay and started shopping it around. The premise of the story was so weird that the script started getting some attention. Oliver Stone was interested in it as a film he might produce for a younger, emerging filmmaker to direct. Jodie Foster considered producing and directing a reworked version of the story.

In spite of all this positive professional momentum, however, Ghazal was struggling with some personal demons. In 1994, he went on a rampage that startled the movie community, which is much more used to conjuring up fake violence than having to confront the real thing. Ghazal killed both his wife and his young daughter, and then he killed himself. At that point, those connected to the nascent project quickly distanced themselves from it. One might think that with this ghoulish history no one would go near *The Brave* again, but soon enough two young producers, Carroll Kemp and Robert Evans Jr. (son of legendary producer Robert Evans, no stranger to controversial projects himself), snapped up the rights to the book and the screenplay.

A little more than a year after the Ghazal murder-suicide, someone gave the screenplay to Johnny Depp's agent. Depp carefully reads all the scripts that Tracey Jacobs puts in his hands. "I hated it immediately," said Depp. "It was full of clichés, a sort of Christ-like allegory that was a long funeral march without the slightest bit of humor." Such a harsh assessment suggests that the script passed right back out of his hands, but there was something about the story that he just couldn't shake. "In spite of everything, I found that central idea compelling," said Depp. "Could you sacrifice your life for love?"

The Brave is a story about a young Native American named Raphael who is living in abject poverty with his wife and two children in a small trailer without running water. He has been in jail and has had a drinking problem. When he answers an ad for a job at a downtown warehouse, a wheelchair-bound sicko named McCarthy (Marlon Brando) gives Raphael a bag full of cash. It's a down payment for the job that Raphael has accepted — to sacrifice his life in a snuff film for a fee of $50,000, which will go to his family once he is gone.

Depp was so fascinated by this story that he decided to talk to the producers about the project. Evans and Kemp were startled that someone of Depp's caliber was interested in their movie, and they were floored by his plan: Depp said he'd consider taking the lead role in the film on the condition that he be allowed to rewrite the script and direct the movie himself and have final cut.

In a televised interview in France in November 1998, Depp told interviewer Chiara Mastroianni (daughter of Catherine Deneuve and Marcello Mastroianni) why he'd decided that this project should be his directorial debut: "The only true reason I wanted to direct *The Brave* was that I was too inarticulate to tell another director what I wanted, you know," he explained. "What I wanted it to look like, or be like, or what the pace should be like, or what the rhythm should be like, or what it should feel like, you know. Just because I couldn't express that, you know."

Depp and his brother, Dan — "D.P. Depp" on the cover page — extensively rewrote the screenplay before presenting it to the young producers. Their draft, dated 30 October 1996, is a compelling read; it is much darker and more dismal than the film ended up being.

Having Depp on board to write, direct, and star, however, didn't mean that the major studios were instantly on the phone with offers. This was still a very difficult story. So Depp, his brother, and the producers headed to the Cannes Film Festival, where they managed to drum up a lot of varied interest in the project and to secure a good chunk of money, estimated at $15 million, for the film. Now it was time to actually make the movie.

No matter how many films you have been involved with, it seems, when you walk onto a set as a first-time director, everything is entirely different. And it's even more difficult if you're starring in the film at the same time.

"To tell you the truth, I found doing both difficult for a lot of reasons, some common, some personal," Depp recalled. "But mostly because as an actor you have to put yourself in a trance, you have to lose contact with reality. But when you direct, it is the exact opposite. Those two opposites are really stressful to be incessantly going back and forth to." On the personal side, Depp found particularly difficult one aspect of directing that he hadn't even considered. "I trusted my feelings and my crew, so I didn't have the classical symptoms of stage fright going on," he explained. "But what really freaked me out was watching myself in the rushes for the first 15 days. That was really painful. I hate seeing myself onscreen, and I never go to the rushes on the films I've just acted in. For those first couple of weeks, I couldn't judge anything because I was blocked. I got used to it. I still didn't like it, but I got used to it."

The complex organizational requirements of big-time moviemaking are something no young director is ever truly prepared for. Depp recalled "dealing with money, with insurance, with trade-union guys. No kidding, can you imagine hearing an assistant yelling 'Lunch break in five minutes!' when you've got an hour's worth of work before losing the light or having someone come onto the set and say that the young actor you are working with has to leave in no more than 10 minutes when you know you have hours of work ahead of you or you will fall behind schedule? I would say that having all those mosquitoes buzzing around and trying to ruin your life — there are fucking rules that make you feel like stopping what you are doing and going home. It really is a nightmare. If I direct again, it will be with five guys and a 16 mm camera. No more hundred-man crew, it's too much to handle."

Depp chose the somewhat seedy Hollywood Suite Motel on the west end of Hollywood Boulevard as his command post and production office because it was near the run-down locations he needed for the film. Then he enlisted the help of his friend Iggy Pop to do the musical score. "As soon as I made the suggestion to Iggy that I would like him to do the music, he immediately started working on the ideas in his head," recalled Depp. "In no time, he brought me a few demos that were very interesting and exactly the kind of thing that I wanted — in some cases, I was listening to the things that were exactly what I wanted before I even really knew that that's what I wanted. It is very strange that Iggy is so very different from the image that most people have of him."

Making the movie was, as they say, a baptism by fire for the rookie director. Most difficult were the seven weeks of location filming in Ridgecrest, a small town outside Los Angeles on the way to Death Valley. Depp has remarked that they were the hottest seven weeks of his life and that he dreamed of heading somewhere cold the minute he could — and staying there. But it wasn't just the sun — that is, after all, why they headed toward Death Valley. Depp also found it tough to handle the heat of being the guy everyone came to with all their questions.

To make things easier, Depp surrounded himself with familiar faces. His director of photography was Vilko Filac, also the DOP on *Arizona Dream*. His set designer was also from *Arizona Dream*. His script supervisor came from *Dead Man*.

Johnny also sponged as much as he could off the directors he'd worked with who had impressed him the most — Emir Kusturica, Tim Burton, John Waters, and Jim Jarmusch. Depp pointed out that his director friends were openly encouraging when he told them he was about to step behind the camera. Jarmusch faxed him a letter of encouragement on the first day of shooting, and Kusturica called. "Emir told me not to hesitate to call him if I had the slightest problem," Depp recalled. "He also wanted to give me one last piece of advice: 'Don't forget, Johnny, fuck them all!'"

"The first day of shooting, I was feeling overwhelmed," said Depp. "Everyone was asking me a lot of questions at the same time, and I had a lot of trouble clearly explaining what I wanted. It was as

if I found myself faced with a colossal mathematical problem. But I didn't panic. Deep inside, I had total confidence in the film."

To start out on the right note, actor Floyd "Red Crow" Westerman performed, at Johnny's request, a Lakota Sioux sunrise ceremony to bless the film. Right after the ceremony, when the sun was coming up, Depp took a seat for the first time in the canvas director's chair, on which his name had been stenciled. At that moment, Depp received an encouraging call on his cell phone from Marlon Brando.

At the end of that first day of shooting, Depp was clearly exhausted — "I've been on a lot of film sets before, but I never knew how physically taxing directing was," he said. But the day didn't end with shooting; afterward, Depp huddled with his crew in the production trailer to plot out the next couple of days. Depp was taking his job as director very seriously, assuring the crew that this was definitely not a vanity project.

In spite of his inexperience, the cast and crew were impressed with their director from the first day of filming. They appreciated the care that he took in speaking with everyone directly rather than having an assistant do it. It wasn't uncommon to see Depp helping the crew members carry equipment. As it turned out, Brando's phone call on the first morning of the shoot was auspicious. Depp said that he'd written the role of McCarthy with Brando in mind but had refused to mention it to him for fear that it would be perceived as taking advantage of their friendship. When Brando called that morning, Depp told him he was about to direct a movie for the first time. Brando was supportive and filled with advice — he has also directed one film so far, *One-Eyed Jacks*, a vastly underrated western from 1960, which Brando decided to direct after both Stanley Kubrick and Sam Peckinpah left the project. Brando then inquired about the theme and story of Depp's film. Johnny filled him in with a brief but fairly detailed description of the movie. Brando wished Depp luck. A week later, Brando called again to see how things were going, and the two ended up talking about the characters in Depp's film at length. Brando asked Depp whom he'd cast in the role of McCarthy. "I told him that I hadn't decided that yet," said Depp. "And then Marlon simply said, 'I'm going to play McCarthy.' I was stunned and delighted." Brando also said he'd appear in the film gratis. He wanted to help his friend in any way he could. Depp was thrilled — having Brando in any movie is bound to make it interesting.

Monday, 8 October 1996, was Brando's first day on the set of *The Brave*. Shooting took place in an old warehouse in downtown Los Angeles. Those on the set said that when Brando arrived the atmosphere became a lot more serious, even though he was jovial and open with the crew members. I know from interviewing actor Karl Malden, who's worked with Brando many times on film and on stage (including starring in *One-Eyed Jacks*), that Brando is one of those actors with that special something that keeps your eyes locked on him at all times when he is working.

There were no schedules or contracts between filmmaker Depp and actor Brando; they were just friends working together — this from an actor who made a French journalist sign a legal document saying that, if anything Brando said to him appeared anywhere other than the French magazine *Studio*, the journalist would have to pay him $100,000. There wasn't a lot of ink connected to Brando's appearance in the film because no one knew Brando was in it. Even the young producers were stunned to learn that their little film was now starring both Depp and Brando.

By Wednesday, October 10th, Brando and Depp were working easily together. As is his custom, Brando remained in his trailer while a stand-in was used to block and light scenes. Brando likes to report to the set at the last possible moment to keep the work as spontaneous as possible. On the day Depp and Brando filmed the first long dialogue between McCarthy and Raphael, it needed to be done several times to get maximum coverage for Depp to use in the editing room. Fortunately, Brando can say his lines over and over without making them sound repetitious; he effortlessly adds something subtle to each take, giving his director a wide array of interpretations to choose from.

After shooting was finally done, Brando headed back to his trailer to relax while Depp and his crew gathered around a video playback unit to view the footage. Everyone was silent — they were all stunned at Brando's ability to use the slightest expressions to convey the most extreme emotions.

Johnny paid close attention to Brando during the shoot, always trying to make him comfortable and discussing every detail of the work with him. Depp had two reasons for being so attentive: he was trying to be a good director by making his star performer as relaxed as possible, and he was an awestruck actor trying to absorb as much as he could from the master.

On the last day of location filming, at a place called Red Mountain, there was a cheer of celebration and relief as "It's a wrap" was finally shouted. There were still some scenes to be shot in Los Angeles, but all the tough location shooting was finished. Before the cast and crew left the area for good, they were invited into the desert to take part in a Native American ceremony to ask the spirits of Red Mountain to protect all those involved with *The Brave*.

As he headed into the final stretch of filming, Depp was asked by Christophe d'Yvoire about the difficulties in translating his own written words to visual images. "Our screenplay was only meant to be the skeleton of the film," answered Depp. "Then you have to give it flesh on the set, depending on the setting and the atmosphere, and its own mood. I would say that 70 percent of what we've shot wasn't written as such in the screenplay."

He's right; there are glaring differences between the two. The first noticeable changes come in the compelling first meeting between Raphael and McCarthy. In the screenplay, McCarthy's intentions are clear, as is Raphael's understanding of the situation. In the final film, Depp has trimmed the scene down to a strangely amorphous conversation. We can sense what is being discussed, but there is room for doubt, which makes the scene a lot more effective and creepy. Can they really be negotiating that?

There are also words and lines taken out of the finished film that change the way the characters are perceived. In the film, McCarthy asks Raphael, "Are you afraid of dying?" Raphael responds, "No, are you?" In the screenplay, the lines read, "Are you afraid to die, of dying?" "Yeah, but it couldn't be much worse than living. Are you?" In the film, Raphael has given up on his own life, but in Depp's screenplay he is still grasping at a faint hope for the future.

Later in the same long sequence in the screenplay, McCarthy uses North American Indian folklore and tradition to communicate with Raphael. There is a long exchange about a ceremony known as the Sundance, performed after braves hung themselves for days by wooden skewers driven through their chest muscles. None of this is in the finished movie. Also absent is the starkness of the language in the screenplay. When McCarthy and Raphael are talking about the remuneration involved, McCarthy tells him, "Well, that depends on how willing you are, how brave you are, because the more you are able to withstand, spiritually, physically, the more money you will be paid." In the film, Raphael answers with an ominous nod and a look of deepening understanding of what he will be subjecting himself to for money. In the screenplay, there is a much more explicit reply: "What do you mean by that? Do you want to fuck me, to torture me, will you kill me?"

At the end of this truly grim sequence is another glaring departure from page to screen. In the script, as Raphael leaves with a paper bag filled with his down payment, he is confronted by the character known as Larry, McCarthy's henchman. Larry spits, "Hey, Tonto, this is a snuff movie. People pay big money to watch people die in pain. He is going to strap you into that fucking chair, scoop out your eyeball with a spoon and carve your dick up the middle with a knife, pull your guts out like a fire hose. You are going to die. You are going to die screaming." Larry then lets out a scream to illustrate his point. The term "snuff movie" is never heard or seen anywhere in the film.

Five pages later in the screenplay, there is a horrifically explicit dream sequence. Raphael is dreaming in sepia, and there is a clutter of sound like "gliding up and down an AM radio dial." The script describes a man's arm being strapped to a rusted metal chair, then a lone crow sitting on a fence. A tongue is slashed, and a penis is cut off. The crow stares back at us in a closer shot. A fingernail is pulled out with pliers, and an eyeball is gouged from its socket with a spoon. In the finished film, no image even remotely that gruesome appears. The director Depp showed a restraint that the writer Depp chose not to exercise.

In their screenplay, the Depp brothers include a subplot about the impending demolition of the squatter trailer village where Raphael and his family live. It is a major concern in the script and is returned to often. This side story is barely mentioned in the finished film; director Depp chose to concentrate on the personal and spiritual problems of the main character and his family.

Toward the end of the screenplay, the Depp brothers once again include a specific reference to Native American tradition and ceremony that doesn't make it into the finished film. It is curious that Depp went this route, because his concern about the treatment of Native Americans is symbolically referenced throughout the film. These omissions bolster the argument that Depp was pressured into delivering the movie before he was ready; if he'd had the time and resources to properly edit and prepare it, it might have been a more even and palatable film.

It is in the ending that the most radical departure from the screenplay is evident. In the film, Raphael comes to terms with the deal he has made with the devil, it seems, and resigns himself to his fate. He simply returns to the warehouse where the bargain was struck and disappears into the guts of the building. The screenplay has a much more complicated and violent ending, which involves a long confrontation between McCarthy and Raphael. Raphael shows up at the warehouse to tell McCarthy that he has no intention of fulfilling his part of the deal. McCarthy tries to bribe him with more money, but Raphael refuses it. McCarthy then rises from his wheelchair to walk, showing Raphael that he has been duped, and leaves him alone in a room with the torture chair and a video monitor showing the torture and murder of a young girl. Raphael ends up killing McCarthy with his own gun.

The trimming of this scene could have had a lot to do with Brando. Although he was open to working with Depp for as long as Johnny needed him, Brando was originally told that it would take no more than two days to film his scenes. He ended up staying much longer after he suggested that McCarthy return at the end of the movie for a coda, but there may not have been time to shoot the entire ending from the screenplay. Brando also may have had moral objections to some of the things he was supposed to say and do, causing the scene to be radically reorganized; Brando had taken a stand while filming The Appaloosa, stipulating on his arrival that he wouldn't appear in any sequence depicting the shooting or killing of Indians, a stand that caused emergency on-the-spot rewrites. In the script's final confrontation, McCarthy spits at Raphael, "Now, listen. I want you to listen to me, you little red nigger spic. There's a lot of coloreds out there, poisoning this country. A lot of decent white Americans who put sweat and blood and tears into the building of this country are not going to let nigger farts like you fuck it up. We're going to burn your churches, and we're going to burn your houses and burn your taco stands. You understand? Get your stink ass up. Come on, sweetheart, get up in the high chair. Up, up, up. Get up in the chair." This venomous speech gets even more vile before McCarthy is killed, and it changes the way that McCarthy is perceived. In the film, however, he is an oddly sympathetic and charismatic character. We are scared of him because of what he represents, but Brando plays him with such a soft voice and a quiet emotion that we can't help but see the tortured being sitting in the wheelchair. In the screenplay, he is nothing but an evil thug. The Depp brothers' McCarthy is a monster who pays the desperate and unfortunate for his own profit and amusement. This starkly written ending would not have fit well with what came before it.

The final sequence was to be shot on Brando's last day on the set. They were supposed to start shooting by 10 AM. By 6 PM, though, Depp and Brando were still huddled in the trailer, rethinking and rewriting the ending. Perhaps they never resolved how the film should end, deciding instead to leave it ambiguous. If you get a chance to see *The Brave*, ask yourself at the end if it would have been trashed by critics the way it was if the credits had read "A film by Wim Wenders" or if it had been the first feature by some highly touted brat from the USC film school. There have been directorial debuts a lot less thoughtful and well made that have received much greater praise for their makers — but, then again, they weren't dating supermodels and being featured on the covers of magazines the world over, so they could be taken more seriously.

Several of Depp's sequences stuck with me after I had watched *The Brave* for the first time. Some of them are obvious symbolic references, but they are captivating nevertheless. Every scene that Brando appears in is riveting. There is a scene by a stream where Raphael is gathering water in jugs, which he carries home on a pole across his shoulders. When he turns around with the water on his shoulders, there is a distinct echo of Christ on the cross.

There is also a nice performance by Clarence Williams III, who, despite doing terrific work for years, will always be known as Linc from *The Mod Squad*. Williams plays a priest who is deeply committed to the community he serves. He has a great moment with Raphael, who confesses to him what he is about to do and asks the priest to make sure that his family gets the promised money. The priest struggles with the implications for a moment and then turns him down.

If there is one performance that stands out for its weakness, it is that of Frederick Forrest, a fine actor who is often given to wildly over-the-top performances, which end up being quite distracting. He does so in *The Brave* and recently in Joel Schumacher's *Falling Down*.

Depp's performance as a self-directed actor is understated and controlled. Johnny could have written himself several major speeches and framed himself glowingly (see *The Horse Whisperer*, directed by and starring Robert Redford), but he deliberately didn't. He keeps the acting simple and straightforward. He effectively portrays hopelessness in a man who is full of love and compassion. The battles he has fought and the obstacles in his path have beaten him down physically and spiritually. The offer he accepts is grue-some, but he sees it as a bizarre ray of light from the depths of hell — it presents him with his one opportunity to do something to save his family.

As a director, Depp handles himself pretty well too. The movie is very languidly paced, but it should be. This isn't an action movie; it is a story about love and death and moral dilemmas. Depp doesn't try to jazz up the proceedings by overstyling the film with camera tricks. He has learned from the great directors he's worked with, and it shows. The ending of the film is especially haunting and well handled.

Depp is quite willing to talk about the movie, and through his words his passion is apparent. Just after filming was completed, he made the extraordinary admission that he hadn't read the novel that served as the original source material for his screenplay. It is hard to imagine writing a screenplay based on a book that you have never read, but Depp and his brother were really working from the existing screenplay by Aziz Ghazal. At the time, Depp said, "I haven't read the book yet; I probably will, though. I did meet the author, Gregory MacDonald. He's a great guy. The strange thing about him is that he is known mainly for writing funny stories. He came to visit the set one day, and I told him that even though I hadn't read the book it strangely served as a real inspiration for me. He smiled and told me it was okay because he hadn't read our screenplay either."

Terry Gilliam, who directed Depp in *Fear and Loathing in Las Vegas*, remembers seeing *The Brave*. "*The Brave* was a painful experience, I think, for Johnny because of the process," he noted. "He had this project that he felt deeply about, he directed it, and then the money guys wanted it at Cannes — but he never really had the chance to finish the film properly." Gilliam went on to assess the film: "If there is a weakness in the film, it is these two sides of Johnny that haven't quite found a middle ground, how you put it together. Because there are scenes in the movie that are like Kusturica's stuff; they're fabulous, outrageous. And then the other part of the film is incredibly dark and real."

What happened to Depp and *The Brave* when the movie was unveiled for the public is an excellent example of some of the things that are wrong with modern moviemaking.

By all accounts, that first showing of *The Brave* at the 1997 Cannes Film Festival was the most agonizing experience of Depp's entire career. "You walk up the red carpet, you know, the whole thing," he recalled, "go up there, wave, go in and sit down and watch the film with 2,500 people. The film goes through the projector. No coughs. No moving shoes. You're charged, you're out of your mind, you're everything. You're dying, you're ready to vomit, you're shaking, you want nothing but to get horribly drunk. And at the same time you are really proud, and you're embarrassed because you feel exposed, you know? You feel like you've just ripped your chest cavity open and begged someone to shit in it."

The film was first shown for the press at 8:30 in the morning — a ridiculous time to watch such a dark and heavy movie. I have done it before; seeing a movie such as Michael Winterbottom's gruelling *Jude* at 8 AM significantly changes the way the film affects you. That first time, I almost ran from the theater, but when I watched the film again, after having interviewed Winterbottom and his cast, and later in the day, it was a completely different experience. I appreciated what I was seeing so much more. The reports out of that early press screening of *The Brave* were that people were booing the film. Maybe they did, but the reaction to the film at its official premiere later that night was much more positive and supportive.

Depp's friend John Waters was at that premiere with Johnny and Kate Moss. Asked about the film, he said, "Well, it's very serious, but it's certainly arty. He didn't make a commercial kind of a movie, which I think is good. People loved it."

Then the scathingly bad reviews started appearing in the major show-business publications. A number of them mentioned that the premiere screening audience had booed the film, which wasn't the case at all. Depp said, "*Hollywood Reporter, Variety,* all these fucking things, they come out and they say, '*The Brave* was booed last night.'

Well, they lied. And the distributors were scared shitless. It was a film that was over two hours long, and they thought it was booed off the screen. It's like, people in . . . [Los Angeles] play follow-the-leader, man. If Joe down the street has a really nice pair of shoes, but, you know, Bob doesn't know if he likes them or not until he sees Sue's boyfriend Lance wearing them. Then, if two people like them, I'm there, you know. That kind of mentality is like a fucking disease." Reading those reviews, you have to wonder about the reviewers' agendas — the movie is a bit confusing at times, and it is dark, to be sure, but it is simply not the breathtakingly bad film that these supposedly big-time critics were telling people it was. "The reviews for *The Brave* were written before the reviewers even saw the movie," explained Depp.

My own reaction to *The Brave* has changed each time I've seen it. On the first viewing, I was prepared to see a work of vanity and self-indulgence that would be difficult to watch. My preconceived notions evaporated almost immediately. There's a lot to admire in this movie. Is it grim? Certainly. Is it ponderous? Definitely. But in forming an opinion of a movie, you have to consider the sum of all its elements — not just those elements that play to your particular tastes. A film has to be evaluated based on what it is, not on what you wanted it to be when you sat down in the theater.

The first thing I noticed about *The Brave* was the striking music by Iggy Pop; the sounds are eerie and ominous but appropriate. My attention was also immediately drawn to the pacing. The movie gets off to a slow start and never really picks up, and this languid pacing accentuates the sense of growing dread and impending horror.

As I watched the film for the first time, I was eagerly anticipating the first appearance of Marlon Brando, and he doesn't disappoint. When he rolls in, he is in a wheelchair and sports a willowy ponytail. He has the same strong presence that Francis Ford Coppola captured so effectively in *Apocalypse Now* — the sense that he is some mysterious, intellectually superior being who has lost touch with the rest of the world. Even though Brando is on the screen for only a fraction of the film's running time, he makes a big impact. He delivers a great, if at times somewhat unintelligible, speech (as in *Apocalypse Now*) that draws us out of our seats and into his space.

Upon reflection, however, the part of the movie that features Brando is indicative of the weakness of the movie overall: that slowness. The lines are delivered slowly. The slowness creates atmosphere at first but quickly becomes tedious. Perhaps with more time and more editing, the pacing could have been tightened up. That said, the points that Johnny and Dan are making with their screenplay came across well. Raphael is a character who cannot outwardly show love because he has never had it shown to him, although that doesn't mean he doesn't have the ability to love very deeply — in fact, he's willing to sacrifice his very life for it. The treatment of Native Americans is also a central issue, from racist remarks casually thrown about as jokes to the depressing squalor in which many Natives are forced to live.

There has been a lot of curiosity about *The Brave* since it was shown at Cannes, but it has yet to pass through a projector in North America. As I write this, a few countries have released the film on videocassette; you can find it with Japanese, German, or Portuguese subtitles, but it is not available yet in North American video stores.

It was reported in *Studio* magazine that Winona Ryder begged her ex for a private showing of the movie, but Depp couldn't oblige, explaining that the film was locked away in a vault somewhere and that he had no access to it. Ryder was very sympathetic toward Depp during this time, saying, "I think what happened to him surrounding the making of the movie strangely echoes the treatment of the

Indians in general." Ryder was raised by hippie parents, so the cause of Native Americans was not a bandwagon she jumped on as it passed. The commune in northern California where she lived when she was young shared its land with California Indian tribes, and she has been a long-time supporter of the American Indian College Fund. Ryder has been quoted as saying, "Native American culture is American culture and we can all learn from it. It is so profoundly important to preserve all of our country's cultures."

Depp discussed how he feels about his own Native blood in a piece in *Studio* in 1992: "I've got Cherokee blood running through my veins but I really didn't start thinking about that until I was a teenager. I was in Florida at the time and there is a lot of racism there. In high school the kids started giving me a hard time — calling me things like 'dirty Indian.' I got completely confused because I have always thought of myself as just being an American. I had completely forgotten about my Indian blood. But those little narrow-minded ignorant guys reminded me of it and I have to say that I am glad they did. Because when I started to get to know more about Indian cultures, I realized that I still had a lot of them in me. Their way of thinking and relating to things is something I inherited."

In the end, Johnny Depp seems to have been reconciled to the experience of making *The Brave*. In some respects, it was an abjectly negative experience; "The film hurt a lot to make," said Depp. "I was very naïve initially. I thought, 'Well, yeah, I can do this. I can direct, and I can do this; I can do both.' But at the same time . . . it's really . . . it's almost impossible. They're opposite things."

This prompts the obvious question: will he direct again? "Yes, definitely. I don't think I would direct a movie that I chose to be in in the lead role, but I will definitely, yeah. I'll do it again."

One of Depp's actors in *The Brave*, Floyd "Red Crow" Westerman, is a Dakota Sioux who plays Raphael's father in the film. Asked about his impressions of the young director, he said, "At first, I thought Johnny was taking on more than he could handle with *The Brave*. I had only seen one other guy who directed and acted in the same film. That was Kevin Costner in *Dances with Wolves*, but I saw Kevin break a couple of times and tear after someone and get angry. I didn't see that in Johnny. He goes beyond getting angry. He likes off-center, arty roles as an actor, and he is that way in his personality too."

The movie has an interesting footnote. There is a strange little symbol in the film: it's a round body with a skeletal face on top of it, and above the face is a question mark. Depp saw the symbol painted on a wall somewhere, and it freaked him out so much that it appeared not only in the film but also on the poster advertising the film. Significantly, what isn't on the poster is a picture of Depp. In these times, when the size of an actor's face or the size of the lettering used to spell his or her name on the poster is a negotiated contract item, Depp's attitude is rare and refreshing.

Although Johnny maintains that he has never worked for the sake of the money, he did put a lot of his own cash into *The Brave*. When you read that a movie cost $16 million or $67 million or $120 million to make, it seems like an abstract notion — until you have to start coming up with the millions yourself. That was the case with *The Brave*. To make the movie he wanted to make, Depp had to use hefty chunks of his own resources. The natural assumption was that he'd recoup that money when the movie was bought for distribution — but it wasn't picked up, and he lost his money.

By this time, Depp had already committed to his next film, the terrific gangster movie *Donnie Brasco*. But the next role he accepted was the lead in a science-fiction/horror movie called *The Astronaut's Wife*, which earned him his heftiest pay packet yet, a reported $8 million.

The Brave

So, as a direct result of making *The Brave*, one of his most interesting pieces of work, Johnny ended up agreeing to be part of a movie that would be the least interesting — with one of the best screen performances of his life sandwiched in between.

Chapter Eleven

Anti-Hero

"It seems I have built a career on being a failure."

Johnny Depp
February 2001

After being a professional actor for 15 years, Johnny Depp finally found a project that got people who'd dismissed him as a flake to reconsider that opinion. It was 1997's *Donnie Brasco*, and in it Depp would play a real person for the first time: Joe Pistone, who was alive and living in the witness protection program. When the film was released, critics remarked that Depp had now reached matu-rity as an actor and was finally playing adults. Those who'd been following his career knew

ALEC MICHAEL/
GLOBE PHOTOS

that this assessment wasn't really accurate, but they were pleased because it represented a step up in the respect that Johnny was getting for his work.

Like many terrific movies — and *Donnie Brasco* is a terrific movie — this one kicked around for a number of years before the right combination of elements allowed it to be made. The movie is based on a book written by former FBI undercover agent Joe Pistone about his infiltration into the Bonnano mafia family in New York. Called *Donnie Brasco: My Undercover Life in the Mafia* and cowritten by Joseph D. Pistone and Richard Woodley, it details the strange situation that Pistone, a.k.a. Donnie Brasco, found himself in when he began to care about the gangsters whose lives he was covertly trying to destroy. He started asking himself questions about his own life and character — was he a good guy pretending to be a bad guy, or was he one of the bad guys who was just pretending to wear a white hat?

Producer Louis DiGiaimo had known Pistone since they were in high school together. Since that time, they'd gotten together a couple of times a week to play basketball or go out for beers. Then Pistone just vanished one day, and DiGiaimo didn't hear from him for six years. When his name finally turned up again, it was in New York newspaper headlines trumpeting his successes as an undercover mafia buster.

Once the cases that Pistone was involved in were blown wide open, he got in touch with his pal DiGiaimo and suggested they have dinner. DiGiaimo was fascinated by what had happened to his friend and suggested that the wild tale be turned into either a book or a movie. Pistone was interested but insisted that they couldn't even begin to discuss it until all the various trials were completed. It would be another four years before the story could be told.

Pistone's book was published in 1989, and DiGiaimo immediately bought film rights to it. He took it to two producers he knew would be interested in such a movie project, Mark Johnson and Gail Mutrux at Barry Levinson's Baltimore Pictures. They were, at the time, working with Levinson on *Rain Man*, but they were impressed enough with the material to put it into active development.

The producers turned to a great screenwriter, Paul Attanasio, who'd written the brilliant *Quiz Show* for director Robert Redford and the pilot episode for Levinson's TV series *Homicide: Life on the Street*, to turn the book into a screenplay. He wrote a detailed script that came in at a whopping 153 pages; it deftly maneuvered through the life-and-death episodes in the book but ended up being more about loyalty and the limits of the human psyche. One particularly striking thing in the book is how Pistone recounts the often horrific events in a very detached, level-headed manner. Depp remarked that it reads like "it was written by a machine." Attanasio was determined to make it human.

The book begins with a case that Pistone was involved with in Florida, which leads him back to New York and the infiltration of the Bonnano crime family (the Bonnano name is never mentioned in the movie). Attanasio streamlined the story, focusing on the New York case, because he was committed to respecting all the real people involved by doing them justice in the film. He spent a lot of time with Pistone doing research. "Joe introduced me to a bunch of different guys involved in this stuff, but I was much less interested in them," said Attanasio. "I also met all of Joe's family, his wife, his kids; I spent a fair amount of time with all of them. They were real people with real feelings and lives — I had to be conscious of that all the time." Later, when Depp became part of the project, he too worked with Pistone. "*Donnie Brasco* was a motherfucker of a movie," said Depp. "I spent a lot of time with Joe Pistone. He's got an interesting rhythm to his speech, I did my best to get that. I put great pressure on myself to make it fucking right for the guy. He lived it. I was just pretending."

When asked if Pistone was allowed to read what Attanasio was writing, Attanasio said, "Yeah, he read everything. He was very, very easygoing about it, which is surprising because it's his life." In the end, Pistone said he was very happy with the finished film and especially with the way Depp portrayed him.

A few directors were considered, and British filmmaker Stephen Frears remained attached to the project for some time. Planning was under way when Martin Scorsese released his gangster film *Goodfellas*, and it set *Donnie Brasco* back a bit. Attanasio felt quite strongly about his script; he considered himself somewhat responsible for making sure that, if a movie were ever made about Pistone's life, Joe be properly represented. As Attanasio explained, "I really did feel responsible for Joe, because all of us could go off on our merry way and onto different things, but he had just one life and one life story to tell." Year after year passed, and Attanasio was called on to write different drafts of his screenplay to appease this producer or that producer at some studio or other, but director Frears kept telling Attanasio that the whole project hinged on Al Pacino. Pacino was fascinated by the Lefty Ruggiero character, maintaining that he wanted to play this guy and would do his best to be available when everything was finally put together.

One of the quirkier elements of moviemaking is that the really worthwhile films always seem to come together exactly when they should, even if years of development have already gone into them. Had *Donnie Brasco* come together earlier than it did, it would have been an entirely different movie. During all those years of development, Frears had left, and a new director had signed on. Mike Newell had made a very cheap but very enjoyable movie called *Four Weddings and a Funeral*, which made a global star of Hugh Grant and a hot property of Newell. Six months before shooting began, Newell — who wouldn't even have been a candidate earlier — agreed to direct *Donnie Brasco*.

When the time finally came to shoot the film, it had grown into a $40-million project for Columbia Pictures. Newell got together with screenwriter Attanasio to plow through the mountain of different drafts. They ended up reverting to the original draft because, as

Attanasio said, "the others went off in the wrong directions — my initial instincts on what this movie should be were correct."

The shooting script for *Donnie Brasco* (dated 22 May 1996) is a nice piece of screenwriting that has earned the respect of everyone who's read it. Newell remained quite faithful to the screenplay, although a few minor characters and situations were excised to improve pacing. For instance, in the screenplay, Sonny Black (Michael Madsen) is constantly hitting on a waitress at their social club who is from Ontario — he keeps telling her to "say something Canadian." The dialogue and even the waitress are gone from the finished film.

Given his previous experience with uniformed authority figures, Depp was initially unsure about the project. It had a lot of positives, including a great true story, but he'd be playing a cop. "I didn't think I would like Joe when I started hanging around with him," said Depp. "I thought he would be this gung-ho cop, this cold, uptight kind of guy, but Joe's a neat person. We actually became friends."

Director Mike Newell was delighted to have Depp as part of the cast; he recognized that this was the perfect part for the actor. "This particular role interested him because the whole character had to run beneath the surface, as it were," Newell explained. "Johnny is one of those actors who acts in a kind of long term. You stay with his characterizations throughout a film because he tells you his story in his own good time — and, more important, you are willing to wait for it."

I chatted with Newell when he was in Toronto making the black comedy *Pushing Tin*, and I asked him what he'd wanted his Donnie Brasco to look like and how Depp worked into that. "Well, Johnny got down deep into this character, a few levels deeper than I thought he would, in the early stages of our working together," said Newell. "That was wonderful because I knew he was capable of it. I was told by a few people who really had no idea that casting Johnny in a role as complex as Donnie Brasco was risky — those people had never either worked with him or really looked at his work. He is not only a good actor on his own, but he can hold it up alongside anyone he acts opposite of."

I told Newell that I thought the chemistry between the actor who played Donnie Brasco and the actor who played Lefty Ruggiero was crucial to the success of the film. "Precisely, yes," he agreed, "and Al Pacino, God, what praise can I heap on Al Pacino that hasn't already been said many times? He is a wonderful presence to have in your film. He is one of the great actors of the century and is also a very nice man and very easy to work with. He gets along with anyone who shows up to work prepared and takes the work as seriously as he does. Chemistry was what allowed Joe Pistone to bond with these guys he was trying to get next to, and it was necessary that Johnny and Al play off one another correctly for the piece. I knew instantly that things were clicking when I watched them do their first couple of scenes together. I saw them playing off one another."

I asked Newell if he'd had the same preconceptions about Depp that had initially clouded John Badham's views. "Only slightly," Newell told me. "I met him before I really developed a lot of preconceived notions about him. I based my opinion on the man who presented himself to the project. He's a nice fellow who happens to be a great actor. He is also more . . . regular than most people think. He is very well read, and he takes his work very seriously." Newell went on to say that some people in Hollywood had told him this was the role that many studio people had wanted to see Depp try — a brutal, strong, manly role — even though that wasn't what had attracted Depp to it. "He is an unplowed field, a man unencumbered by ego, and increasingly confident of his gift for transforming himself into anything he wants to be," said Newell of Depp — but he could just as easily have been talking about Joe Pistone or Donnie Brasco.

Just before the shooting began on *Donnie Brasco*, Al Pacino was asked about working with Johnny Depp. "I like him," Pacino responded. "He knows what he is doing, and he is easy to be around. Depp is a lot better actor than he is given credit for."

Donnie Brasco was released to resoundingly positive reviews. Depp was showered with accolades for his controlled, witty, and subtle performance as a guy who pretends to be another guy. His dilemma is slowly revealed until the audience feels sympathy not only for Joe/Donnie but also for the poor dumb gangster Lefty. Pacino's performance was accurately described as one of the best of his career, and predictions of Oscar nominations rang out — which, unjustly, didn't come true. The film did reasonably well at the box office; it was no blockbuster, but it was never expected to be one. *Donnie Brasco* can easily be listed as one of the best American gangster movies in the past 20 years, fitting into the category of hard-hitting American films made by non-Americans (e.g., John Schlesinger's *Midnight Cowboy*).

Probably the most important endorsement of the movie — and the only opinion important to Depp — came from the real-life Donnie Brasco, Joe Pistone. "He brought a sensitivity to the part. That's a side of me that a lot of people don't see," said Pistone. "It was amazing — a lot of times during the shoot I'd close my eyes and say, 'Christ, that's me talking!' It was eerie. The kid's a good actor. He doesn't seem to put much effort in it, he just does it."

In what is probably his strangest attempt at commercial success, Johnny Depp made his least interesting and least satisfying movie so far, *The Astronaut's Wife*. Even though Depp kept his chin up before, during, and after the movie, it was clear that he did it almost entirely for the money. He'd found himself in something of a hole after the enormous financial drain of *The Brave,* and *The Astronaut's Wife* presented a great opportunity to make some money.

The film has an interesting premise, but unfortunately it just never gels into anything very scary or interesting. Written and directed by Rand Ravich, it is about an astronaut named Spencer Armacost (Johnny Depp) and his partner Alex Streck (Nick Cassavetes) who are on a space shuttle mission. They are walking in space to repair a satellite when they are overwhelmed by some kind of weird energy that knocks them both out, putting them completely out of contact with Earth for two solid minutes. They make it home safely but are badly shaken up, unable to answer any questions about what happened to them during those missing minutes.

Not long after his return, Spencer's schoolteacher wife, Jill (Charlize Theron), starts having strange dreams and thinking weird thoughts about her husband — that he isn't the same person anymore, for instance. Her fears multiply when both Alex and his wife suffer untimely deaths within days of one another.

Spencer abruptly resigns from NASA and takes a high-paying job with an aerospace firm in New York City, a place he has always claimed to profoundly hate. Shortly after the Armacosts move into a ridiculously large apartment in New York, Jill learns that she is pregnant with twins. Her sense of unease keeps growing, and she starts feeling like there is something wrong with the babies growing inside her.

An ex-NASA man named Sherman Reese (Joe Morton) knows that something terrible happened in space and that the space agency is covering it up. He approaches Jill to get her to side with him. Reese is an interesting character, but the fact that he never really discloses anything or answers any of the questions the movie raises is frustrating. The incident in space is only ever referred to as "what happened up there" — we never find out what that was.

Such movies try to get by under the "psychological thriller" moniker, but they only work when they get us asking questions and then give us answers that we weren't expecting. The central question in *The Astronaut's Wife* has to do with how well spouses really know each other. As a filmmaker, if you can take the paranoia everyone has felt about a spouse and amplify it into dark, gut-wrenching terror, then you have a great psychological thriller. But *The Astronaut's Wife* doesn't do that; it sets up a scenario that makes us wonder what is going on without ever giving us any real answers or a satisfying payoff.

Writer-director Rand Ravich said, "In *The Astronaut's Wife*, we witness the unsettling terror of a woman who senses something unnatural is taking over her life and her pregnancy — and the one person she loves is at the center of it. . . . I wanted to write a story that would carry the audience along on an impending sense of doom." Ravich managed that part, but because the characters are flat we don't really care what happens to them.

There are several red herrings too, including one that has Jill admitting to a doctor that in the past she had a rather serious bout with mental illness and would probably not have gotten through it without her husband's help. Instead of making the story more complex, this stuff just confuses the issue.

Producer Andrew Lazar romanticized this horror-movie plot even further: "I immediately saw this as a story that revives the intense, sophisticated psychological horror movie. I think what really sets us apart is that it's not just a very scary movie; it's a tragic and passionate love story about a romance that goes terribly wrong, a romance that becomes something terrifying, evoking our most basic and primal fears." Lazar explained that he was drawn to this project because "the story keeps you guessing as to who the people really are, what is real, and what is not. You cannot be sure if Jill is going through her own internal nightmare or something far more malicious. Up until the last moment, you are caught up in her desperate anxiety, until the truth is revealed." Now, that sounds good, but it's just another example of how movie producers tend to underestimate audience sensibilities. If you go to the trouble of setting up this eerie story, and it ends up that nothing happened in space, that Armacost is a good guy after all, and that everything was in the pregnant woman's head, how much fun would the movie be to sit through? There has to be something sinister at work or it isn't a horror movie.

Depp was offered this movie for the right reasons — whether he accepted it for the right reasons is entirely his business. Ravich said, "Johnny Depp is, in my mind, the best actor of his generation. I felt that he would bring the necessary element to the role of Spencer Armacost: truth." Executive producer Mark Johnson went even further with his praise for Depp: "Depp's classic rugged American good looks combined with a sense of mystery going on behind the eyes works incredibly well for his character. He brings that quality of underlying danger to Spencer, the sense of unpredictability, the feeling of never really knowing who this man is and what his true intentions are." Producer Lazar elaborated: "Depp can be both the consummate gentleman and the most sinister source of evil at the same time."

I spoke to Charlize Theron about the movie during a visit she made to Toronto. She has a chameleon-like appearance; her short blonde look in *The Astronaut's Wife* had been transformed into a stunning, glamorous '40s movie star look, for her role in *The Legend of Bagger Vance*. When the subject of Johnny Depp came up, she grinned and spoke very highly of him. "He is a really gorgeous man," she said, "but he is also a wonderful, instinctive actor. I loved watching him work, watching him layering on the complexities of his character." What she liked most about the movie, she added, was "the idea that a great horror movie, or a great horror novel for that matter, works a lot better when it taps into normal everyday fears as well as the huge unimaginable ones."

Theron does respectably well in the role of the terrorized wife; she mainly has to frown and look scared throughout the film. As for Depp, he seems to just walk through this one. He's not really believable as an astronaut, and once he is no longer an astronaut he only pops up now and again as the film becomes more about his wife looking scared.

Depp always chooses his jobs based on the scripts, the stories being told, the characters he'll play, and the people he'll be working with. He has said that he decided to play Spencer Armacost because he liked the perversity of the character. "It was fun to play a redneck, an all-American gone wrong," said Depp. "What interested me was not the idea of some kind of being possibly inhabiting his body. It was that whatever happened in space just allowed him to reveal who he really is. He's got this image of being an all-American guy with bleached white teeth and sun-kissed hair, but he's an awful person."

When asked what he thinks the movie is about, Depp said, "I'm not so good at talking about my own movies. Go see it; it's worthwhile, and I don't say this out of promotional considerations. Okay, it's a thriller in layers. I play an astronaut, my wife is a schoolteacher who notices something weird about her husband after a mishap in space . . . what the hell, just go see it."

The Astronaut's Wife was shot in Los Angeles and New York by cinematographer Allen Daviau. Daviau has been nominated for five Oscars and has shot such wonderful-looking films as *The Color Purple, E.T. the Extraterrestrial, Empire of the Sun, Avalon,* and *Bugsy.* He's also part of an interesting footnote to movie history; in 1968, he shot an experimental short film called *Amblin'* for a kid named Spielberg. When Universal Pictures boss Sid Sheinberg saw the film, he immediately offered young Steven Spielberg a directing contract — he was so impressed with the look of the film that he offered Allen Daviau a contract too. Daviau deserves praise for his work on *The Astronaut's Wife*; he gives it a wonderfully lush look that creates a creepy, unsettled atmosphere. It's just too bad the story can't sustain it.

The Astronaut's Wife wasn't released in theaters until August 1999. It took a critical drubbing, coming and going without being noticed at all by audiences.

By this time, the relationship between Johnny Depp and Kate Moss was over. The breakup was, of course, subject to countless rumors. One claimed that he'd moved into her New York apartment to make a serious commitment and that they couldn't get along. Another rumor held that Kate had called off the romance but publicly stated that she wanted to continue seeing Depp off and on — an arrangement that didn't interest him. Someone close to Moss said that the two had called it off because they were having too many fights. And "official spokespersons" continued to deny that anything was wrong.

In the end, the relationship was over, and Depp later shouldered the blame. "We would still be together if I had not behaved like such an idiot," he once admitted. "She was the best thing that ever happened to me, but I blew it because I was too moody and too miserable to be around. I hated myself, and she couldn't take it anymore. I don't blame her one bit. I would give anything to have Kate back in my life. I don't blame her one bit."

The next couple of years would bring many ups and downs for Depp. He'd make a movie that would lead him down a weird and twisted path, taking him deeper inside a character than he'd ever gone before. Once it was over, he'd head to Europe, where his life, as he describes it, would start.

Chapter Twelve

When the Going Gets Weird, the Weird Turn Pro

"... just another freak in the Freak Kingdom."

Hunter S. Thompson
Fear and Loathing in Las Vegas

Perhaps the most extreme piece of work Johnny Depp has done is the 1998 Terry Gilliam film *Fear and Loathing in Las Vegas*, based on the landmark book by journalist-provocateur Hunter S. Thompson, Doctor of Gonzo Journalism. Although the movie tells a largely true story, it was written as a novel to avoid possible criminal prosecution. It first appeared in 1971 in serial form in the pages of *Rolling Stone* magazine, and it has been required reading for hipsters ever since. Therein lies the basic problem with trying to turn this book into a

Johnny Depp on the road with
Dr. Hunter S. Thompson
ROSE HARTMAN/GLOBE PHOTOS

popular film — it is simply too well known. In fact, the novel has been elevated to cult status; it has become the definitive combat-zone documentary of the dying days of drug culture.

The book originally began as a 250-word job captioning photos of a desert motorcycle race for *Sports Illustrated.* Thompson, however, had something else in mind. He decided to take a thick notebook and just fill it with notes about his road trip to Las Vegas — and just publish it as it was. "That way," he explains in the book's jacket copy, "I felt the eye and the mind of the journalist would be functioning as a camera. The writing would be selective and necessarily interpretive — but once the image was written, the words would be final."

In the novel, a journalist named Raoul Duke (a thinly veiled Thompson) is on assignment for *Rolling Stone*; he is supposed to go to Las Vegas to cover a motorcycle race across the desert. While having drinks at a Beverly Hills hotel with his lawyer, Oscar Acosta, they decide to make the weekend more fun by loading up their car with booze and dope before heading to Las Vegas. Duke is also asked to cover a Las Vegas convention of American district attorneys. But the weekend turns into a drug-hazed freakout, a kind of wake for that strong, glorious, and confused time known as the '60s. The book ends with Duke heading back to Beverly Hills after "laying a savage burn" on Las Vegas — "just another freak in the Freak Kingdom."

There was interest from the start in making a film from *Fear and Loathing in Las Vegas,* but no one had been able to do so. Jack Nicholson showed early interest in the book, as did esteemed novelist Larry McMurtry attempted to write a screenplay. Nothing came of either man's interest.

Then, in 1980, a curious movie called *Where the Buffalo Roam* was released by Universal Pictures. The movie wasn't based specifically on *Fear and Loathing in Las Vegas,* but it was about the wild exploits of Dr. Hunter S. Thompson and his lawyer. The poster for the movie read "Based on the twisted legend of Dr. Hunter S.

Thompson." *Saturday Night Live* comic actor Bill Murray played Raoul Duke (Thompson), and Peter Boyle was Acosta, the lawyer. Murray, a fine actor when he is allowed to play to his strengths, had had some success with low-budget comedies such as *Meatballs* and *Stripes*, and he was ready to try to stretch his career out a bit. As for whether he did a credible job as Thompson, the word from Thompson himself is that "I'm still friends with Bill Murray."

In the end, however, the movie was eccentric and pointless. It bombed, making the idea of a movie version of *Fear and Loathing in Las Vegas* — which would probably be only a variation on what was done with *Where the Buffalo Roam* — considerably less appealing.

Another 15 years would go by before the idea of filming this book — still popular enough to be repeatedly reprinted — surfaced once again. In 1992, young producers Stephen Nemeth and Harold Bronson teamed up to start a production company called Rhino Films. They wanted *Fear and Loathing in Las Vegas* to be the first movie produced under their banner. Nemeth and Bronson talked to a young director named Jeff Stein who had no feature-film experience but had directed a number of award-winning music videos; they also considered a Cuban filmmaker named Leon Ichaso (*Sugar Hill*). But when they were asked whom they'd most like to direct the movie, they said British director Alex Cox.

Cox is no stranger to cult status, having made *Repo Man*, starring Emilio Estevez, and the brilliant *Sid and Nancy*, about the late Sid Vicious (a movie that introduced to the world a truly great actor, Gary Oldman), one of the best films released in 1986. My favorite among the films directed by Cox is a little-seen 1988 gem with Ed Harris called *Walker*. This bizarre film is based on the true story of a man named William Walker who walked into Nicaragua in 1855 with a band of mercenaries and declared himself president of the country. Unfortunately, although Harris delivered one of his best screen performances, only about two dozen people have ever seen the film.

Cox and his writing partner, Ted Davies, were very interested, but they weren't about to start work until the situation was more certain. Two solid years of negotiations with Hunter S. Thompson followed; he finally granted Nemeth and Bronson the proper rights in 1994. The film appeared to be set to go, and it was given a $5-million budget.

Given the imagination and ingenuity that go into Cox's films, it was hardly a stretch to imagine that Cox could pull off a film version of *Fear and Loathing in Las Vegas*. But there was a stumbling block — Thompson.

It was on 12 January 1997 that the weirdness really got rolling. Cox and Davies went to Owl Farm, Thompson's house, for their first meeting with the eccentric writer. Thompson was ready for the event. He had the football game on and was cooking up a batch of his favorite sausages. To make sure that Cox and Davies knew which house was his, Thompson placed a blow-up sex doll covered with fake blood in his front yard.

Cox and Davies arrived with an attitude. "It didn't go very well," Depp reported. "I think it could have gotten much uglier than it did. As far as I understand it, Alex and Tod went up to Woody Creek, and, like a person could easily do when you spend time with Hunter and you know his day-to-day routine and intake, a person could think he is a madman and try to overtake him in a condescending way. They were very precious about their script, whereas Hunter has written one of the greatest pieces of 20th-century literature — I would say that that is something to be precious about, not a screenplay."

When Thompson was asked about the meeting, he responded with wonder. He first commented on the bloody blow-up doll: "I keep all these things around — good-humored." Furthermore, Thompson believed they didn't appreciate his efforts at hospitality: "I cooked my special sausage, and the ball game was on. And, Jesus

Christ, it was the classic example of how not to work, as a director, with writers," he said. "First, . . . [Cox] hated football — he refused to watch football. And then I cooked real good sausages, which I prize, and he disdained that — vegetarian. Here in my house comes this adder, this asp. And he persisted to soil the best parts of the book. It's just a miracle I didn't fucking stab him with a fork."

The version of this story told by Alex Cox and Tod Davies has a considerably different slant. Cox remembers being summoned to Thompson's house for a meeting at 2 AM on the night the pair arrived in Colorado. Cox refused, saying he wanted some sleep and preferred to begin work fresh the next morning. This ticked Thompson off, because he, according to Cox, "isn't used to getting anything but his own way."

When they arrived at the house the next day, they found a videographer following Thompson around, taping everything he said and did. "When they [Thompson and the videographer] weren't watching football, they would put on videotapes of dinners that had been held in the past to honor Thompson. It was really a deeply pathetic scene," recalled Cox. He observed that, whenever Thompson coughed, he'd insist that the videographer turn off the camera so that Thompson wouldn't appear weak on the tape. "And his head is just one big bucket of alcohol," said Cox. "From about 10 in the morning on, he had a giant beaker of ice and cheap liquor. Then he would go off in his car and come back claiming that he had driven over a hundred miles per hour. All we would say was, 'I bet that was fun for you.' It was as if he was desperate to impress us. But what is really worrying is that he was suffering. He was in a really bad way. Even though he has all these pilgrims and admirers going over to tell him how great he is, the guy needed to check in to a hospital. He's an alcoholic, and he needs to get better. It's too bad because he is a great writer, and the worst thing for a writer is to not write."

When it came time to discuss their script, Cox and Davies reported, Thompson was hostile, threatening to veto it — although he had not even read it. "He kept sitting there all morning trying to read the first three pages," said Davies. "He'd then get up and get another drink and say, 'Let's do some acid.'"

At this point, the film rights to *Fear and Loathing in Las Vegas* were held by Rhino Films. Everything was developing slowly but surely, in spite of the obstinate relationship between Thompson and the filmmakers. Then Universal Pictures stepped in and made a deal with Rhino to bolster the financing and distribute the film world-wide. The movie now had a budget of about $17 million and was starting to look like a studio movie.

Alex Cox was growing more and more unhappy about how things were shaping up with this movie, which he'd originally envisioned as a tight little film that would reflect the wildly independent nature of the book. He was also resentful of the way Rhino Films, a company run by neophytes, was handling the development of the movie. The newcomers had brought Cox into the project, but it was Cox and his partner who'd gotten the script together and attracted the top-notch cast (Depp was keen, and actor Benecio Del Toro was committed to playing Acosta, Thompson's lawyer and sidekick). Cox and Davies were dismayed to see the two young hucksters take this attractively developed film property — their hard work — and shop it around to the studios for as much money as they could get. Cox and Davies decided to walk away before the project turned into a big-budget, commercially driven movie.

Soon Nemeth and Bronson were racing against the calendar. The pair would lose the film rights if they weren't shooting by January 1997; in October 1996, they had no script and no director firmly attached to the project.

The cast was more certain. Keanu Reeves had been considered as

When the Going Gets Weird, the Weird Turn Pro

a possible Raoul Duke, but the producers knew they couldn't afford him. John Cusack was then approached; he is a fine young actor, and he'd directed a stage version of *Fear and Loathing in Las Vegas* for his theater company in Chicago. The producers also loved the choices that Johnny Depp had been making with his career, so they decided to offer the role to him and see what happened. But, being inexperienced producers, they made the mistake of offering it to both Depp and Cusack at the same time. Cusack's schedule, however, was booked solid, and the role went to Depp — who'd been Thompson's choice in the first place.

When Depp was approached about the project, it wasn't his first encounter with Thompson. The first-ever meeting between Thompson and Depp was, as one might expect, strange. "At the time, I would have done just about anything to be in a film version of *Fear and Loathing in Las Vegas* — I loved the book that much," said Depp. "But that first meeting had nothing to do with the film at all." In fact, their initial meeting took place in Aspen, Colorado, of all places, during the Christmas holiday of 1995. Depp and Kate Moss had headed out of L.A. in search of snow. "We were with a friend of ours in the Woody Creek Tavern, and another guy nearby says, 'I just got off the phone with Hunter, and he says he's coming right down,'" recalled Depp. "So I was thinking, 'My God, I'm finally going to meet Hunter S. Thompson, someone I have admired for so many years.'" Depp wasn't disappointed. Soon the tavern doors burst open, and in strode the larger-than-life Doctor of Gonzo Journalism. As Depp recalled, "He was wearing a hunting jacket, sunglasses, and a hat and was flailing his arms around constantly. He had a stun gun in his right hand and a three-foot cattle prod that was fully electrified in his left hand. He was swinging them around as he talked to people, and the other patrons were scurrying about trying to get out of his way." Thompson made his way over to the table where Depp was sitting. He joined them. "He didn't zap me with the cattle prod, thankfully. But we did explode a can of mace all over the tavern wall. We then headed back to his house, where we built a bomb, and I shot at it with a 12-gauge shotgun. That was within the first two hours of knowing him."

Next, Thompson accepted an invitation from Depp to appear on stage at the Viper Room on 29 September 1996 for an evening of oration with the Sunset Boulevard crowd. The small club was packed to the rafters as Depp took to the stage to introduce Thompson; he stayed on as a host and moderator. Thompson rambled on for hours, and the audience loved every minute of what they were hearing.

Thompson then invited Depp to join him in New York for a special 25th-anniversary party for the book; everyone from Tom Wolfe to Mick Jagger was there. Talk of the movie buzzed through the party, with the main topic of debate being who should play the lead role. Consensus indicated that the choices were down to John Cusack, Matt Dillon, and Johnny Depp, but Thompson, who believed he had a greater measure of control over the choice than he actually had, had already decided. Thompson said, "I told him [Depp], 'Don't worry, son, I'll make you a Kentucky color'" — which, in the language of Hunter S. Thompson, means "You've got the part."

Getting to know Thompson made Depp even more enthusiastic to play him on-screen. At the time, Thompson was only slightly aware of Depp's work: "I saw part of *Cry-Baby*; I didn't see all of it because I was doing acid, and the whole thing was incredibly long." Yet he wanted Depp to play him on-screen because he felt a freakish kinship with him. Depp had the support of Thompson, but Thompson didn't have the contractual authority to choose the actor for the lead role — although his endorsement certainly didn't hurt.

Depp observed the producers' scramble from a distance. The intrusion of commerce into art is his least favorite part of the world that he inhabits. He was fairly certain that the role of Duke was his, so he decided to ignore the mess and simply stay focused on the task at hand — becoming Hunter S. Thompson. Depp and Thompson had already started spending time together, so Depp decided to stay the course and hope for the best. "Johnny is a very cool guy, a great actor, and a committed pro," said Cox. "He had wanted to play this character for a long time, so he simply concentrated on that. He did a good job in a movie that should have been so much more than it was."

Thompson wasn't losing any sleep over the departure of Cox and Davies from the project, and the search for a replacement began. It was suggested to Depp that Terry Gilliam of Monty Python fame might connect with the material; Depp was very keen to work with him; and Gilliam was quite interested in working with Depp on this project. It wasn't, of course, Depp's decision to make, but Johnny was pretty firmly attached to the project by this time, so his opinion was valued. Before Gilliam and his writing partner, Tony Grisoni, would go any further with negotiations, however, they insisted on meeting with Johnny Depp, Del Toro, and Hunter S. Thompson.

Gilliam remembers that first meeting with Thompson. "It was very late one night, and I was told that Hunter was at the Chateau Marmont Hotel and wanted to talk about the project. I wasn't sure if he was actually going to be there because I had heard that he had been arrested the night before for some mischief charge or another," Gilliam recalled. But Thompson was there, and he did want to talk seriously about the movie. "I remember him telling me that the one thing he wanted understood was the fact that he was a serious journalist at the time of the writing of the book, and Acosta was a serious lawyer; what was written in the book was a detailing of the happenings of one weekend. Once he saw that I got that, we were all right, and we moved forward."

Once Gilliam was officially attached to the movie, the budget swelled again, and he and Grisoni rewrote the screenplay. Then the shit really hit the arbitration fan of the Writers Guild.

After they left, Cox and Davies held no ill will toward the project; in fact, they were very curious as to how Gilliam's interpretation of the book would differ from theirs. Davies said, "Terry Gilliam has a very unique and individual vision, and we were looking forward to seeing his script, which we thought would be very interesting and completely different from our take on it." When they managed to get their hands on the script, they read it with increasing chagrin. The first 36 pages, according to Davies, were almost exactly as they had written them. Their original structure had been followed like a road map. Cox and Davies had been particularly proud of the way they'd reconstructed the ending of the book for their screenplay; they claimed that Gilliam and Grisoni used the same ending they had, even though that ending differs from the one in Thompson's book. "It was so blatant," said Davies. "I thought they had just used our script to make the producers angry for some reason. Gilliam and Grisoni must have literally just put our script on a disk, put it in the computer, and typed over it."

Cox put the episode in perspective. "It is because so many directors working for the studios feel their positions are insecure," he explained. "The director is just an employee with no job security. You can't be a maverick when you are directing a movie with Johnny Depp, because he calls the shots. I feel sorry for Terry Gilliam, because working on a movie like this with a big studio must have been an anxiety-filled occasion. If he puts one foot wrong, they will fire him and bring in Peter Medak to finish it up."

When the Going Gets Weird, the Weird Turn Pro

Gilliam was less philosophical about the situation. When I asked him if he and Grisoni rewrote the Cox-Davies script from scratch, his response was quick and adamant. "No, to say we *rewrote* the screenplay is not an accurate way of describing it. I never even read their fucking script in the first place. When I signed on to do the film, I told the studio that I wanted to go through the book with Tony Grisoni, and we would fashion a screenplay that we thought would work. I was already familiar with the book, so I already had definite ideas of where I wanted to go with it."

Gilliam lost the Writers Guild arbitration; the committee ruled that the screenplay credit for the film would go to Alex Cox and Tod Davies. I asked Gilliam how an arbitration committee could rule that he used a large chunk of the previous screenplay when both sets of writers were using the same source material. Of course, there would be similarities — even verbatim dialogue sequences — since both were using Thompson's words. "Thank you, that was exactly my fucking point," said Gilliam. The explanation of the Writers Guild "was a kind of 'rules are rules' bullshit response. I guess because they adapted the book first or something." Gilliam and Grisoni got something of a last laugh when Applause Books published their *Fear and Loathing in Las Vegas* screenplay and the subtitle read "NOT the screenplay by Terry Gilliam and Tony Grisoni."

Even without the screenplay fiasco, Gilliam had an interesting job ahead of him. He was taking on a well-known book, and he wasn't the first director chosen for the project. He was also working with a star whom he'd never worked with before, and he'd had no say in the casting decision. I asked Gilliam if he'd thought Depp could pull this off. "I was completely sure," he said. "I had to be, or I would not have gone forward. He was a part of this before I was, so it might be better asked of him if he thought I could pull it off. But I saw how he threw himself into the role and into that weird plane of existence that Hunter Thompson inhabits. I knew that I didn't have to worry about him at all, and I didn't."

I wanted to know if Gilliam's ideas about the book and Johnny's take on Thompson clashed. "I don't know it happened quite as starkly as your question implies," Gilliam responded. "We had disagreements on certain things; I would have been disappointed in him if he hadn't banged heads with me at least a few times — that is how the creative process works. But I found that when these disagreements happened we both ended up agreeing to each do it the other way, and then we would decide together what way worked the best. He is a great collaborator that way — extremely cooperative."

Johnny Depp's perspective on the development of the movie was a bit different. Depp agreed to do the movie almost immediately when it was mentioned to him, even though the project looked a bit shaky at the time. The book is one of his favorites, and he is very intrigued by the era it so accurately depicts. "I was only eight years old when the book came out, so obviously I didn't read it when it first came out, but I can vividly remember the time," said Depp. "I can remember watching Vietnam on TV as we sat down to dinner. I remember very vividly watching the Watergate hearings on TV as a little kid. Those were pretty strong images for me." The other pivotal event of that era especially captured his imagination. "I can remember standing with my next-door neighbor as the men were landing on the moon. It was dark, and we were looking up at the moon. The guy was saying — and this was very heavy for a kid to hear — 'When the first man steps onto the moon, the moon will turn to blood.' That was our neighbor!"

When Depp was officially offered the role, he immediately accepted it. Soon Thompson was asking him to accompany him to Louisville, where Thompson was going to do a reading from his

When the Going Gets Weird, the Weird Turn Pro

Promoting *Fear and Loathing in Las Vegas* at Cannes with
Benicio Del Toro and Terry Gilliam

work. It was originally planned as a small event to honor a native son, but when Thompson described it to Depp in a fax it turned into "a huge historic event where the mayor will present me with a key to the city onstage at Memorial Auditorium with a SRO crowd of 8,000 and flutes playing and nymphets dancing on perfect gold-strung hearts and teenage winos fighting in the aisles for autographs. The scene is set for a beautiful public drama about Right and Wrong and about what happens to the high-life in Bluegrass County when Billy the Kid returns more or less from the dead to settle many old scores. And never mind the fact that he might be certifiably insane ye gods they're giving him the key to the fucking city."

This event turned out to be another piece in the puzzle of the character of Raoul Duke that Depp was assembling. After the key ceremony, Thompson took Depp on a tour of Louisville. Depp drank it all in. "I was so fucking excited to be part of that whole Louisville extravaganza," he raved. "It was fantastic."

From here, Depp went in full tilt. He actually asked Thompson if he could move into the basement of Owl Farm, Thompson's home. He'd spend just over a week there, absorbing every detail of Thompson's life. It was really important to Depp to get it perfect. As he explained, "Hunter was the deepest I've ever gotten into a character. I love and admire the guy. I really wanted to get him down right."

Once inside the house, Depp became a bit apprehensive; he wasn't sure how much he could tolerate or how well Thompson would tolerate him. "I told Hunter that I intended on becoming a pain in the ass," Depp said, meaning he'd ask a lot of questions, take notes, and record conversations. He told Thompson that he would become like his "parole officer." Depp later said, "He never kicked me out, which was good."

At the time that Depp was living at Owl Farm, Thompson was preparing the first volume of his letters for publication in a book called *The Proud Highway: Saga of a Desperate Southern Gentleman 1955–1967* (*The Fear and Loathing Letters, Vol. 1*). Thompson informed Depp that if he was going to stay in his house he'd be put to work helping to organize and edit the papers.

That kind of intense scrutiny can't be comfortable, but Thompson didn't mind Depp playing Body Snatcher. "I was aware of what he was doing," Thompson said. "If I hadn't liked him. . . ." In other words, had Depp been a "waterhead," as Thompson likes to describe a person he doesn't have time for, he wouldn't have put up with the suffocating attention for a minute.

Of his living quarters at Owl Farm, Depp said, "I called it the dungeon. It was this little room with these makeshift bookshelves and a lot of spiders, and a small little sofa thing that folds out into a bed, and this enormous keg of gunpowder which he let me know about only after I had been smoking in bed next to it for about five days."

Becoming this character would involve more pure research than

Depp had ever done before for a movie. He was thrilled to discover that Thompson had kept all the material he'd used in writing the book — including the original notebooks, the clothes he'd worn, the car he'd driven, and even the souvenirs he'd taken from Las Vegas.

Depp used his time with Thompson to absorb the rhythm of his life. "A normal day with Hunter has him getting up at about eight or nine at night, watching ESPN, watching sports, or watching CNN," explained Depp. "Deborah Fuller [Thompson's trusted assistant] would cook breakfast and give us vitamins — she's a saint. Not much dialogue for the first hour or so while he wakes up. And then we would sit around and talk for hours and hours, and then we might drive into a nearby town and have a drink or two, then come back and talk and talk until about three or four in the afternoon."

Depp was trying to study Thompson by osmosis. Johnny explained that he spent a lot of time "watching the way he thinks; you can actually see the wheels turning and see the ideas coming. That was really the key for me because he is thinking constantly, there are no lulls, and he is very quick-witted."

One thing that Depp decided to do — which took considerable humility — was to read pieces of Thompson's own writing in front of Thompson and let him critique the performance. This is how Depp managed to capture Thompson's odd half-mumble around his cigarette holder.

One day, while rooting around in boxes of papers in the basement, Depp struck gold. He came across three cartons that were marked "1971 — The Vegas Book." As he sat in Thompson's kitchen going through the papers and souvenirs, he came across the spiral notebooks that contained the original notes for *Fear and Loathing in Las Vegas*. Depp devoured the pages. "It's all true, and there's more," he marveled. "There is much more. The notebooks and the actual manuscript, it's more insane than the published book."

Depp got his own notebooks and copied out Thompson's notes. He dug out the clothes that Hunter had worn during that trip in 1971 and started wearing them — even though they probably hadn't been washed since then. And to cap off his transformation into Thompson, Depp borrowed, with Hunter's blessing, the Red Shark, the big red Chevrolet convertible that is such an integral part of the story. Depp drove the beast from Colorado to Los Angeles; he left the Owl Farm at 3 AM on a freezing morning in a convertible with the top stuck open. Depp even listened to the same music that Thompson and Acosta had listened to on their epic journey across the desert. The excursion succeeded in putting the final pieces of the puzzle together for the actor — when he finally arrived in Los Angeles, Depp *was* Raoul Duke. He had dinner with a flabbergasted Terry Gilliam, who noted, "He was wearing Thompson's clothes, and he was speaking like Thompson speaks. It was very strange and exciting at the same time."

Depp would visit Thompson once more before the film went into production. This time he arrived with his head shaved to match Thompson's bald pate. This both impressed and, according to *Rolling Stone* writer Chris Heath, "freaked Thompson out a little." Depp was wearing a hat, and Thompson initially asked him not to remove it. He soon relented because his curiosity got the best of him. Thompson inspected Depp's bald head, and then both decided that the hairstylist in Los Angeles hadn't shaved it closely enough. Hunter said, "I can fix this," getting a can of shaving foam and a couple of blue plastic disposable razors. He quickly got down to business. "I trusted him completely," recalled Depp. "I really did. He was very gentle. No cuts. No weirdness. He wore a mining light so he could see. He's prepared for fucking everything."

As an aside, Depp told a funny story about being bald to interviewer Chiara Mastroianni in their TV interview in November 1998. Depp and Chiara sat cross-legged on the floor in what looked like a comfortable sitting room as Depp smoked and they both sipped wine — this was in France. "I got an offer to do a shampoo commercial during the shooting of *Fear and Loathing*," Depp said. "I can't remember where it was from, but it was for a lot of money. My agent calls me and says, 'Listen,' and she tells me about this commercial offer for a ton of money that will only be shown in the one European country. I kept telling her, 'Tracey, I'm bald. Listen to me, *I'm bald!*'"

Depp's research was thorough, but it was hardly difficult. In fact, half of it was pure pleasure, especially since Depp and Thompson clicked. When asked if he sees any similarities between himself and the good doctor, Depp replied, "Actually, I do. We sort of connect on many levels. But the initial bonding was in the idea that he is from Louisville, Kentucky, and I was from Owensboro, Kentucky. So there was that initial connection; there is a kind of innate understanding between Kentuckians — we are from the dark and bloody ground, as they say." They continued to correspond after Depp's visit, and they created a flurry of letters by fax that was quite funny on both sides.

Depp did some costume tests for the film and faxed the images to Thompson for his opinion. Thompson faxed back a tirade against the look the movie Raoul Duke was assuming: "Clothes all wrong — ugly, screwy, flashy." About the body language that Depp had chosen, he wrote, "Jesus! The stance is too exaggerated." Thompson finished off his fax by describing how their correspondence would unfold. "Any formal, polite correspondence would be false. It's in keeping with the nature of the rapport we've founded. A little beating here and there is good for you." Depp, to his credit, did not let Thompson's mad-hatter persona intimidate him. He fired back, "Doctor, Too late . . . fuck you! The Colonel." Thompson responded, "Okay, Go ahead and make an ass of me on the screen — your turn will come + history will not absolve you. Beware." Depp's carefully worded answer was meant to be only partly humorous.

Hunter, Please know that I am not, in any way, 1) trying to make an ass of you on film, 2) turn you into some over-the-top caricature, 3) fuck you over in some cartoony kind of way, 4) treat this material like an episode of *The Red Skelton Show*, 5) disappoint you, or anything close to any of those things. I am doing the best to combine pieces of you (the you of today that I have gotten to know), the you that I have studied from some older video material, and the character from the book, Raoul Duke.

We are at the beginning of a hideous ride, and things are starting to take shape, only starting! So don't freak out. Give it, and me, a chance. The wardrobe is not where it needs to be yet, and I want your help with it. Fuckin' A! Understand that I am not a scumbag and that all I want out of this thing is for you to be proud of my work, and the film. Nobody's getting fucking rich here, believe me. I am an actor and can only do what I can do. I am NOT and CANNOT be you. But I can come pretty fucking close, and will. This is *my* work!!! If you remember back about a year or so ago, I asked you if you were sure that I should be the actor to play you in the film. Your reply was "yes." Well, it was at that point that I told you that if I was able to do it properly, and do even a remotely good job or accurate portrayal, that you would most likely hate me for the rest of your life. That is the risk that I run here, and okay fine, I'll deal with that. But don't ever think that you can throw a bunch of shit at me and expect that I'll eat it. You've got the wrong boy in that case. I respect and admire you greatly and hold our friendship in very high regard, but don't treat me as if I were a weaker animal, because I will surprise you. Your work is yours. My work is mine. We need to remember that. Call or write or not. Yours in love and war, The Colonel.

To this wordy statement, Thompson fired back only a short reply: "Cheer up. I was just answering your questions about the wardrobe. Yr. real fears are still to come." It went unsigned.

I first saw *Fear and Loathing in Las Vegas* in a screening room on the Universal Pictures lot several weeks before its release. The movie starts with a black screen and Johnny Depp's voice-over quoting Thompson: "We were somewhere around Barstow on the edge of the desert when the drugs began to take hold." I was immediately encouraged, hopeful that Gilliam and Grisoni had crafted a starkly literal translation of the book, like John Huston did when he adapted *The Maltese Falcon.* Since it is all there in the book, why change anything? *Fear and Loathing in Las Vegas* was that — almost.

I spent the next couple of days after seeing the film talking with Depp, Gilliam, and Benecio Del Toro about the film. Depp arrived for our interview wearing a nice brown suit with an open shirt; he'd already taken on most of the physical characteristics he would need for his next role, Dean Corso in Roman Polanski's *The Ninth Gate.* I asked him about his concern for Thompson's opinion of the film. "I wanted him to be proud of it in a strange way," said Depp. "I wanted him to feel that his work was properly represented by us."

Thompson's approval, however, couldn't have been a consideration on a daily basis when they were making the film. "That would have driven me out of my fucking mind. I had to make sure of all that stuff before we started so I was sure that we were paying Hunter and his work the proper respect. This is a great piece of literature after all; we weren't making a movie based on a novel by some kid that the producers bought in galley form before anyone had read it.

That really goes for all the work I do. I keep the audience out of the equation. I'm thinking about that moment and getting that little piece of work done properly."

Depp isn't entirely sure how Thompson reacted to the film in the end. "I think he has seen it, I know he has seen at least part of it," Depp said. "He must think it is all right because he told me earlier on that if he didn't he would come after me. I think he called me a 'fucking little hillbilly' or something right after that."

Depp very much wanted to please Thompson. "He had the most beautiful line [in the book]," said Depp. "It was 'It's an eerie trumpet call over a lost battlefield.' Which I thought was just so beautiful." Depp wanted to do justice to his words — and he did.

I also talked with Depp about the process of translating an abstract book into a film; when you are reading a book, your mind can create any images you choose to help you interpret what is happening on the page, but when you present that abstract material on film you are reducing it to the specific images of the director and the actors. "It certainly is, as you say, completely abstract," Depp agreed, "not only visually but verbally as well. From my point of view, I have to rely on my director to keep me on track. Again, we were trying to make the movie as the best version we could make of Hunter's book." I speculated that that would be tough given the collaborative nature of filmmaking, that there must be numerous interpretations swirling around. "Not several," he explained. "A few, but that stuff is all sorted out in the script development stage."

I asked Depp about his working relationship with Gilliam. "I connected with Terry Gilliam right away," he answered. "I am hoping to actually work with him again sooner rather than later on a project called *The Man Who Killed Don Quixote* [that film went into production in October 2000, but shooting was suspended when one of the lead actors, Frenchman Jean Rochefort, badly injured his back halfway through shooting]. Terry has a real sense of uniqueness and a great sense of noncompromise in a place that specializes in the opposite of both those things. If a studio guy doesn't like his vision or his take on something, he simply says 'Fuck 'em' and goes out and raises the money for his films for himself. I have enormous respect for that way of doing things; I wish there was a lot more of it out there."

I wondered if Depp was familiar with Gilliam's work before this film. He was. "Well, I had met him a couple of times a couple of years before we worked together, and, yes, I was very familiar with his work — I just loved the TV stuff he did with Monty Python — and his early films fucking killed me. I remember laughing all the way through *Monty Python and the Holy Grail* and then seeing it years later and laughing just as hard even though I knew where each laugh was coming."

I told Depp that I knew he loved Thompson's book and had read it a number of times, so I asked him what it was about the book that he loved. "I actually love just about everything Hunter has written," Depp said. "His stuff really makes me laugh out loud when I am reading him. There is only one other writer I've read that can do that — Terry Southern. [*Fear and Loathing in Las Vegas*] . . . fascinated me because it was like reading a firsthand account of a time and an attitude that simply doesn't exist anymore." Depp will have another chance to film his hero's words; he will produce and star in an adaptation of Thompson's "long-lost novel," *The Rum Diary*.

I spoke with the brilliant Benecio Del Toro about working with Depp on the film. Del Toro had to go through a remarkable transformation for his role as Acosta in *Fear and Loathing in Las Vegas*; he gained 50 or 60 flabby pounds and grew his hair into a bushy, unruly mop. When I sat down with him, he'd already shed the pounds and was somewhat better groomed. "I loved working with Johnny," said Del Toro. "It is always great to work with another actor who you can see putting the same stuff into a role that you are. He had the head shaved, and he did this weird thing with his walk. What is great about working with him also is the fact that he respects everyone around him. He respects his fellow actors and the director and the crew guys. He had a great respect for Hunter that was quite tangible on a daily basis."

Terry Gilliam also had good things to say about Depp, and talking with him was a treat. Gilliam has a wide-eyed enthusiasm about everything and an easy, infectious laugh. When I talked with him, he was wearing white linen pants and a blindingly bright flowered shirt. I asked him about Thompson's relationship to his movie — did Hunter make suggestions, was he a consultant, was he an on-set presence? "Are you kidding? I didn't want him around. Having him around the set would have meant chaos would have been a daily expectation. We couldn't have that. I knew how to reach him if I needed his input — that was good enough."

As well as having to undergo Writers Guild arbitration and losing the writing credit, Gilliam had to fight a battle even after the grueling process of shooting the film. He and his editors cut together a promotional trailer for use on television and in theaters. Even trailers must be submitted to the Motion Picture Association of America for scrutiny. The MPAA determined that the trailer could not run on television during the evening hours because the association believed the book to be "pro–drug use." Gilliam was told that he'd have to prove to the association that his film did not reflect the philosophy of the book if the trailer was to be allowed. He was stunned. Why would he make a movie that wasn't reflective of the book that it was based on? And why did he have to prove himself to this army of bureaucrats? He later told talk show host Charlie Rose about the incident: "It worries me because it's that kind of censorship which is one of the things that we used to fight very hard against. And one feels that creeping back in. I don't know how much it has to do with the 'Mouse,' y'know, owning ABC and things like that, but it's worrisome."

When the movie finally reached the movie screens of the world in the early summer of 1998, reaction was mixed but generally negative. It's a savagely funny retelling of the novel, but it strays from the intellectual — which the novel ultimately is — and into the surreal and the gross far too often. Depp does a fantastic job, perfectly capturing Hunter S. Thompson physically, and he proves without a doubt that he was the perfect actor to play this part. But the movie itself became too mixed up in drug and alcohol consumption, hangovers, and weirdness — too much for an audience to stomach.

You'll have noticed that when Depp speaks about Thompson it is not merely as one friend talks about another; when the subject of Thompson arises, Depp's voice takes on a tone of respect, even reverence. "He's very original, I think he is a genius. I really believe that he is one of the greatest minds of the 20th century," said Depp. "I put him right up there with Jack Kerouac, Allen Ginsberg, William Burroughs, all those guys."

Speaking of Ginsberg, one of Depp's next projects was to turn his momentous meeting with one of his idols into a piece for *Rolling Stone*'s 8 July 1999 issue called "The Night I Met Allen Ginsberg." In it, Depp documents the profound impact that Kerouac and the Beat poets had on his life. "I had the honor of meeting and getting to know Allen Ginsberg for a short time. The initial meeting was a soundstage in New York City, where we were all doing a bit in the film *The United States of Poetry*. I was reading a piece from Kerouac's *Mexico City Blues*, "the 2nd Chorus," and I was rehearsing it for the camera, I could see a familiar face out of the corner of my eye: 'Fuck me,' I thought, 'that's Ginsberg!' We were introduced and he immediately launched into a blistering rendition of said chorus, so as how to show me the proper way for it to be done. 'As Jack would have done it,' he emphasized. I was looking straight down the barrel at one of the most gifted and important poets of the 20th century, and with all the truth and guts I could muster up, I said in response, 'Yeah, but I'm not reading it as him, I'm reading it as me, it's my interpretation of the piece.'" Depp goes on to describe how he waited out the endless moments it took Ginsberg to answer him and his deep relief when Ginsberg simply smiled and nodded in agreement. At the end of the piece, Depp describes the Beats as "angels and devils who once walked among us, though maybe just a bit higher off the ground." I've always held the opinion that comparing Johnny Depp to James Dean or Marlon Brando isn't entirely accurate — comparing him to Kerouac, Cassady, and Ginsberg hits closer to the mark.

When the troupe headed to the desert for the shooting, things proceeded in a wild and wacky way. It was hot and dusty in the desert and strange and colorful in Las Vegas. When asked for his impression of Las Vegas, Johnny Depp said "I actually find Las Vegas very sad. You can see people there wasting their social security, their pensions, inserting their last nickel into a slot machine and sitting at them endlessly." Depp admitted to gambling in a casino only once and that was "just to say that I've played against a Vegas dealer."

By the time *Fear and Loathing in Las Vegas* reached theaters, Johnny Depp was starting a new life. He was working on a film with Roman Polanski, and he was finally becoming happy about who he was away from the screen. Depp was in Paris, and he wasn't looking back.

Chapter Thirteen

Leaving Home

In 1998, Johnny Depp headed to Paris to star in Roman Polanski's super-natural thriller *The Ninth Gate*. Depp had been an admirer of Polanski's work for some time, so he was eager to be in the film. It was also a chance to get out of Los Angeles and spend time in Paris. He would never look back.

For Depp, *The Ninth Gate* began at the Cannes Film Festival in 1997. "I met Roman at that festival, and he told me about this script he was writing based on this novel," recalled Depp. "He asked me if he could send it over to me to read when he finished it." Depp was a huge Polanski fan already — "I think within the first three minutes of watching a Roman Polanski film, you feel some kind of uneasiness, a sense of instability in the center of your body — he is the king at that," said Depp. Of course, he said he'd be delighted to read the script.

Outside the Ed Sullivan Theatre in New York
HENRY MCGEE/
GLOBE PHOTOS

A few months went by before the screenplay arrived on Depp's doorstep. Shortly thereafter, Polanski called Depp. "Johnny, what did you think of the script?" the director asked. "Do you want to do it?" Depp paused for a moment before saying "Yes," and then he headed to France. "Roman was, yeah, instrumental in this transformation, this change in my life," Depp commented. The experience would give him new maturity as an actor; it would also give him a new family and new happiness.

Roman Polanski has led a life more fascinating than any movie could ever be. He fled Nazi persecution in Poland as a child only to wind up in Los Angeles as a revered Hollywood filmmaker. He made the horror masterpiece *Rosemary's Baby* and the classic *Chinatown*, which is often on lists of the top American films of all time. Between these films, Polanski's wife, actress Sharon Tate, was brutally murdered by the Manson "family" on their rampage. Several years later, Polanski was charged in an incident of sexual activity with a minor in a hot tub in the home of his friend Jack Nicholson. A trial, a psychiatric evaluation, and jail time followed. During a work release, Polanski fled the country for Paris and has lived there ever since. In the ensuing years, he has made some interesting films, such as *Frantic*, with Harrison Ford, and *Death and the Maiden*, with Sigourney Weaver. And he almost made a big-budget film called *Double*, with John Travolta.

Double collapsed when Travolta backed out at the last minute, allegedly because the nudity and sex in the film made him uncomfortable. This wasn't the first time that he'd backed out of a film for this reason. In 1980, he was all set to play *American Gigolo's* Julian Kay. Giorgio Armani had outfitted him, and the shooting schedule had been set. Then he had second thoughts about what playing a male prostitute would do to his image and left the project; Richard Gere stepped in and has had a successful career ever since.

Messy lawsuits are still pending involving that nonexistent

movie, so Polanski decided to return to the realm of the macabre, where he'd already had great success — *Repulsion*, *The Fearless Vampire Killers*, *Rosemary's Baby*, and *The Tenant*. But it wasn't the macabre theme that attracted him to *The Ninth Gate*; "This is simply a good, interesting story," he explained. "I liked the novel. I liked the idea of a mystery story set in the world of books. Simple as that."

The Ninth Gate is not the most exciting movie you'll ever see, but it does deliver on its promise. It's a creepy, very European, macabre mystery that is a nice change for movie fans sick of the likes of *End of Days* and *American Pie*.

The film is based on a terrific novel called *El club Dumas* by Spanish author Arturo Pérez-Reverte. Polanski is a perfect match for the book; it begins with a line that might have come from one of his movies: "The flash projected the outline of the hanged man onto the wall." In fact, when Polanski first read the novel, he immediately thought of making it into a movie. Pérez-Reverte's tale is, he said, "a fun story — right up my alley. Devils and vampires and such make great stories." He also immediately saw Depp as the main character, Dean Corso, a rare-book dealer on the hunt for a book said to be able to conjure up the devil. "Reading, you imagine the characters in the book as physical beings," said Polanski. "I realized right away that the character was very close to what Johnny looks like: his smile, his charm, and his wickedness combined." Polanski also appreciates Depp's talent: "It is rare that you find such a good-looking man with his abilities."

Depp arrived at the set of *The Ninth Gate* filled with enthusiasm even though he'd heard the charges made by departing *Double* star John Travolta that Polanski was a tyrant and impossible to work with. Travolta claimed that Polanski was making demands on him that were far in excess of what he was contractually obligated to do.

When I asked Depp if he'd had any apprehensions about working with Polanski after hearing the stories, he said, "I had heard that Roman could be pretty focused and rigid, but he never actually tried to give me line readings [something that Travolta strongly objected to during the early shooting on *Double*]. If he had, I'd probably still be in jail." Depp found working with Polanski more challenging than he'd anticipated. "It was not an easy film to make," noted Depp. "Roman is pretty set in his ways. There isn't much room for collaboration or discussion. He was definitely a bit too rigid for my liking."

That said, Depp enjoyed playing Dean Corso. "I think Corso is very passionate about books, but he is also a hard-nosed businessman and a great cynic," said Depp. "I think he is probably a failed writer, so he has great hatred for that thing that he loves in a strange way."

Polanski was thrilled with Depp's work. "The way he played it gave an unexpected color to the character," he said. "I imagined Corso a bit differently, but Johnny always sounded right when he was saying a line. He never sounds phony, there was never a wrong tone in his delivery." Polanski was grateful that as soon as they'd started working, Depp's instincts as an actor revealed themselves in full force. "With some actors, you have to be very specific and explain every detail to get the performance out of them," noted Polanski. "With Johnny, there is no need to do that — his approach is completely instinctual."

Depp's performance in *The Ninth Gate* was critically well accepted even though the movie wasn't. Charles Taylor of *Salon* remarked that "Nothing seems impossible for Depp as an actor. . . . [F]rom our first glimpse of him, as he screws a greedy, bourgeois couple out of a book collection, Depp is right in tune with Polanski's beat. Depp's performance here is so understated it is nearly subterranean." Indeed, in *The Ninth Gate*, Depp gives one of his most controlled performances. Because the movie hinges on the believability of his performance, it's important that it both stands out from and fits in with the tone and the theme of the movie. He succeeds, and his acting creates the atmosphere that Polanski wanted.

Dean Corso (Lucas Corso in the novel) is a well-known mercenary in the world of buying, selling, and tracking down rare books. He is a slightly rumpled character who is always digging in his well-worn canvas shoulder bag for something. Corso, like Depp, is a chain smoker, and the character is always searching his well-worn clothes for a cigarette. But he is also charming and witty and well spoken, and he knows the book world intimately. When Corso takes notes, he does so with a Mont Blanc pen. When he buys a book, he does so with a wad of cash from an envelope he fishes out of his pocket.

Corso is hired by a mysterious American businessman named Boris Balkan (a character that is radically changed from the novel) to hunt down two remaining copies of a book called *The Nine Gates of the Kingdom of Shadows*. Balkan is a scholar of demonology and the devil — the key code to his library is 666. He is a dark character, and his true intentions aren't revealed until the end of the film. He hires Corso because he knows him to be a bit of a buccaneer: "There is nothing more reliable than a man whose loyalty can be bought for hard cash," Balkan tells Corso. As he travels through Europe, Corso manages to stay one step ahead of a growing trail of people connected to the books who are turning up dead. He then finds himself in a fight not only for his life but also for his very soul.

Polanski was correct when he described the Dean Corso role as the most mature of Depp's career — "He tried to grow what would be generously called a beard for the role," Polanski noted — in the sense that this isn't a quirky outsider or a dark and brooding fringe dweller. He plays someone you could be waiting with in a checkout line and not look at twice. Even though Depp was moving into his late 30s during the making of the movie, he retains his boyish appearance, and he had to have some of the hair at his temples colored gray in an attempt to make him look somewhat older. A strong testament to the effectiveness of his performance is that, although Corso smokes too much and reaches for the liquor bottle frequently, although he will do anything for money and cannot be trusted even by those whom he considers friends, he evokes enough sympathy that we hope he makes it safely through his ordeal and ultimately finds what he seeks.

Polanski enjoyed working with Depp, and the two were often seen out for drinks or dinners even when they weren't working. Polanski commented on his working relationship with his star by saying, "He [Depp] was very easy to work with once he was on the set. But it was a bit of a struggle getting him out of his trailer. He was quite comfortable in his trailer — reading, talking on the phone, drinking."

The novel, *El club Dumas*, connects the events surrounding the hunt for the books with the plot of the Alexandre Dumas novel *The Three Musketeers*. The red herring in the novel concerns some pages that might be written in Dumas's own handwriting. While this plot line is a large part of the book, it doesn't make it into the movie; Polanski trimmed the movie into a more manageable detective story. Likewise, just about every character, with the exception of Corso and the devilish young woman, was extensively rewritten.

Terrific American actor Frank Langella adds his strength to *The Ninth Gate* by playing Boris Balkan, the incredibly rich collector of books about the devil who sends Corso on his satanic adventures. Langella first gained notice 20 years ago with his Broadway and film incarnations of Dracula, and he has since played a variety of character roles made unforgettable by his deeply resonant voice and regal disposition. Langella has positive memories of the experience of making *The Ninth Gate*. "You see Roman Polanski's passion every day on the set — great, great passion. There isn't a cynical bone in his body when he is making a movie; he is a child still, in the best sense of the word."

During a recent conversation I had with Langella, I asked him about working with Depp. Langella was impressed with him: "He [Depp] really is a committed, serious actor who has been painted with this brush of celebrity gossip icon. He is so uncomfortable with that aspect of his life that you can see him struggling with it often."

If there is a major weakness in the movie, it is supporting actor Emmanuelle Seigner, who plays the amorphous devil. It's a very interesting and potentially workable idea to cast a beautiful young woman as the devil incarnate, a being who adapts her appearance according to the person she is pursuing. But Seigner isn't much of an actor. She was introduced to American audiences when Polanski cast her opposite Harrison Ford in the big-budget film *Frantic*; she is probably in these movies because she is married to Polanski. In the novel, the young woman is a pretty 19-year-old innocent who slowly seduces Corso, but Seigner is well into her 30s and doesn't quite pull off that innocence in her portrayal.

Production on *The Ninth Gate* began in Paris in June 1998. Shooting took place at the Plaza Athénée Hotel, the Île St.-Louis, and the shores of the Seine. The scenes at the Telfer Château were shot at the 19th-century home of the Rothschild family. Polanski also decided to shoot scenes in some of the locations described in the novel, Sintra in Portugal and Toledo in Spain. The home serving as the beaten-up Spanish estate of book collector Vargas is actually a beautiful, well-kept estate made to look decrepit by production designer Dean Taveularis and art director Philippe Turlure. The early scenes that are supposed to take place in New York, as well as every time the

New York City skyline appears, are really just elaborate prints and paintings created as backdrops in the Studio Epinay in Paris.

A large part of the intrigue of the story involves several etchings from these rare devilish editions. Polanski wanted the books and the etchings in the film to look authentic because they are crucial to the movie's ability to convince audiences. So he asked Francesco Sole, who illustrated the French and Spanish editions of *El club Dumas*, to create woodcuts and etchings. As Polanski said, "The more fantastic a story becomes, the more convincing it has to be in the telling, which means a more realistic style. It all comes down to creating the right atmosphere."

One thing that makes this a much better movie than it could have been is the work of Darius Khondji, the director of photography. Khondji worked his magic on *Se7en* a few years ago and left his dark, indelible impression on that film. When he first read the script for *The Ninth Gate*, he was delighted that Polanski had asked him to be a part of the movie: "I thought of it as a very modern story but at the same time a very old, classical film about books. I saw Dean Corso as a character who could be in an old Jean-Pierre Melville film — uncompromising, with cold eyes. He is very cynical, like the main character in Melville's *Le Samouraï*."

Khondji got along well with Polanski because they approach filmmaking in the same way. Preproduction was a whirlwind of absorbing inspiration from everything and everywhere. "Roman kept reminding me of *Touch of Evil* by Orson Welles. We watched the film together, and we both liked its sense of darkness. We decided that that kind of darkness would make up one side of *The Ninth Gate*."

Khondji knew that he had to shoot Depp carefully because he was the central figure in the story. "Johnny nearly always lent a warm, slightly reddish glow — even in otherwise cool scenes," he explained. "The actor is also groomed appropriately in a devilish fashion, sporting both an earring and a goatee," said Khondji. "I always had to take into account that Johnny was playing a character with two sides. We present the Corso character as very ambiguous. He definitely has a dark side, but there is also a side that we don't know very much about." To heighten that sense of conflict, Khondji uses increasingly striking red tones as Corso's journey progresses.

There is something refreshing about a big movie starring a famous Hollywood actor that is about books and writing instead of hype and special effects, which are fine in measure, but it is reassuring to know that there is still room for a movie such as *The Ninth Gate*. It's the very antithesis of an action movie, but it manages to click along at a reasonable pace and to be captivating. Polanski does get a bit strange, even for him, at the end of the movie when Corso and Balkan square off in a fiery climax, but the movie does need a big payoff for it to be satisfying. Upon its release, *The Ninth Gate* received mixed reviews. They swung from mildly positive to somewhat indifferent. The movie cost just over $30 million to make and earned back just $18.5 million during its domestic release.

But there has been fallout of a different kind connected with *The Ninth Gate*. On 19 July 2000, it was announced that Artisan Entertainment, backers of *The Ninth Gate* (and reapers of *The Blair Witch Project* windfall), had filed a suit against Roman Polanski for allegedly absconding with over $1 million of French tax-credit money that should have gone into the production's bank accounts. Because the movie was shot entirely in Europe, it qualified for a VAT (value-added tax) refund from the French government. The first payment was $619,000, and the second was $577,000. Rather than turning the money over to the production company, Polanski allegedly put the money into a private bank account in the name of R.P. Productions. Artisan Entertainment maintains that it repeatedly asked that the money be transferred to its accounts, but a transfer was never done. Whatever the truth, this case proves once again that the one common factor in show business is greed.

Chapter Fourteen

Paradis and Paradise in Paris

"I think I have finally understood what attracted me to Paris — it was Vanessa and Lily-Rose. In a sense, it was as if part of me was in Paris and I just didn't know it yet."

Johnny Depp, 7 January 2000

The Johnny Depp story has two parts. Part One begins in 1963 and extends to 1999. The second stanza begins on 27 May 1999 at 8:35 PM, when Lily-Rose Melody was born in Paris to proud parents Johnny Depp and French singer/actress Vanessa Paradis. But Depp didn't end up in Paris by accident.

He made his first trip there for the sole purpose of sleeping in the bed Oscar Wilde died in. From his first visit he felt an odd pull towards the City of Lights.

Johnny with Vanessa Paradis,
GARY MARSHALL/
SHOOTING STAR

In the early '90s, Depp gave an interview in which he said he probably would "live in another country, probably France" some-time in the future. He also said that if he ever bought a house in Los

Angeles he wanted it "to be a house with a history, like Errol Flynn's old house, or Bela Lugosi's old house." Four years later, Depp bought and moved into Lugosi's 9,000-square-foot mansion in the hills above Sunset Boulevard. His first prophecy would be realized, too.

Depp's love affair with France continued with the making of *The Ninth Gate*. Since then, he has gone off to make one movie in London and one in Los Angeles, but he has also made a few small films in a row with European locations. Paris is now his home.

Much of the reason Depp is in love with the City of Love is that he has found true love with one of its citizens. Depp's relationship with Polanski had been contentious during the on-set work of *The Ninth Gate*, but they got along very well off the set and often went out for drinks or dinner after work to talk about Paris and the work they would do the next day. One night, after Depp had been shooting scenes all day with Polanski's wife Emmanuelle Seigner, he headed out to hook up with some pals. It would be a night that would change Johnny Depp's life.

Depp ended up in the smoke-filled red lounge in the Hotel Costes in Paris. A lovely French actress and singer named Vanessa Paradis was also in the lounge with a few friends.

During the evening Depp found himself repeatedly glancing in the direction of Paradis's table, although not only had he never met her, but he had never even heard of her. She was getting ready to begin work on a film called *The Girl on a Bridge*, Depp was told by a friend at his table who knew the people at the other table. Depp asked his friend introduce him to the redheaded, gap-toothed beauty. Since Paradis speaks very good English and Depp speaks no French, the two ended up speaking almost exclusively to one another during the evening.

Vanessa Paradis let Depp know, in both her words and her actions, that she likes men who are a little on the dreamier side, men who are a bit more uncompromising — like Depp.

After work the next day Vanessa stopped by Johnny's suite where, as the story goes, the two stayed up talking until dawn. Before long they were seeing each other every day, and by the end of that month Johnny had rented an apartment in Montmartre.

A few months later Vanessa discovered that she was pregnant with what Johnny hoped would be a daughter.

Vanessa Paradis has quite an interesting story herself. She comes from a stable family; her a mother and father have been happily married for three decades and run their own interior design business. She is close with them and her sister, who is 12 years Vanessa's senior. In fact, as Vanessa's pregnancy progressed, she and Johnny lived with her parents in their house in Seine-et-Marne.

Paradis was only 14 years old when her life took a radical turn. During a get-together with her uncle, a French record producer and sometime actor named Didier Pain, Vanessa was introduced to a young songwriter who had written a song about a Parisian cab driver and his exploits. Vanessa asked if she might be allowed to sing "Joe le taxi." She sang it in such an endearing way that she was asked to record it. The song was released in 1987 and was a big hit in France almost instantly. It went on to make the charts all over the world and hit Number One in at least 14 countries. She became an overnight pop star.

Like most pop stars, Paradis was approached by movie producers who were interested in capitalizing on her popularity. Vanessa was bombarded by film offers until she finally settled on one, called *Noce Blanche (White Wedding)*, for her screen debut when she was 16. In the film Paradis plays the teenage object of desire for a much older man. She was so convincing as the home-wrecking teenager that a number of her intellectually inferior fans turned on her in a violent way — there were reports of "Die Vanessa" being scrawled on the walls outside her apartment. Her acting was good enough to earn her a César Award as Best New Actress.

Paradis is a lot like Depp in that she doesn't float from movie to movie; she only does a film when it profoundly touches her. In 1995 she made a film called *Elisa*, in which she starred opposite French star Gérard Depardieu, who says of her, "I was constantly surprised by the force which she gave off. She has all it takes to be a really great actress."

The natural assumption would be that Johnny Depp is the big star and has all the attendant pressures, but Vanessa Paradis has gone through just as much. Her life has been as fascinating and as much the subject of tabloid harassment as Johnny's has been. "I remember when I went on my first concert tour," says Paradis. "It was in 1993 and it was after the release of my first album. It was the only tour I've done and it was the most intense thing that I have ever been through. The applause was so touching night after night that I found myself constantly crying."

She has also had the strange experience of living with the renowned singer/poet/philosopher Serge Gainsbourg for three months. She was 17 and he was 61, but Vanessa remembers him as being "as frail as a little seven-year-old boy. I regretted that I didn't constantly tell him how much I admired him." Before meeting Depp Paradis had very public relationships with a couple of high-profile guys from the music world — including French singer Florent Pagny and American rocker Lenny Kravitz, who wrote a number of songs for her — so being followed by paparazzi is familiar territory for her.

Paradis has found peace with Depp — and in being a mother. She enjoyed her pregnancy, during which she and Depp played their guitars, hoping their child would have an instinct for music. On 27 May 1999 Vanessa gave birth to Lily-Rose. Johnny was in the delivery room the entire time, even asking that he be allowed to cut the

Paradis and Paradise in Paris

Paradis in concert
SHOOTING STAR

umbilical cord — "I didn't want a stranger to cut this link between our daughter and us," he explains. The event was not without its frustration, though. As news of Vanessa going into labor spread, photographers descended on the hospital. When Depp went outside for a smoke, he had to hunker down behind an umbrella, "so they didn't get a picture of Johnny Depp waiting for his baby to be born," he complained to *Premiere* magazine's Johanna Schneller. "Now that is no way to live," he continued. "That's a sick thing to have mixed in with the beautiful memories of your life. It's like being in jail."

After the birth Johnny called his family back in the United States, and his mother and stepfather immediately made the trip to Paris to see the new addition to the family. From the start Depp did his share of bottle feeding and diaper changing, proudly proclaiming, "I'm pretty gifted."

In an interview Vanessa Paradis gave to the French *Elle* magazine for their March 2000 issue, she speaks of her daughter in glowing terms. "[Lily-Rose] looks like her father very much. She has a gap in her teeth like me, poor girl! She is absolutely sublime and smart, but particularly she is a good person. She is extremely generous, I can already see it. Kids are often very selfish, but her, she shares all that she has. She's very special, very, very easy to get on with, she never cries. Children, even the children of others, have always moved me. Often I wondered, 'But how will it be when I have a baby?' You know what? It is even more wonderful than I imagined." Asked in the same piece if she wanted more children, she answers, "I want her to have lots of little sisters and little brothers, many of them."

Lily-Rose's birth had also brought Paradis a deep sense of fulfillment. "Since Lily-Rose is in our life, we really need for nothing. Nobody else," she says. "We are self-supporting. Before I had my amoureau and my daughter, I thought routine must be boring and insipid, it scares me a little. It's the contrary, things are even more beautiful, getting stronger and stronger. We've organized our schedules so we will always be together."

About her day-to-day life with Johnny Depp, Vanessa says, "We are good for each other. I'm not sure we inspire each other for our work, but we help each other, and that's important. We are best friends, and you are never going to leave your best friend, are you?" She adds that they "leave each other a lot of space and have a lot of respect for each other."

Contrast this with the piece that was written in the UK *Mail,* also in March 2000 that quotes comments Depp supposedly made — when his daughter was just a couple of weeks old — about his attitude towards marriage, "Fidelity is fine in theory, but if it runs against your nature, you have to change. I can't be faithful. Half of me loves the idea of having two kids and spending every evening watching TV, but the other half of me will always need to stay out all night." Now, Depp may have said this, perhaps during one of the blow-ups he and Vanessa have had — "They are always my fault," says Depp. Or perhaps he never said it at all. When Vanessa heard the quote she responded by saying, "He has as much of his life as I have of mine. I'm not going to eat it all. I don't want to know it all. Like anyone's relationship we have talked about the past. All I can say is that what happened with us was all very natural and felt so right. There is no real problem between us."

Depp has also said, "My girl and I gave Lily-Rose life, and she gave us life. She gave us the opportunity to breathe differently. It's a huge and beautiful situation."

If you are still wondering why a guy like Johnny Depp turns so violently against the press, the treatment he and Vanessa have received at the hands of the tabloid press provides further explanation. Caroline Graham wrote a piece in the 19 March 2000 *Day and Night* supplement to the *Mail on Sunday* in England in which Vanessa Paradis is asked if she has ever met Kate Moss. Paradis replies, "Oh, you cannot ask me such a thing!" The journalist goes on to inform Paradis that Moss ended up in London's Priory Clinic, suffering from depression and stress after she found out that Depp had been "stolen" away from her by Vanessa Paradis (Moss was a patient in the clinic, and Depp, still a loyal friend, did visit her there, allegedly leaving a new white BMW as a gift for when she was released). In the next paragraph she asks Paradis about a story that was published in yet another British tabloid about Depp having dinner with Moss in London while Paradis was carrying their child in London. An increasingly angry Paradis answers, "I know who he is and I know what we have, and I am secure with that."

The reporter continues to hammer away, regurgitating more British gossip rags. She mentions a story about Depp and 18-year-old Christina Ricci in a club being "terribly indiscreet" and "all over each other." Paradis shrugs, "Oh, my God, I won't answer that."

This drawn-out piece ends with another nasty swipe. Paradis is asked if she wishes to have more children and she answers that she would gladly give up her career to look after a house full of children. The journalist asks the question again, this time adding a snarky "with Johnny as the father?"

Exasperated, Paradis says of her tabloid battle-scarred beau, "There is the person that everyone sees, and then there is the Johnny that I see, who nobody else sees, that is the person that matters to me."

The film that Vanessa Paradis was working on when she met Depp, *The Girl on the Bridge*, was finally released in North America in August 2000. Critics, with sound reason, praised the movie. Paradis is quite good as the emotionally wrought young woman who attempts suicide only to be saved by a carnival knife thrower who has made a habit of rescuing desperate women whom he then recruits for his act. The knife thrower is played by French actor Daniel Auteuil (looking like Al Pacino as Tony Montana), who won the César Award for Best Actor for his work. *The Girl on the Bridge* is a moody, thoughtful movie shot in atmospheric black and white and directed with sensual style by French director Patrice Leconte.

Johnny Depp wrote an emotional entry in the February 2000 issue of the French magazine *Studio* about Vanessa and *The Girl on the Bridge*. "We were already going out when [Vanessa] finished shooting *The Girl on the Bridge*, around the same time I was shooting *The Ninth Gate*," writes Depp. "We saw each other every night and every day. We couldn't stay far away from each other for very long. You couldn't possibly tear us apart. When I finally saw *The Girl on the Bridge* I was deeply impressed by what I saw — it went beyond the images I was seeing on screen. You can't see her acting, there appears to be no effort — she's just so alive, so genuine. I was truly and deeply impressed by her. I'm quite sure that one day our daughter will be of an age to understand this movie and she will feel the same pride for her mother that I feel. There is something rare and precious in Vanessa and it comes through in this movie."

Johnny Depp seems to have found true happiness in Paris, and the reasons are simple. He has started a family with a Parisian and has gotten to know the place and the culture. It is very much to his liking. "What's great about Paris," he raves, "is that people don't give a shit who you are. They appreciate art, they read a lot, and they make movies about people rather than killer asteroids. It is interesting being here."

When Depp first arrived in Paris to begin work on *The Ninth Gate*, Polanski took him aside for a quiet chat. "I told him that here in Paris you have rights that you really don't have anywhere else," Polanski recalls. "His whole career he has been a hunted man, the press and the photographers have been all over him. I feel sorry for him for that reason and I told him that he could relax because that is not the way it is here."

As much as Johnny Depp digs Paris, the feeling seems to be mutual. The Parisian film magazine *Studio* has been a huge supporter of Depp throughout his career. In the March 1997 issue of the magazine French writer Christophe d'Yvoire wrote the only major piece of journalism devoted to Depp's little-seen directorial debut, *The Brave*; Depp deeply appreciated it. He has appeared on its cover numerous times, including the fascinating February 2000 cover, which featured his hand-drawn self-portrait. The issue also features 40 pages of material on Depp's career and his likes and dislikes, all written by Depp himself. He writes about Allen Ginsberg, Iggy Pop, and French singer Serge Gainsbourg. ("His work is so multi-dimensional. He had one of the most beautiful sentences I have ever heard in my life — 'Ugliness is far superior to beauty in that it lasts forever,' isn't that wonderful"). He explains why he prefers Buster Keaton to Chaplin and speculates that absinthe may have been outlawed only because it threatened the profits of the powerful wine barons. But the most telling part of the article is the page that features a hand-scrawled note, "Vanessa & Lily-Rose — My reason to live," written over and over again all the way down the page.

The annual César Awards in Paris in April 1999 provide clear evidence of how France seems to have embraced Depp and his family. Johnny Depp was honored at the ceremony, which is simplistically referred to as "the French Oscars," for his body of work and his contribution to cinema. It is somewhat odd to give such an honor to someone who is so young and still very hard at work, but it is something that the Frnech like to do. If a great actor or director is scorned or ignored by the intelligentsia in America, then the French will embrace him or her to inform the world that they know what is cool and that they are willing to unapologetically celebrate it.

On the evening Depp was to be honored he was still in awe. He had won awards before, but this was something else. When his name was announced, the crowd applauded wildly. He came out onto the stage looking somewhat bewildered, his hair long and lank, and he gave a nice smile to the crowd, acknowledging his friend Roman Polanski who had made the introduction. He was wearing a black jacket over a brown shirt with a black tie. As is his custom when he appears in front of crowds, he scratched the back of his head vigorously as he stepped up to the microphone. "Wow, merci," he said quietly. The camera panned to the crowd to find Paradis, then back to the man of the hour. Depp spoke nervously. "To everybody who followed me on this strange road, I'm, ah, deeply grateful. Merci," he said quickly. He then tapped the gold award a couple of times, picked it up, and headed offstage.

Paradis and Paradise in Paris

With Depp's love of the rhythm and texture of life in France, it can be safely assumed that he will remain there for the foreseeable future. As of November 2000, Depp shot five of his last six major film roles in Europe. Apart from the comfortable apartment in Montmartre in Paris, Depp and his family also have a large stucco house with a tiled roof in Saint Aygulf, near the ritzy enclave of St. Tropez; the home is surrounded by trees and is set quite far back from the road.

Lily-Rose is a good part of the reason Depp doesn't want to return to live in America. "America frightens me now, the guns and the violence, especially the violence in the schools, it means something different to me now," says Depp. "I used to think maybe I could do it in the middle of the States, Colorado or somewhere. But no, the States is out of control. It's becoming dirty. I think it's imploding."

Depp is especially thrilled to be away from Hollywood. "I'm happy to be removed," he says. "I'm happy that I made the decision to stop looking at magazines, that I don't see any movies, that I don't know who people are in terms of movie executives or actors and actresses." Roman Polanski echoes, "Europe becomes Johnny. He doesn't look like an expatriate. He looks like he really lives here. He's very much at ease."

It is evident that Johnny Depp, former wild man and all-night-party guy, is living a different life in Paris. He can often be seen wandering the streets in the early morning looking for fresh bread. Johnny and Vanessa often dine out in small restaurants with candlelit tables, eating early and returning home early. Depp also walks his daughter and can be seen doting on her constantly.

And the French seem to have adopted Depp. To them, Depp is just another cool artist, choosing to live among them, where, in their estimation, he belongs.

Chapter Fifteen

Depp and Burton, Burton and Depp: Part 3

Burton, Christina Ricci, Depp, and Casper Van Dien
at the *Sleepy Hollow* premiere
AP PHOTO/MARK J. TERRILL

"There was a young man

everybody thought was quite handsome.

So he tied up his face

and held it for ransom."

*Tim Burton,
poem about his
friend Johnny Depp,
from the book*
Double Exposure

Sleepy Hollow began in the head of a special-effects ace named Kevin Yagher. He came up with the idea of resurrecting the story of the headless horseman in 1993 and hoped to make the film on his own, but he found no takers. "Then my agent introduced me to a new writer named Andrew Kevin Walker who had just got into town and was shopping around a script called *Se7en*," recalled Yagher. Yagher and Walker got to know each other and began kicking around ideas; they got stuck on the notion of reworking Washington Irving's *The Legend of Sleepy Hollow* in the manner of the old Hammer Studios horror movies from Britain in the '50s and '60s. They worked on the script together and started pitching it with the idea that Yagher would direct it. He'd directed a sequel, *Hellraiser: Bloodline*, but had been so disappointed with it that he'd had his name taken off the credits. "I used to joke around that the only way I would not direct this movie was if someone the caliber of Tim Burton were to attach himself to it," laughed Yagher. "And that was exactly what ended up happening" — but not for a few years.

Walker's screenplay is ghoulish and violent but also very respectful of its literary roots. On paper, it's a good read, but making the transition to the big screen required a sure hand and a stylish, almost outrageous, imagination — a job tailor-made for Tim Burton. At that time, however, Burton was unavailable, and the script didn't have much heat anyway. The property was bought by megaproducer Scott Rudin, and it lay dormant for a few years. Burton hadn't directed a movie since *Mars Attacks!* in 1996. He'd spent the next couple of years involved in the revamping of the Superman franchise, but *Superman Reborn* suddenly, although not unexpectedly, became such a mammoth challenge in logistics and cost that Warner Brothers decided to simply suspend the project indefinitely. Burton sent out word that he was looking for a new project, and the scripts started pouring in. One that got his immediate attention was *Sleepy Hollow*.

In Walker's version, Ichabod Crane has been transformed from the meek and mild schoolteacher Washington Irving described as "tall, but exceedingly lank, with narrow shoulders, long arms and legs, hands that dangled a mile out of his sleeves, feet that might have served as shovels, and his whole frame most loosely hung together.

His head was small, and flat at top, with huge ears, large green glassy eyes, and a long snipe nose, so that it looked like a weathercock, perched upon his spindly neck." Crane became a New York City police detective trying to introduce modern scientific forensics to a backward force on the eve of the millennium in 1799.

Yagher's experience of turning over to another director a movie that he'd been so close to for so long was, surprisingly, pretty painless, mainly because Burton was a perfect fit. "It was interesting to stand back and watch it happening," Yagher said, "the script was always scary and dramatic, but Tim's quirkiness took it beyond our expectations and made it into something better. With all the death in the story, it does get kind of gruesome, but Tim's humor lightened all that up. If I'd have ended up directing it, I would have probably gone further into the darkness and horror. I now see that that would have been a wrong turn to take."

"I'm a big fan of the Hammer horror films of the '50s and '60s, and this script had a lot of classically beautiful horror images," said Burton. "What I also liked about this script is that it's respectful to the original story, but it takes it to new territory. It has a great mix of humor and drama. I had known the story of the headless horseman mainly from the Disney cartoon. It's one of the few great American classic horror stories. I don't know what its power is exactly, but there is a certain reason why people remember the headless horseman. He's a great symbol."

There was another influence at work, which Burton described as "a major influence over my decision to even make *Sleepy Hollow* at all" — the 1949 Disney cartoon *The Adventures of Ichabod and Mr. Toad*, memorably narrated by Bing Crosby. "I really like that cartoon," said Burton. "And I now think it was one of the reasons why I wanted to go to work for Disney in the first place. The artists, Wolfgang Reitherman and John Sibley, created a wonderful sense of a story which was funny, scary, and visceral all at the same time. The layout and the color design were so beautiful too, and it had a great energy. Plus, it captured the feeling of upstate New York very well for an animated featurette . . . it's such a haunted place, and I love it."

As much as Burton liked the Walker screenplay, he decided to take a quick whack at it himself. He then turned it over to Academy Award–winning screenwriter and master playwright Tom Stoppard for an uncredited brushup. Walker, however, would end up with sole screenplay credit.

Casting the Ichabod Crane character was very important, but right away Burton thought his pal Johnny Depp would be perfect. Depp agreed almost immediately, yet he remained cautious; he wasn't sure that Paramount would allow an actor of dubious box-office reputation to carry the lead role in what was becoming a big-budget film for release in the all-important holiday season of 1999. But Burton convinced the executives at Paramount that Depp was the actor for the job, and they trusted his instincts.

From the work they produce together, it's obvious that Johnny Depp and Tim Burton are on the same wavelength. Both are repeatedly asked about their symbiotic relationship; Depp gave perhaps his most succinct explanation to a French journalist, Christophe d'Yvoire. "I think the way we work with one another is as close to ideal as a working relationship can get. It is something I really can't explain, something that is probably best left unexplained," said Depp. "From the beginning our connection is based on affinity, a confidence and trust in one another. We share the same visions and the sense of absurdity in things, a similar perspective on life in general, but also a common point of view, twisted almost, on the comprehension or incomprehension of the world around us."

When Burton is asked the same question, he responds similarly: "We've worked together a couple of times before, so we know what each other is about. It is also fun watching him work at doing different things each time out — it gives me a renewed energy," said Burton. "I appreciate actors who like to transform and are not afraid to get messy, dirty, and dragged through the mud. Johnny has always been one of those guys. . . . Johnny is willing to try anything, and it's what I love about him. I know he's not the traditional image of the Ichabod Crane character, but Johnny has that in-and-out-of-it thing. I felt that was important for the role. He's sort of in tune with things on one level but not attuned to them on another. That's a very human quality to me, and Johnny exactly captures the spirit of what I have always believed Ichabod Crane to be about."

Burton likes the Crane character, describing him as "someone who is basically behind the times and ahead of the times, and it's the contradictory aspects of the character that make him fun and interesting. One of the images that I had in my mind is a character who lives in his head versus the character with no head, which I always thought was a wonderful symbol."

Burton's casting choice had the support of the producers of the project as well. Even before Burton had officially signed on with the project, producers Adam Schroeder and Scott Rudin had considered Depp for the lead role. Said Schroeder, "Johnny's name had come up in discussions before. It was thought that someone like John Malkovich might make a perfect Crane, and he would, but not the Ichabod Crane that we wanted for this version. Johnny is a physically dynamic character who has that obsessive quality combined with a very sexy brashness we thought would be really important to the success of the film." Producer Rudin went as far as saying that "Johnny is as much a design element in the movie as any piece of the scenery" — which I am sure Depp would probably not want to hear, no matter how generously it was intended.

Depp's initial enthusiasm was for the opportunity to work with

Burton again, which is usually enough to convince Johnny to join a project. But he was equally excited about the film itself. "I've always loved this story, and I knew that with Tim's twist on the story it would be something cool, something very special," he said. "What's exciting for me about playing this character is the idea of riding the fine line between honest acting and going just a bit over the top, the style of the Hammer horror film starring Peter Cushing and the great Christopher Lee. I also liked the idea of playing a romantic lead who is not your typical romantic lead. Ichabod has a lot of nervous ticks. He's squeamish. He's extremely uptight. It's as if there's a very fine piano wire running through him that could snap at any second."

Depp's talent as an actor makes it seem that his characterizations are instinctive, but in fact Johnny thinks his characters out very carefully, drawing influences from diverse and sometimes eccentric sources. For Crane, Depp says that he was inspired by the late Roddy McDowall, a longtime friend of his. "Roddy was one of the main ingredients, one of the great inspirations for what I saw as Ichabod Crane," Depp noted. "I thought that Roddy would have made a great Ichabod Crane if they'd have done the movie in the '60s." He also, bizarrely enough, studied Angela Lansbury's performance in *Death on the Nile*, saying, "In that movie, she just kind of rattles on and on, and you never really know what she is talking about, and neither does she." He also used the performance of Basil Rathbone as Sherlock Holmes.

Depp began his preparation for the role by "renting many of the Hammer horror films — the ones I couldn't find, Tim offered to lend me out of his extensive personal collection. Films with Christopher Lee and Peter Cushing mostly. I wanted to analyze their acting from that era. The style is very different, so specific; that was the most intriguing thing to me, and the more I watched the more I was able to appreciate the real technique involved in their acting. It was very risky because it starts out looking like bad acting, but before long you are no longer sure. But that is where the challenge of that [and this] kind of performance lies — the barrier between what is good and bad and what is funny and what isn't is never clearly defined."

As a direct homage to the Hammer tradition, one of the first actors we see in *Sleepy Hollow* is the towering Christopher Lee, who was cast in a cameo as the burgomaster who sends Crane upstate to Sleepy Hollow. Both Burton and Depp were huge fans of Lee and quite taken with him when they finally met him. Burton enthused, "I've been very lucky to meet people like Vincent Price and now Christopher Lee. These are people who basically inspired me to do this stuff, and it's really amazing to work with them. Christopher is hypnotic. He just looks at you with those eyes, and you are compelled." Depp found himself initially intimidated by Lee. "Christopher truly is a force to be reckoned with," he said, awestruck. "Doing that scene with him and having him peering down at you, screaming in your face, all you can think of is, 'My God, that's Dracula!'"

Incidentally, there is another bit of casting fun in *Sleepy Hollow*. The Hessian villain is that perennial bad guy Christopher Walken, who has no dialogue in the movie; he just snarls and growls. One of the stuntmen hired to play the headless horseman in combat was actor-stuntman Ray Park, who will now forever be known as the red-faced Darth Maul in *Star Wars Episode I: The Phantom Menace* and more recently as Toad in *X-Men*.

The cast also includes Christina Ricci, who had a small role in *Fear and Loathing in Las Vegas*. Ricci is among the brightest of the young crop of actors coming of age in Hollywood. In *Sleepy Hollow*, she plays Katrina Van Tassel, the object of Crane's affection; unfortunately, however, the love story is one of the weakest aspects of what is an otherwise completely enjoyable movie. Ricci is not to be blamed. She remembers her first meeting with Depp. "I first met him when I was nine years old, and he has always been so kind and considerate to me," she said. "He remembers my mother's name every time he meets her, which to her makes her life worth living. He's also an amazing actor, and look at him — he's beautiful!" When I asked Depp about Ricci, particularly about her playing his love interest, he said, "Oh, I thought it would be fine at first, but then it kept popping into my head that I had known her since she was nine years old, and we were going to be kissing and stuff! That was a little odd at first. But, you know, we're both pretty calm, we're not walking bags of neurosis."

An actor known more for his action roles, Casper Van Dien, played the hulking Brom Van Brunt. Van Dien is best known for his roles in *Starship Troopers* and *Tarzan and the Lost City*. He saw *Sleepy Hollow* as a chance to be in a movie with some of the coolest people in the business, and he willingly put on 20 pounds of bulk for his role. Van Dien enjoyed working with Depp: "He is so professional. He comes and does his stuff, then he snaps out of it. Some actors like to stay in character, but he doesn't have to. He's very generous and giving, but he also likes to keep to himself a lot of the time. I had a lot of respect for him beforehand, and that has only increased. I really appreciate the choices he's made as an actor."

The filming of *Sleepy Hollow* went smoothly in spite of Depp's lighthearted attempts to shake things up. One story had Depp arriving on the set one night wearing a Bill Clinton mask and carrying a giant pump-action water rifle, then dousing the crew as he stepped out from his Mercedes.

Depp was content. He was working on a fun project with his pal Burton. He had a new life in Paris with a great woman who was then still pregnant with his child. Then, one night after shooting, Depp found himself involved in yet another "incident." He and Vanessa were having a quiet dinner in a London restaurant with a couple of friends to celebrate the pregnancy. Before long, photographers started peering in the window, looking for photo ops. "They wanted some pictures of me and my pregnant girlfriend, and that angered me," explained Depp. "They were turning something sacred into a product." Depp went to the door, where a group of photographers had gathered. He acted like a gentleman as he pled his case. "I asked them nicely, 'Please, I can't be what you want me to be tonight — I can't be novelty boy, a product. Please leave me alone for just this one night.'" The photographers laughed at this, making comments such as "We'll be waiting right here when you leave, mate." This blatant disregard for his wishes made Depp's blood boil. Johnny stepped into the rear doorway of the restaurant and grabbed a three-foot section of wood that was being used to prop the door open. He headed back to the gaggle of photographers in a rage and swung the plank at the first photographer he saw, catching him hard across the hand. Depp then squared off with the remaining six photographers, shouting, "The next flash I see, the guy is going to be on the receiving end of this." No one snapped a picture. Not one. "The beauty, the poetry of fear in their eyes, in their filthy, maggoty little faces was worth it. I didn't mind going to jail for what, six hours? It was absolutely worth it."

Jail is exactly where Johnny ended up. The police were called, and the quiet evening came to an end when he was escorted away in handcuffs yet again for defending his right to privacy. He was released the next morning by a police force he described as very friendly. They even arranged for him to be released through a different door so he wouldn't have to face the photographers waiting for him yet again. When his friend Roman Polanski heard about this incident, he commented, "He would come to our set [on *The Ninth Gate*] quite shaken up by stuff like that, quite disturbed by the photographers. . . . He acts viscerally, and that is just what they are

Depp, with his mother, stepfather, and Vanessa,
receiving his star on the Hollywood
Walk of Fame.
LISA ROSE/GLOBE PHOTOS

waiting for. He falls into their trap. That is a teenage reaction. He should shake it off."

The decision was made early on that *Sleepy Hollow* would be shot entirely in England during the winter, which guaranteed a perpetually gloomy sky for the exterior shots. Most of the interior work was done at Leavesden Studios, just outside London, a WWII-era airplane-engine factory. It was converted into studio space for use by George Lucas on *Star Wars Episode I* before *Sleepy Hollow* moved in.

Sleepy Hollow had the look of a Burton movie: dark and gothic, and just bordering on the surreal, yet still comfortably identifiable. Depp is terrific as Ichabod Crane. He uses a mid-Atlantic accent and is delightful in scenes that require him to shy away from something frightful. In one sequence, as he is examining a headless corpse, he physically shrinks away from the ghoulish sight a couple of times, all the while wearing a high-tech (for 1799) magnifying rig on his head.

Sleepy Hollow's November 1999 release was the biggest opening in Depp's career. It made a whopping $38 million in its first weekend of release and went on to earn a respectable $90 million in its domestic release. One can only hope that the success of *Sleepy Hollow*, both artistically and on the suit-pleasing financial front, means that there will be at least a fourth collaboration between two of cinema's most interesting talents, Johnny Depp and Tim Burton.

After finishing the film, Depp found himself in Los Angeles to receive an honor that was strange given the nature of his career. He was awarded with a star on the Hollywood Walk of Fame. At first, one might assume that Depp would avoid such iconic Hollywood displays, but his reaction was the antithesis of disdain. He showed up to the ceremony with a beaming Vanessa Paradis, his mother, his stepfather, and his two sisters. Depp was dressed in jeans and a loose-fitting shirt. His long hair was held back under a striped wool hat, and he wore sunglasses through a lot of it. He smiled and posed for pictures. Vanessa laughed, obviously very proud of her mate. In his brief speech, Depp emphasized his appreciation of the fans and supporters who have stayed with him during his weird journey.

Chapter Sixteen

Absinthe, Croissants, and Cigarettes

"This is the happiest I've ever been in my life, the most together I have been in my life."

Johnny Depp,
Los Angeles, April 2001

As 2001 rolled around, the movies that Johnny Depp had filmed during 2000 were starting to find their way into theaters. And once again his idiosyncratic choices were received with critical accolades.

During the 2000 Toronto International Film Festival, the first of these, *Before Night Falls*, was one of *the* films to see. The film is the second feature from New York artist-turned-filmmaker Julian Schnabel, who first made a splash in 1995

Depp wearing the cause
YORAM KAHANA/
SHOOTING STAR

with his wonderful debut, *Basquiat. Before Night Falls* is based on the memoir of exiled Cuban author Reinaldo Arenas. Arenas was a truly gifted writer, winning a National Book Award when he was only 20 years old. But because he was a homosexual, Arenas soon fell from being celebrated to being persecuted. He was thrown in prison for publishing material outside Cuba without the permission of the government. Upon his release, he was allowed to leave Cuba on the condition that he never return. Arenas lived in exile until he died of AIDS in 1990. *Before Night Falls* was published posthumously three years later.

Depp wanted to be in this movie because of his fondness for Schnabel and because he felt passionate about the subject matter and wanted to help bring it to life. His part in the film amounts to a double cameo: he plays both a slick-haired lieutenant and a Carmen Miranda-like transvestite named Bon Bon who helps Arenas smuggle his writing out of prison. Schnabel told me during the Toronto International Film Festival that "Johnny could not have been cooler about the whole thing — I told him what I wanted him to do, and he did it. He really loved the story we were telling and wanted to help get it told. I really admire him for it and really am grateful that he took the time to work with me on this." Depp's involvement in the film is a bit jarring at first — Johnny is easily recognized as himself — but Schnabel wisely chose not to concentrate on him. The focus of the film is on Spanish actor Javier Bardem, who delivers a truly magnificent performance as the tortured writer. His depiction of Arenas is smart, conveying both style and charisma; in fact, Bardem was awarded with a well-deserved albeit surprise Academy Award nomination in the Best Actor category. I asked him if he noticed any difference on the set when Depp was working. Bardem frowned slightly and asked, "In what way?" I explained that it could have been awkward with a big American movie star who'd agreed to lend his name and talent to the low-budget film. "Johnny was not a movie star on this movie," Bardem responded. "He was another actor who believed in the beauty of what we were doing, in the meaningfulness of what we were doing."

The reviews for *Before Night Falls* were almost unanimously

Absinthe, Croissants, and Cigarettes

Depp with *Chocolat* costars Lena Olin, Juliette Binoche, and Alfred Molina
SONIA MOKOWITZ/GLOBE PHOTOS

positive. Because his screen time was minimal, Depp was mentioned only in passing in most reviews. When reviewers chose a still to run with their reviews, however, it was often one of Depp in his colorful drag regalia. This would happen again in the next film in which Depp had a small role — *Chocolat*.

Chocolat was released in November 2000 — Miramax thought that it might have an Oscar contender, so it rolled the film out at the end of 2000 to qualify it for the Oscars, then put it into much wider release in the early weeks of 2001, kicking up the heat on the advertising campaign then as well. The strategy worked like a charm. The film grossed solidly for several weeks and ultimately earned five Academy Award nominations, including a surprising Best Picture nod. After the nominations were announced, the ad campaign was changed yet again to further sway those involved in the voting — in the new ads, Depp is featured prominently in interview segments describing how wonderful Judi Dench and Juliette Binoche are. Both actresses were nominated for Oscars for the film.

Depp's performance in *Chocolat* is simple and charming. Despite his heavy presence in posters and trailers, Depp is only on the screen for 17 minutes of the two-hour-plus running time. His Roux has an Irish accent — instead of the French gypsy accent in the novel by Joanne Harris — and smiles easily, charming every woman he meets. One aspect of the role that particularly delighted Depp was Roux's guitar playing; the music in the film is actually Johnny playing. Thematically, the attraction to this movie for Depp and director Lasse Hallström was virtually the same; as Hallström explains, "*Chocolat* is a very funny fable about temptation and the importance of not denying oneself the good things in life. It's about the constant conflict in life between tradition and change. And at its very center it is about intolerance and the consequences of not letting other people live out their own lives and beliefs." Compare this view to what Depp told *Today Show* reporter Jill Rappaport: "It kind of represents the idea of change and allowing yourself to step outside the confines of your normal everyday life and seek out plea-sure, and live a little again. It's a very romantic idea that you can just live simply — just go and do what you want and live how you want to live without hurting anybody else, just taking life how it comes."

The story is set in a quaint French village, Lansquenet, where everything is pretty much as it was a hundred years ago. A chilly wind blows through the town one day and brings with it a young woman and her daughter. This woman, Vianne, opens a chocolaterie, offering the townspeople tasty delights that seem to arouse more cravings than they satisfy. Her confections start to awaken things the repressed townsfolk have long since forgotten. The noble Comte de Reynaud is convinced that Vianne is the devil incarnate and that her candy will cause social unrest and the decay of the town's morals. Almost immediately the people in the town start feeling differently about things. Less repressed, more expressive, more open-minded, as if by magic. And, as the townspeople loosen up, it is Vianne who seems to be the one with something missing from her life. A mysterious, smiling riverboat gypsy named Roux arrives in town with his tribe — he is the one who finally shows Vianne what she had been looking for.

Screenwriter Robert Nelson Jacobs was hired to adapt Harris's novel, and he did so with a great amount of diligence and gusto. Rather than simply take the novel and turn it into a screenplay, he chose to research the historical and mythological associations of chocolate. But even though he indulged in chocolate from all over the world in his search for authenticity, he did keep the emphasis of the story on prejudice and repression and the dangers of valuing tradition over choice and freedom.

The movie plays out in a very European manner, the pacing is slow and languid, and we are allowed to get to know the characters so well we know where they fit into each other's life. This kind of meticulous storytelling allows viewers to become part of the story rather than have the story thrust upon them. The casting of the film was almost perfect, from lead actress Juliette Binoche, who'd score a Best Actress Oscar nomination, to Depp's *The Ninth Gate* costar Lena Olin (who's married to Lasse Hallström), from Alfred Molina as the very picture of repression to Judi Dench, who'd also receive an Oscar nomination in the Best Supporting Actress category, and finally to Johnny Depp, who slides into the movie seamlessly and enhances it without overpowering it.

Even though Depp's part in the finished film isn't that long, his Roux can be accurately described as the romantic lead — not a role that Johnny usually associates himself with. But he trusted his director's judgment. "I would do just about anything Lasse asked of me," said Depp. "But this was easy — it was such a beautiful story, such a beautifully written script. And it fits so well with Lasse and his interest in telling stories that actually try to say something in an entertaining, funny, and different way."

Depp eagerly anticipated working with Juliette Binoche, but he describes the experience as something he couldn't have prepared himself for. "She is so beautiful and deep, she makes you fall instantly in love with her," raved Depp. "She's an intensely committed actress, and if art is possible in cinema I think she comes as close as anyone can."

Roux's musical side was very appealing to Depp, and it gave him a great way into the character. "He's the kind of guy who lands his boat in a village and busks for a while, then moves on," said Depp. "I figured that Roux would be the sort who was really into old blues. This is the first time I have ever actually played the guitar on film."

Hallström, an early and loyal admirer of Depp's work, said, "He brought a wonderful leading-man quality, a true presence, to the movie." Hallström genuinely likes Depp, referring to him as "a wonderful, kind man whose choices are always tasteful and accurate." He added, "I am always impressed by what he does."

Both *Chocolat* and *Before Night Falls* were nominated for Academy Awards, and by the time the ceremony took place there was already a healthy buzz around Depp's next release (although his small role in Sally Potter's *The Man Who Cried* was next in chronological order as far as shooting goes). The explosive true story of an ordinary man named George Jung, who played a significant role in one of the worst public-health catastrophes in U.S. history, the film was called *Blow*, and it was about the first wave of cocaine into North America in the '70s.

Absinthe, Croissants, and Cigarettes

Blow was a book before it was a movie. Written by Bruce Porter and published in 1993, it was subtitled *How a Smalltown Boy Made $100 Million with the Medellin Cocaine Cartel and Lost It All.* A young director named Ted Demme read it and immediately saw the movie in it. It's a story about a young man from Massachusetts who vows in his youth that he will never fall into the working-class life that trapped his parents. This determination takes him in the late '60s to California, where he becomes involved in distributing marijuana in the Manhattan Beach area. But the easy money and the infamy that this new career brings only fuel his ambition; his involvement in the drug trade grows, and so does the risk, and, as is the case with many drug dealers, he is arrested and sentenced to three years in prison. George shares his cell with another drug lord on the rise — Carlos Lehder — and he soon moves from marijuana to cocaine.

When George gets out of prison, he goes to Colombia to hook up with Carlos, who then introduces him to "the man" — Pablo Escobar, the king of cocaine. This alliance brings a wave of cocaine into North America, ripping apart countless lives and making millions of dollars for the importers.

But, like most crime-czar stories, this one ends with the $100 million that George made being stolen by Panamanian president/thug Manuel Noriega, another couple of long jail stretches, and despair. The real George Jung is currently in prison, with no hope of seeing the outside until at least 2014.

Demme's film version of this story is two things: first, it is a very loose adaptation of the book; second, it is one of the best films released in 2001, containing one of the greatest performances ever given by the already very distinguished Johnny Depp.

Demme chose to change the name of Carlos Lehder for obvious legal reasons, but he also scaled down the story by eliminating the parts of the book in which Jung lived with up-and-coming director-writer Barry Levinson in Los Angeles and the stories of how, when he was at the height of his marijuana trading, Jung would hang out with Elizabeth Taylor and Richard Burton in Puerto Vallarta. Demme keeps his story simple, and in doing so he raises it to the level of Shakespearean tragedy. Demme's George is a remarkable character, a greedy drug dealer with redeeming qualities. In fact, at the end of the film, we find ourselves pulling for him, hoping that he will turn himself around in time. This odd reaction to the film can be credited both to Demme for his direction and to Depp for his exceptional performance.

Demme decided to select a cast with a wildly international flavor, which was ultimately to the benefit of the film. Costarring with Depp were German actress Franka Potente and Spanish firecracker Penélope Cruz as his women, Spanish actor Jordi Mollà as the Carlos Lehder character Diego Delgado, and Australian actress Rachel Griffiths, who brilliantly plays George's mother. Ray Liotta turns in a terrific performance as George's father. Interestingly, Liotta is only six years older than Depp, and Griffiths is five years Depp's junior. Liotta plays the father with such passion and grace that his character ends up being the hero of the film. He is a man who loves his son so unconditionally that our hearts break more for him than for George.

Paul Reubens, a.k.a. Pee-wee Herman, does a fantastic job of playing Derek Foreal, the flamboyant Manhattan Beach ex-marine/hairdresser who introduces George to the dealer life, becoming his partner and then his betrayer. Reubens has had his own ups and downs in the past few years, both in his career and in his personal life, but he comes back strong in *Blow*. His Derek is a swishy character but one who can't be trusted.

When I spoke to *Blow*'s director at the ultrahip Standard Hotel on Sunset Boulevard in March 2001, I asked him about the decision to cast Depp as George. "You know, he was really the only guy I

Absinthe, Croissants, and Cigarettes

Ted Demme, Penelope Cruz and Johnny at the premiere for *Blow*
PAUL SKIPPER/GLOBE PHOTOS

thought of," said Demme. "When I was first thinking about this story as a film five years ago, I thought that it needed an actor like Johnny — a guy who takes a lot of chances and a guy who would be able to bite into this story more than other actors might be able to." I mentioned to Demme that when I was reading Porter's book I was struck by the line about Jung loving *On the Road* by Kerouac. "Yeah, exactly, man," said Demme. "It is that little stuff, those little points of identification, that Johnny was able to latch on to. No matter how many fucking takes we did of any of the scenes, Johnny was always honest — each take had something real in it. He was easy to direct."

The film was made on a relatively low budget and shot in California (Beverly Hills, Long Beach, Manhattan Beach, Pasadena, Malibu, and Whittier) and Mexico (Morelos and Guerrero). It's very much a character-driven movie but one that is set 30 years ago, so physical authenticity is crucial to the believability of the entire movie. Demme told me, "This had to look right, man. I had to accurately reflect the clothing and the hairstyles of the time without being clichéd and obvious. That would have produced laughter, and I really didn't want that." I suggested to Demme that making a movie such as *Blow* isn't a lot different than making one such as *Braveheart* in that they are both set in bygone times. "You're right," boomed Demme. "I had to make sure I had the right production designer — and production designers rarely get a lot of credit, but this one deserves all the credit for the look. His name is Michael Hanan, and he worked the same magic on *Boogie Nights* and *Magnolia*, among other things." The look of the film is quite good, especially considering that the story takes place over five decades and uses more than 60 different locations.

Cinematographer Ellen Kuras, known for her work with Spike Lee, had her work cut out for her in shooting Depp in particular because he had to age — subtly — throughout the film. Like every cinematographer who's filmed Depp, Kuras had to deal with the shadows cast by his angular cheekbones. "We had to make sure that we always had a special rig on hand just for Johnny to light his face," said Kuras. But some of the locations were too cramped to allow for additional lights. Kuras persevered, however, and Depp looks great in the film.

I asked Franka Potente about *Blow*. She mentioned how she almost missed out on the film when there was a mix-up in getting her the script; Demme assumed that she'd received the script he'd sent her, and when she didn't respond to it he assumed that she wasn't interested in the project. When he hand-delivered a second copy, she read it and agreed immediately to be in the film. I asked Franka, looking startlingly beautiful with her hair cut very short, about working with an actor of Depp's stature. "I have to tell you that I only knew Johnny Depp from his other movies, which I loved," said Potente. "I loved the fact that he chose to do movies that he wanted to be proud of. What I wasn't prepared for was how quiet and humble and funny he was. He is the star of the movie, and he had the weight of the film on his shoulders, but he was always very concerned about my performance and helping me and trying to make me feel relaxed."

Penélope Cruz echoed those sentiments to me later the same day. "This character I play, Mirtha, was a lot different than the kind of character I have played before," said Cruz. "I was nervous about this movie, but Johnny really helped me. He kept telling me, 'You can do it, you can do it, you are doing great.' He was wonderful." Cruz is riding a huge wave of popularity in North America after starring opposite Matt Damon (*All the Pretty Horses*) and Nicolas Cage (*Captain Corelli's Mandolin*), but she has also turned in some spectacular performances in her native Spain. Her work in *Blow* is brief but effective; she plays a Colombian cocaine baroness who marries George Jung when things are great but can't accept that the bubble has burst when their fortunes turn.

Depp, as was the case when he played Raoul Duke/Hunter S. Thompson, took the responsibility of playing a real person who is still alive quite seriously. "Where George is concerned, yeah, I feel a deep responsibility to him," said Depp. "He is sitting in prison for God knows how long, and even though I didn't get to spend all that much time with him there came a moment, an exciting moment, when it all just clicked into place and I was George. It can't be explained or analyzed, it just happens." And while Depp doesn't want to scrutinize the process of creating the character, he is passionate about Jung's story. "After reading the story and speaking to George a few times, I started to see a lot of similarities between the two of us," said Depp. "When I started acting, I didn't really want all of this, but then money started rolling in at a rate that I never could have imagined. One thing led to another, and I was suddenly on this kind of a rise, and there was no stopping it. That is what happened to George; he saw what he was doing as a business, a lucrative business that was risky and illegal, so he would stay in for a while, make the money, then retire." Just how strongly did Depp identify with Jung? With a few wrong turns here and there, might Depp himself have gone down the same road that George did? "You better believe it!" said Johnny. "Had things not worked out for me the way that they did, had I not found music, I certainly could see myself taking the same directions that George did."

Depp sees Jung as a modern-day pirate, a guy who looked at his hard-working parents and didn't want that kind of life for himself. He wanted freedom and all the good things in life. He knew that what he was doing was ultimately wrong, that the people he was associating with were dangerous, that he could end up in prison for a long time. But he was good at dealing, and he genuinely loved the adrenaline rush of breaking the law. Jung will sit in prison until he is at least 72. He knows he fucked up, but he also lived the kind of life he always dreamed of living — it just didn't last.

Depp's identification with Jung led to a spectacularly accurate performance. When Ted Demme showed the finished film to Jung in prison, George cried. He told Demme that Depp was "dead on" in his portrayal, especially in the final third of the film, which chronicles Jung's downfall.

Blow opened on 6 April 2001 and received terrific reviews across the board; the performances of Johnny Depp and Paul Reubens were singled out for their excellence.

Next on Depp's list of wildly diverse film roles is *The Man Who Cried*, by British director Sally Potter. It hit theaters on 8 June 2001, a small film released into the same pond as *Tomb Raider, The*

Mummy Returns, and *Rollerball. The Man Who Cried* stars Christina Ricci as a young German woman who ends up in Paris during the dark days of World War II, hoping to make her way to America to escape the violence. Johnny Depp plays, once again, a gypsy; he has a brief but inspiring interlude with Ricci's character.

Ricci told Lawrence Grobel in the May 2001 issue of *Movieline*, "I have never seen anyone more moved by her own material than Sally Potter. Our rehearsals consisted of two hours of talking about everything. The first couple of weeks on that film made me feel weird, and I began to feel that nothing I did had any honesty. So I stopped talking about it. To talk about it makes me self-conscious." When asked about her relationship with Depp, Ricci responded, "*Sleepy Hollow* was great because we had so much fun together. But in this movie it's weird because we're having sex in almost every scene we're in, and it's rough sex. The first time we tried to be serious about it, we both started laughing, saying, 'This is ridiculous.'"

From Hell built the same kind of anticipation that *Blow* did. *From Hell* is a period piece, a reexamination of the infamous Whitechapel/Jack the Ripper murders, and it was scheduled for release on 19 October 2001. Depp plays a London detective, Inspector Frederick Abberline, on the trail of the Ripper — but in this version of the story, the investigation leads right to Buckingham Palace.

A report during the shoot at Prague's National Museum said that Depp and the crew were having a lot of fun re-creating this gruesome piece of history. One story had the fully costumed Depp approaching a group of high-society men, introducing himself, then flubbing his lines and breaking into laughter, which then had the rest of the cast and crew in stitches as well. Director Allen Hughes said that levity on the set was fine with him; the darkness of the material would get overwhelming without it.

Twentieth Century Fox has high hopes for *From Hell*, and Hughes thinks that it will attract a large and curious audience. "The fact that this famous case is unsolved is a big part of the fascination with the story," said Hughes. "The obvious comparison to it would be the assassination of John F. Kennedy. A lot of people think there is something fishy with the official explanation — the same has held true for the Jack the Ripper case. And talk about an identifiable phrase — Jack the Ripper is a part of the common lexicon the world over."

Johnny Depp's predilection for choosing eccentric projects that would be unappealing or inaccessible to less talented actors continues. But choosing more off-the-beaten-track projects means that there will be more cases like that of *Divine Rapture*. Shades of that debacle have shown themselves in two of Depp's current projects — the first being his reteaming with Terry Gilliam. *The Man Who Killed Don Quixote* would have been the first film to costar Johnny Depp and Vanessa Paradis. Production was shut down after only a week of shooting, however, because French actor Jean Rochefort was injured — and irreplaceable. Weather, financial uncertainty, and Johnny Depp demanding that every actor on the set be given the same sized trailer as he had (something that wasn't practical given their Spanish location) all contributed to a project that seemed doomed from day one. Paradis was very disappointed, commenting to journalist Marcel Anders, "It's on hold. I didn't shoot any scenes at all, I just rehearsed my lines. It is too bad because it is a beautiful project, very special." The project is, as Paradis said, on hold — but not cancelled. Once Rochefort has recovered, the trick will be to reconfigure the schedules of all those involved with the project.

The second big uncertainty, which has received much press, is Depp's chance to play *Gong Show* host and tv impresario Chuck

Absinthe, Croissants, and Cigarettes

Barris. The script is called *Confessions of a Dangerous Mind*, and it is based on Barris's almost entirely fictional autobiography, in which Barris describes himself as a CIA operative in his off-hours. The film was supposed to be directed by the mercurial young Bryan Singer (*The Usual Suspects*, *X-Men*) and still might be. It was written in the Hollywood trades that the film was about to go into production on 13 March 2001, but when the producers failed to secure the budget the project was called off. Now it looks as though Depp will shoot director Griffin Dunne's gangster film *Nailed Right In* before thinking about playing Barris if financing for the film can be reorganized.

There is also serious talk — though in Hollywood serious talk can only be taken slightly seriously — of a fourth collaboration between Johnny Depp and Tim Burton. The two have discussed the possibility of making a film based on the novel *Geek Love*, which is currently owned by Warner Brothers. Depp wants to play the lead character, Arturo, a murdering circus freak with flippers for feet. But what is absolutely certain is Johnny Depp's small role in Robert Rodriquez's new project called *Once Upon a Time in Mexico* — a sequel of sorts to *Desperado* which itself was a remake/expansion of Rodriquez's breakout film *El Mariachi*. Also starring in the film is Depp's pal and fellow tabloid target Mickey Rourke.

Depp has dutifully fulfilled the publicity expectations placed upon him in Los Angeles for all these films, even though he'd have much rather been back in France with Lily-Rose and Vanessa.

Johnny showed up at the Hollywood premiere of *Blow* with shock-rocker Marilyn Manson, and he appeared to be relaxed and happy. In fact, friends have described his life as being much calmer and more focused of late. He can often be seen strolling the streets of Saint-Tropez with fresh bread in hand. Evenings out now consist of quiet dinners with Vanessa or a few close friends.

On 20 March 2001, Vanessa Paradis took to the concert stage for the first time in years. It was to support her new album, *Bliss*. Depp played a role in the making of the album and is given comusic credits on the ᴅ's eighth track ("St. Germain") and again on the title track — an obvious love song that Vanessa has written to Depp. He also plays lead guitar on the song "Firmaman." To top it off, he also took the photograph of Vanessa that decorates the cover of the ᴅ. While Vanessa may not be that well known in North America, one couldn't turn on a radio in France in the winter of 2000 and the spring of 2001 without hearing the catchy single from the album called "Commando."

Depp was asked by a Parisian journalist about Vanessa's return to music. He responded that he was very proud of her and loved her music and that he "would not miss the concert for anything in the world." And he didn't. Depp attended all three of the concerts and made a surprise on-stage visit at the end of the final one. After the encore, the musicians returned to the stage for what appeared to be a second encore — only this time Depp and his guitar were there. They played a French song called "Fais pas ci, fais pas ça." Vanessa was so moved that she cried when the band got into the song. Johnny kissed his girl as he left the stage.

Johnny Depp is now closing in on 40. He lives in France, where he believes "there is still the possibility of living a simple life." He has a new family, which has provided him with stability and focus. And the result of this domesticity is that he is now doing the best work of his already highly distinguished career. Who would have thought that Depp would become a living example of the benefits of stability, monogamy, and traditional family life as the path to happiness and renewed professional satisfaction? I'll tell you who — anyone who really knows him.

Filmography

A Nightmare on Elm Street (1984)
Directed by Wes Craven
Written By Wes Craven
Starring John Saxon, Ronee Blakley,
Heather Langenkamp, Robert Englund.

Private Resort (1985)
Directed by George Bowers
Written by Gordon Mitchell
Starring Rob Morrow, Hector Elizondo,
Leslie Easterbrook

Slow Burn (Made for TV 1986)
Directed by Matthew Chapman
Written by Matthew Chapman
Starring Eric Roberts, Beverly D'Angelo,
Raymond J. Barry

Platoon (1986)
Directed by Oliver Stone
Written by Oliver Stone
Starring Charlie Sheen, Tom Berenger,
Willem Dafoe, Forest Whitaker

21 Jump Street (Weekly TV show 1987–1991)

Cry-Baby (1990)
Directed by John Waters
Written by John Waters
Starring Amy Locane, Iggy Pop,
Ricki Lake, Susan Tyrrell

Edward Scissorhands (1990)
Directed by Tim Burton
Written by Caroline Thompson, based on a story
by Tim Burton and Caroline Thomspon
Starring Winona Ryder, Dianne Weist, Alan Arkin

Freddy's Dead: The Final Nightmare (1991)
Directed by Rachel Talalay
Written by Michael DeLuca, based on a story
by Rachel Talalay
Starring Robert Englund, Lisa Zane,
Yaphet Kotto

Arizona Dream (1991)
Directed by Emir Kusturica
Written by David Atkins, from a story
by Emir Kusturica and David Atkins
Starring Jerry Lewis,
Faye Dunaway, Lili Taylor

Benny & Joon (1993)
Directed by Jeremiah S. Chechik
Written by Barry Berman, from a story by
Barry Berman and Leslie McNeil
Starring Mary Stuart Masterson,
Aidan Quinn, Julianne Moore

What's Eating Gilbert Grape? (1993)
Directed by Lasse Hallström
Written by Peter Hedges, based on his novel
Starring Leonardo DiCaprio,
Juliette Lewis, Darlene Cates

Filmography

Ed Wood (1994)
Directed by Tim Burton
Written by Scott Alexander and
Larry Karaszewski
Starring Martin Landau,
Sarah Jessica Parker, Bill Murray

Don Juan DeMarco (1994)
Directed by Jeremy Leven
Written by Jeremy Leven
Starring Marlon Brando,
Faye Dunaway, Bob Dishy

Dead Man (1995)
Directed by Jim Jarmusch
Written by Jim Jarmusch
Starring Crispin Glover, Robert Mitchum,
Gary Farmer, Iggy Pop

Nick of Time (1995)
Directed by John Badham
Written by Ebbe Roe Smith and
Patrick Sheane Duncan
Starring Christopher Walken,
Roma Maffia, Charles Dutton

The Brave (1996)
Directed by Johnny Depp
Written by Johnny Depp and D.P. Depp
Starring Marlon Brando, Elpidia Carrillo,
Clarence Williams III

Donnie Brasco (1997)
Directed by Mike Newell
Written by Paul Attanasio
Starring Al Pacino, Michael Madsen,
Anne Heche, James Russo

LA Without a Map (1998)
Directed by Mika Kaurismäki
Written by Richard Rayner and Mika Kaurismäki,
based on the novel by Richard Rayner
Starring David Tenant, Vanessa Shaw, Julie Delpy

Fear and Loathing in Las Vegas (1998)
Directed by Terry Gilliam
Written by Alex Cox, Tod Davies,
Terry Gilliam and Tony Grisoni, based on
the novel by Hunter S. Thompson
Starring Benicio Del Toro, Tobey Maguire,
Christina Ricci

The Astronaut's Wife (1999)
Directed by Rand Ravich
Written by Rand Ravich
Starring Charlize Theron, Joe Morton,
Nick Cassavetes

The Ninth Gate (1999)
Directed by Roman Polanski,
Written by John Brownjohn, Roman Polanski,
Enrique Urbizu, based on *The Club Dumas*
by Arturo Pérez-Reverte
Starring Frank Langella, Lena Olin,
Emmanuelle Seigner, James Russo

Sleepy Hollow (1999)
Directed by Tim Burton
Written by Andrew Kevin Walker,
based on the novella by Washington Irving,
Starring Christina Ricci, Michael Gambon,
Casper Van Dien, Christopher Lee

Filmography

Before Night Falls (2000)
Directed by Julian Schnabel
Written by Cunningham O'Keefe,
Lázaro Gómez Carriles, and Julian Schnabel,
based on the memoir by Reimaldo Arenas
Starring Javier Bardem, Sean Penn, Oliver Martinez

The Man Who Cried (2000)
Directed by Sally Potter
Written by Sally Potter
Starring Christina Ricci, Cate Blanchett,
John Turturro, Harry Dean Stanton

Chocolat (2000)
Directed by Lasse Hallström
Written by Robert Nelson Jacobs,
based on the novel by Joanne Harris
Starring Juliette Binoche, Lena Olin,
Carrie-Anne Moss, Judi Dench

Blow (2001)
Directed by Ted Demme
Written by Nick Cassavetes and David McKenna,
based on the book by Bruce Porter
Starring Penélope Cruz, Ray Liotta, Paul Reubens

From Hell (2001)
Directed by Allen and Albert Hughes
Written by Terry Hayes and Rafael Yglesias, based on the comic
book series by Alan Moore and Eddie Campbell
Starring Heather Graham, Ian Holm, Robbie Coltrane

The Man Who Killed Don Quixote
(Production started, then suspended in early 2001)
Director Terry Gilliam
Written by Terry Gilliam and Tony Grisoni
Starring Jean Rochefort, Vanessa Paradis.

Sources

Articles

Brinkley, Douglas. *George.* June 1998.

Calkin, Jessamy. "Johnny Depp. Esquire." *Esquire, British Edition.* February 2000.

Cook, Kevin. "Playboy Interview." *Playboy.* January 1996.

Depp, Johnny. "The Night I Met Allen Ginsberg." *Rolling Stone.* 9 July 1999.

Diamond, Janice. "Johnny Depp." *Cosmopolitan.* May 1993.

d'Yvoire, Christophe. "Johnny Depp par Johnny Depp." *Studio.* February 2000.

Frankel, Martha. "A Man Apart." *Moveline.* March 2001.

Galvin, Peter. "Johnny Depp, Drag Superstar." *Advocate.* November 1994.

Georgiades, William. "An American in Paris." *Detour.* December/January 2000.

Heath, Chris. "Johnny Depp's Savage Journey." *Rolling Stone.* 11 June 1998.

Jacuaird, Darcy. "The Happiness of Vanessa Paradis." Translated by Karelle. *French Elle.* 20 March 2000.

Jones, Alan. "Sleepy Hollow." *Cinefantastique*. December 1999.

Koch, William. "A Window Into His Soul." *Los Angeles Times*. 1 April 2001.

Lennon, Brandon. "Johnny Depp." *Interview*. December 1995.

Levin, Brenda. "Johnny Depp." *Interview*. December 1995.

McCracken, Elizabeth. "Depp Charge." *Elle*. June 1998.

Morgan, Susan. "Depp Perception." *Harper's Bazaar*. May 1993.

Peters, Jenny. "Narcotics Synonymous." *GQ, Australian Edition*. June 1998.

Pizello, Chris. "Satanic Verses." *American Cinematographer*. April 2000.

Pond, Steve. "Depp Perception." *US*. 26 June 1989.

Schickel, Richard. "Depp Charge." *Time*. 3 March 1997.

Schneller, Johanna. "Johnny Angel." *GQ*. October 1993.

———. "Where's Johnny?" *Premiere*. December 1999.

Schoemer, Karen. "A Little Respect Please." *Newsweek*. 3 March 1997.

Sessums, Kevin. "Johnny Be Good." *Vanity Fair*. February 1997.

Shone, Tom. "Johnny Depp Isn't Johnny Depp Anymore." *Talk*. October 1999.

Vaz, Mark Cotta. "A Region of Shadows." *Cinefex*. January 2000.

Warren, Elaine. "Bad Boy Role Model." *TV Guide*. 23 January 1988.

Weiner, David. "Life in the Fast Lane." *American Cinematographer*. March 2001.

Zehme, Bill. "Sweet Sensation." *Rolling Stone*. 10 January 1991.

Books

Burton, Tim. *Burton on Burton.* Ed. by Mark Salisbury: Faber & Faber, 1996.

Davies, Stephen Paul. *Alex Cox: Film Anarchist.* Batsford Film Books, 2000.

Dunaway, Faye. *Looking For Gatsby.* New York: Simon & Shuster, 1995.

Hunter, Jack, Editor. *Johnny Depp: Movie Top Ten.* Creation Books, Great Britain.